THE WORLD'S SIXTEEN CRUCIFIED SAVIORS

OR,

CHRISTIANITY BEFORE CHRIST

by

Kersey Graves

ISBN 9781631828188

THE WORLD'S SIXTEEN CRUCIFIED SAVIORS

OR,

CHRISTIANITY BEFORE CHRIST

Printed January, 2014
Published and Distributed By:
Lushena Books
607 Country Club Drive, Unit E
Bensenville, IL 60106
www.lushenabks.com
ISBN: 9781631828188

Printed in the United States of America

THE WORLD'S SIXTEEN CRUCIFIED SAVIORS

OR,

CHRISTIANITY BEFORE CHRIST

CONTAINING NEW, STARTLING, AND EXTRAORDINARY REVELATIONS IN
RELIGIOUS HISTORY, WHICH DISCLOSE THE ORIENTAL ORIGIN OF ALL THE
DOCTRINES, PRINCIPLES, PRECEPTS, AND MIRACLES OF THE CHRISTIAN NEW
TESTAMENT, AND FURNISHING A KEY FOR UNLOCKING MANY OF ITS SACRED
MYSTERIES, BESIDES COMPRISING THE HISTORY OF 16 HEATHEN CRUCIFIED
GODS.

By Kersey Graves

1

CONTENTS

THE WORLD'S SIXTEEN CRUCIFIED SAVIORS.

3

PREFACE.

INVERSELY to the remoteness of time has been man's ascent toward the temple of knowledge. Truth has made its ingress into the human mind in the ratio by which man has attained the capacity to receive and appreciate it Hence, as we tread back the meandering pathway of human history, every step in the receding process brings us to a lower plane of intelligence and a state of mind more thoroughly encrusted with ignorance and superstition. It is, therefore, no source of surprise to learn, when we take a survey of the world two or three thousand years in the past, that every religious writer of that era committed errors on every subject which employed his pen, involving a scientific principle. Hence, the bible, or sacred book, to which he was a contributor,

4

is now found to bear the marks of human imperfection. For the temple of knowledge was but partially reared, and its chambers but dimly lighted up. The intellectual brain was in a dark, feeble and dormant condition. Hence, the moral and religious feelings were drifted about without a pilot on the turbulent waves of superstition, and finally stranded on the shoals of bigotry. The Christian bible, like other bibles, having been written in an age when science was but budding into life, and philosophy had attained but a feeble growth, should be expected to teach many things incompatible with the principles of modern science. And accordingly it is found to contain, like other bibles, numerous statements so obviously at war with present established scientific truths that almost any school-boy, at the present day, can demonstrate their falsity. Let the unbiased reader examine and compare the oriental and Christian bibles together, and he will note the following facts, viz:—

1. That the cardinal religious conceptions of all bibles are essentially the same—all running in parable grooves.

2. That every chapter of every bible is but a transcript of the mental chart of the writer.

3. That no bible, pagan or Christian, contains anything surpassing the natural, mental and moral capacity of the writer to originate. And hence no divine aid or inspiration was necessary for its production.

4. That the moral and religious teachings of no bible reach a higher altitude than the intelligence and mental development of the age and country which produced it.

5. That the Christian bible, in some respects, is superior to some of the other bibles, but only to the extent to which the age in which it was written was superior in intelligence and natural mental capacity to the era in which the older bibles were penned; and that this superiority consists not its more exalted religious conceptions, but only in the fact that, being of more modern origin, the progress of mind had worn away some of the legendary rubbish of the past. Being written in a later and more enlightened age, it is consequently a little less encrusted with mythological tradition and oriental imagery. Though not free from these elements, it possesses them in less degree. And by comparing Christ's history with those of the oriental Gods, it will be found:—

1. That he taught no new doctrine or moral precept.

2. That he inculcated the same religion and morality, which he elaborated, as other moral teachers, to great extremes.

3. That Christ differs so little in his character, preaching, and practical life from some of the oriental Gods, that no person whose mind is not deplorably warped and biased by early training can call one divine while he considers the other human.

4. That if Christ was a God, then all were Gods.

The Author.

5

PREFACE TO THE SECOND EDITION.

The author desires to say that this work has been carefully reviewed and corrected, and some additions made, embracing two chapters from "the Bible of Bibles," and some explanatory notes, and is now able to place before the reader a greatly improved edition.

The author also desires to say here, that the many flattering letters he has received from various parts of the country, from those who have supplied themselves with the work, excites in his mind the hope it will ultimately effect something towards achieving the important end sought to be attained by its publication—the banishment of that wide-spread delusion comprehended in the belief in an incarnate, virgin-born God, called Jesus Christ, and the infallibility of his teachings, with the numerous evils growing legitimately out of this belief—among the most important of which is, its cramping effect upon the mind of the possessor, which interdicts its growth, and thus constitutes a serious obstacle to the progress both of the individual and of society. And such has been the blinding effect of this delusion upon all who have fallen victims to its influence, that the numerous errors and evils of our popular system of religious faith, which constitutes its legitimate fruits, have passed from age to age, unnoticed by all except scientific and progressive minds, who are constantly bringing these errors and evils to light. This state of things has been a source of sorrow and regret to every philanthropist desiring the welfare of the race. And if this work shall achieve anything towards arresting this great evil, the author will feel that he is amply compensated for the years of toil and mental labor spent in its preparation.

Note.—As the different works consulted have assigned different dates for the same event, the author has, in one or two cases, followed their example, accepting them as authority; as in the date of the birth and death of the Gods of Mexico. The reader will also notice that the name of the same God is found in different countries. Example—Adonis and Bacchus are found amongst the Gods of both Greece and Egypt.

6

EXPLANATION

"The World's Sixteen Crucified Saviors." What an imposing title for a book! What startling developments of religious history it implies! Is it founded on fact or on fiction? If it has a basis of truth, where was such an extraordinary mine of sacred lore discovered? Where were such startling facts obtained as the title of the work suggests. These queries will doubtless arise as soliloquies in the minds of many readers on glancing at the title-page. And the author is disposed to gratify this natural and most probable, in some cases, excited curiosity by a brief explanation. In doing this, he deems it only necessary, to state that many of the most important facts collated in this work were derived from Sir Godfrey Higgins' Anacalypsis, a work as valuable as it is rare—a work comprising the result of twenty years' labor, devoted to the investigation of religious history. And although embodying many important historical facts which should have commanded for it a word-wide circulation, but a few copies of this invaluable treasury of religious knowledge have ever found their way into this country. One of these copies the author of this work obtained, at no inconsiderable expense, long enough to glean from its pages such facts as he presumed would be most interesting and instructive to the general reader, some of which will be found in nearly every chapter of this volume. With the facts and materials derived from this source, and two hundred other unimpeachable historical records, the present work might have been swelled to fourfold its present size without exhausting the author's ample store of materials and would have possessed such unwieldy dimensions but for a strict conformity to the most rigid rules of eclecticism and condensation. Encouraged by the extensive demand for his former work, "The Biography of Satan," which has passed through seven editions, the author cherishes the hope that the present work will meet with a circulation commensurate with the importance of the many invaluable facts which it contains. For he possesses the sad conviction that the many religious errors and evils which it is the object of this work to expose, operate very seriously to retard the moral and intellectual growth and prosperity of all Christian countries. They have the effect to injure mentally, morally and religiously the great body of Christian professors.

Dr. Prince, of Long Island (now deceased), wrote to the author, respecting the thirty-fifth chapter of this work, entitled "The Logical View of the Incarnation," after he had seen it in the columns of a newspaper, "It is a masterly piece of logic, and will startle, if it does not revolutionize, the orthodox world. And the chapters comprising 'The Philosophical View,' and 'The Physiological View,' were afterward pronounced specimens of profound and unanswerable logical reasoning." We thus call the reader's attention to these chapters in advance, in order to induce that thorough attention to their facts and arguments which will result in banishing from his mind the last vestiges of a belief (if he entertain any) in the doctrine of the divine incarnation.

IMPORTANT FACTS CONSTITUTING THE BASIS OF THIS WORK.

IGNORANCE of science and ignorance of history are the two great bulwarks of religious error. There is scarcely a tenet of religious faith now propagated to the world by the professed disciples of Christ but that, if subjected to a rigid test in the ordeal of modern science would be found to contain more or less error. Vast acquisitions have been made in the fields of science and history within the last half century, the moral lessons of which have done much to undermine and unsettle our popular system of religious faith, and to bring into disrepute or effectually change many of its long-cherished dogmas. The scientific and historical facts thus brought before the intelligent public, have served as keys for explaining many of the doctrines comprised in the popular creed. They have poured a flood of light upon our whole system of religion as now taught by its popular representatives, which have had the effect to reveal many of its errors to those who have had the temerity, or the curiosity, to investigate it upon these grounds. Many of the doctrines and miraculous events which have always been assigned a divine emanation by the disciples of the Christian faith, are, by these scientific and historical disclosures, shown to be explainable upon natural grounds, and to have exclusively a natural basis. Some of them are shown to be solvable by recently developed spiritual laws, while others are proven to be founded wholly in error. The intelligent community are now acquainted with many of these important facts, so that no man of science can be found in this enlightened age who can popularly be termed a Christian. No man can be found in any Christian country who has the established reputation of being a man of science, or who has made any proficiency in the whole curriculum of the sciences, whose creed, when examined by an orthodox committee, would not be pronounced unsound. It is true that many of the scientific class, not possessing the conviction that duty imposes the moral necessity of making living martyrs of themselves, have refrained from fully avowing or disclosing to the public their real convictions of the popular faith.

The changes and improvements in religious ideas now observant in the most intelligent portion of the community, are due in part to the rapid progress of scientific discovery and the dissemination of scientific knowledge in Christian countries. The explorer in the field of religious history, however, comes in here for his meed of praise. New stores of historic facts and data may be reckoned among the recent acquisitions of the laborious archeologist; new fountains of religious history have recently been unsealed, which have had the effect to reveal many errors and false claims set up for the current religion of Christendom—a religion long regarded as settled and stereotyped. For many centuries subsequent to the establishment of the Christian religion, but little was known by its disciples of the character, claims and doctrines of the oriental systems of worship. These religions, in fact, were scarcely known to exist, because they had long been veiled in secrecy. They were found, in some cases, enshrined in religious books printed or written in a language so very ancient and obscure, as to bid defiance for centuries to the labors of the most indefatigable, profound and erudite archeological scholar to decipher it. That obstacle is now partially surmounted.

The recent translation for the first time of the Hindoo Vedas into the English language (the oldest bible now extant or ever written) has revealed to the unwelcome gaze of the Christian reader the startling fact that "the heathen" had long been in possession of "holy books," possessing essentially the same character, and teaching essentially the same doctrines as the Christian

8

bible—there being, as Horace Greeley expressed it, "No doctrine of Christianity but what has been anticipated by the Vedas." (See Vol II., Chap. i, of this work.)

If, then, this heathen bible (compiled, according to the Christian missionary, Rev. D. G Allen, 1400 B. C.), contains all the doctrines of Christianity, then away goes over the dam all claim for the Christian bible as an original bible as an original revelation, or a work of divine inspiration.

Bibles are thus shown to be of heathen and human origin, instead of heavenly and divine authorship, as claimed for them by their respective disciples—the Christian bible forming no exception to this statement. The latter, being essentially like other bibles, it must, of course, have had the same or a similar origin—a fact which, though it may be new and startling to millions, will be universally accepted as truth before the lapse of many generations, and a fact which confronts with open denial the claims of two hundred millions of Christian professors, who assert with unscrupulous boldness that every doctrine, principle and precept of their bible is of divine emanation.

How utterly groundless and untenable is such a claim when arranged by the side of modern discoveries in religious history!

Equally unsupportable is the declaration that "there is no other name given under heaven whereby men can be saved, than that of Jesus Christ and him crucified," when viewed in the light of the modern explorations of Sir Godfrey Higgins, which have disclosed the history of nearly a score of crucified Gods and sin-atoning Saviors, who, we have equal proof, died for the sins of mankind.

Thus, the two prime articles of the Christian faith—Revelation and Crucifixion—are forever established as human and heathen conceptions. And the hope might be reasonably entertained that the important historical facts disclosed in this work will have the effect to open the eyes of the professors of the Christian religion to see their serious error in putting forth such exalted claims for their bible and their religion as that of being perfect products of infinite wisdom, did not the past history of all religious countries furnish sad proof that reason and logic, and even the most cogent and convincing facts of science and history often prove powerless when arrayed against a religious conviction, enstamped upon the mind for thousands of years in the past, and transmitted from parent to child until it has grown to a colossal stature, and become a part of the living tissues of the soul.

No matter how glaringly absurd, how palpably erroneous, or how demonstrably false an opinion or doctrine is shown to be, they cannot see it, but will still continue to hug it to their bosoms as a divinely-revealed truth. No facts or evidence can prove an overmatch for the inherited convictions of a thousand generations. In this respect the Mahomedan, the Hindoo and the Christian all stand upon a level. It is about as easy to convince one as the other of their easily demonstrated errors.

RELIGION OF NATURAL ORIGIN.

Among the numerous errors traceable in the history of every religious sect, commemorated in the annals of the world, none possesses a more serious character, or has been attended with more deplorable consequences, than that of assigning a wrong origin to religion. Every bible, every sect, every creed, every catechism, and every orthodox sermon teaches that "religion is the gift of God," that "it is infused into the soul by the spirit and power of the Lord." Never was a greater mistake ever committed. Every student of anthropology, every person who has read any of the numerous modern works on mental science, and tested their easily-demonstrated facts, knows that religion is of *natural* and not *supernatural* origin; that it is a natural element of the *human mind*, and not a "*direct gift from God*;" that it grows as spontaneously out of the soul as flowers spring out of the ground. It is as natural as eating, sleeping or breathing. This conclusion is not the offspring of mere imagination. It is no hastily-concocted theory, but an oft-demonstrated and scientifically-established fact, which any person can test the truth of for himself.

And this modern discovery will, at no distant day, revolutionize all systems of religious faith in existence, and either dissolve and dissipate them, or modify and establish them upon a more natural and enduring basis, expurgated of their dogmatic errors.

Let us, then, labor to banish the wide-spread delusion believed and taught by a thousand systems of worship—Jew, Pagan and Christian—that "religion is of supernatural or divine origin," and the many ruinous errors; senseless dogmas and deplorable soul-crushing superstitions so thoroughly inwrought into the Christian system will vanish like fog before the morning sun, and be replaced by a religion which sensible, intelligent and scientific men and women can accept, and will delight to honor and practice.

ADDRESS TO THE CLERGY.

FRIENDS and brethren—teachers of the Christian faith: Will you believe us when we tell you the divine claims of your religion are gone—all swept away by the "logic of history," and nullified by the demonstrations of science?

The recently opened fountains of historic law, many of whose potent facts will be found interspersed through the pages of this work, sweep away the last inch of ground on which can be predicated the least show for either the divine origin of the Christian religion, or the divinity of Jesus Christ.

For these facts demonstrate beyond all cavil and criticism, and with a logical force which can leave not the vestige of a doubt upon any unbiased mind, that all its doctrines are an outgrowth from older heathen systems. Several systems of religion essentially the same in character and spirit as that religion now known as Christianity, and setting forth the same doctrines, principles and precepts, and several personages filling a chapter in history almost identical with that of Jesus Christ, it is now known to those who are up with the discoveries and intelligence of the age, were venerated in the East centuries before a religion called Christian, or a personage called Jesus Christ were known to history.

Will you not, then, give it up that your religion is merely a human production, reconstructed from heathen materials—from oriental systems several thousand years older than yours—or will you continue, in spite of the unanimous and unalterable verdict of history, science, facts and logic, to proclaim to the world the now historically demonstrated error which you have so long preached, that God is the author of your religion, and Jesus Christ a Deity-begotten Messiah? Though you may have heretofore honestly believed these doctrines to be true, you can now no longer plead ignorance as an excuse for propagating such gigantic and serious errors, as they are now overwhelmingly demonstrated by a thousand facts of history to be untrue. You must abandon such exalted claims for your religion. or posterity will mark you as being "blind leaders of the blind." They will heap upon your honored names their unmitigated ridicule and condemnation. They will charge you as being either deplorably ignorant, or disloyal to the cause of truth. And shame and ignominy will be your portion.

The following propositions (fatal to your claims for Christianity) are established beyond confutation by the historical facts cited in this work, viz:—

1. There were many cases of the miraculous birth of Gods reported in history before the case of Jesus Christ.

2 Also many other cases of Gods being born of virgin mothers.

3. Many of these Gods, like Christ, were (reputedly) born on the 25th of December.

4. Their advent into the world, like that of Jesus Christ, is in many cases claimed to have been foretold by "inspired prophets."

5. Stars figured at the birth of several of them, as in the case of Christ.

6. Also angels, shepherds, and magi, or "wise men."

7. Many of them, like Christ, were claimed to be of royal or princely descent.

8. Their lives, like his, were also threatened in infancy by the ruler of the country.

9. Several of them, like him, gave early proof of divinity.

10. And, like him, retired from the world and fasted.

11

11. Also, like him, declared, "My kingdom is not of this world."

12. Some of them preached a spiritual religion, too, like his.

13. And were "anointed with oil," like him.

14. Many of them, like him, were "crucified for the sins of the world."

15. And after three days' interment "rose from the dead."

16. And, finally, like him, are reported as ascending back to heaven.

17. The same violent convulsions of nature at the crucifixion of several are reported.

18. They were nearly all called "Saviors," "Son of God," "Messiah," "Redeemer," "Lord," &c.

19. Each one was the second member of the trinity of "Father, Son and Holy Ghost."

20. The doctrines of "Original Sin," "Fall of Man," "The Atonement," "The Trinity," "The Word," "Forgiveness," "An Angry God," "Future Endless Punishment," etc., etc. (see the author's "Biography of Satan,") were a part of the religion of each of these sin-atoning Gods, as found set forth in several oriental bibles and "holy books," similar in character and spirit to the Christian's bible, and written, like it, by "inspired and holy men" before the time of either Christ or Moses (before Moses, in some cases, at least). All these doctrines and declarations, and many others not here enumerated, the historical citations of this work abundantly prove, were taught in various oriental heathen nations centuries before the birth of Christ, or before Christianity, as a religion, was known in the world.

Will you, then, after learning these facts, longer dare assert that Christianity is of divine emanation, or claim a special divine paternity for its author. Only the priest, who loves his *salary* more than the cause of *truth* (and I fear this class are numerous,) or who is deplorably ignorant of history, will have the effrontery or audacity to do so. For the historical facts herein set forth as clearly prove such assumptions to be false, as figures can demonstrate the truth of any mathematical problem. And no logic can overthrow, and no sophistry can set aside these facts.

They will stand till the end of time in spite of your efforts either to evade, ignore, or invalidate them.

We will here briefly state:—

WHY ALL THE ANCIENT RELIGIONS WERE ALIKE.

Two causes are obviously assignable for Christianity in all its essential features and phases, being so strikingly similar to the ancient pagan systems which preceded it, as also the close analogies of all the principal systems, whose doctrines and practical teachings have found a place on the pages of history.

1. The primary and constituent elements and properties of human nature being essentially the same in all countries and all centuries, and the feeling called Religion being a spontaneous outgrowth of the devotional elements of the human mind, the coincidence would naturally produce similar feelings, similar thoughts, similar views and similar doctrines on the subject of religion in different countries, however widely separated. This accounts in part for the analogous features observable in all the primary systems of religious faith, which have flourished in the past ages.

2. A more potent cause, however, for the proximate identity extending to such an elaborate detail, as is evinced by the foregoing schedule, is found in the historical incident which brought the disciples of the various systems of worship together, face to face, in the then grand religious emporium of the world—the royal and renowned city of Alexandria, the capital of Egypt Here, drawn together by various motives and influences, the devotee of India (the devout disciple of Buddhism), the ever-prayerful worshipper of "Mithra, the Mediator," the representatives of the crucified Quexalcoate of Mexico, the self-denying Essene, the superstitious Egyptian, the godly Chaldean, the imitative Judean founders of Christianity, and the disciples of other sin-atoning Gods, met and interchanged ideas, discussed their various dogmas, remolded their doctrines, and recast and rehabilitated their systems of religious faith by borrowing from each other, and from other systems there represented. In this way all became remarkably similar and alike in all their doctrines and details. And thus the mystery is solved, and the singular resemblance of all the ancient systems of religion satisfactorily accounted for. (For a fuller explanation of this matter, see Chapters XXX. and XXXI. of this work.)

In conclusion, please note the following points:—

1. The religious conceptions of the Old Testament are as easily traced to heathen sources as those of the New Testament. But we are compelled to exclude such an exposition from this work.

2. The comparative exhibition of the doctrines and teachings of twenty bibles which proves them to be in their leading features essentially alike (originally designed for this volume), is found to be, when completed, of sufficient magnitude to constitute a volume of itself.

3. Here I desire to impress upon the minds of my clerical brethren the important fact, that the gospel histories of Christ were written by men who had formerly been Jews (see Acts xxi. 20), and probably possessing the strong proclivity to imitate and borrow which their bible shows was characteristic of that nation; and being written many years after Christ's death, according to that standard Christian author, Dr. Lardner, it was impossible, under such circumstances, for them to separate (if they had desired to) the real facts and events of his life from the innumerable fictions and fables then afloat everywhere relative to the heathen Gods who had pre-enacted a similar history. Two reasons are thus furnished for their constructing a history of Christ almost identical with that of other Gods, as shown in chapters XXX., XXXI. and XXXII. of this work.

4. The singular and senseless defense of your now tottering system we have known to be attempted by members of your order, by the self-complacent soliloquy "Christianity, whether divine or human, is good enough for me." But such a subterfuge betrays both a weak mind and a weak cause. The disciples of all the oriental systems cherished a similar feeling and a similar

13

sentiment. And the deluded followers of Brigham Young exclaimed in like manner, "I want nothing better than Mormonism." "Snakes, lizards and frogs are good enough for me," a South Sea Islander once exclaimed to a missionary, when a reform diet was proposed. Such logic, if universally adopted, would keep the world eternally in barbarism. No progress can be made where such sentiments prevail. The truth is, no system of religion, whatever its ostensible marks of perfection, can long remain "good enough" for aspiring and progressive minds, unless occasionally improved, like other institutions. And then it should be borne in mind, that our controversy does not appertain so much to the character as to the origin of the Christian religion. Our many incontrovertible proofs, that it is of human and heathen origin, proves at the same time that it is an imperfect system, and as such, needing occasional improvement, like other institutions. And its assumed perfection and divine origin which have always guarded it from improvement, amply accounts for its present corrupt, immoral, declining and dying condition. And it will ere long die with paralysis, unless its assumption of divine perfection is soon exchanged for the principles of improvement and reconstruction. This policy alone can save it.

5. We will here notice another feeble, futile and foolish expedient we have known resorted to by persons of your order to save your sinking cause when the evidence is presented with such cogency as to admit of no disproof, that all the important doctrines of Christianity were taught by older heathen systems before the era of Christ The plea is, that those systems were mere types, or ante-types, of the Christian religion. But this plea is of itself a borrowed subterfuge of heathenism, and is moreover devoid of evidence. The ancient Egyptians, also the Greeks, claimed that Brahminism was a type, or ante-type, of their religious systems. And Mahomedans now claim that both Judaism and Christianity were designed by God as foreshadowing types of religion of the Koran. And the disciples of more than a thousand systems of religion which have flourished in past ages, could have made such logic equally available in showing, in each case, that every system preceding theirs was designed by Infinite Wisdom as simply a typical or ante-typical forerunner of theirs. How ridiculous and senseless, therefore, is the argument thus shown to be when critically examined in the light of history! So much so as scarcely to merit a serious notice.

6. Here permit us to say that we believe Christianity to be not only of human origin, but of natural origin also; I that is, a natural outgrowth, like other systems, of the religious elements of the human mind—a hypothesis which accounts most beautifully for the numerous human imperfections now visible in nearly every line of its teachings.

Those imperfections correspond exactly to the imperfect minds which produced it.

7. And we believe that the principle teacher of Christianity, "the man Christ Jesus," possessed a very exalted and superior mind for that age in the moral and religious departments, and in the intellectual to some extent also. But his superiority in these respects was not probably greater than that of Zera Colburn or Henry Salford in the mathematical department. And all probably derived their peculiar extraordinary traits of mind from the same causes—that of strong psychological influence impressed upon the mind of the mothers prior to their births. Had these ante-natal influences been as well understood then as now, we presume Christ would have escaped the fate of an exaltation to the Godhead.

        [The author, stating the above, demonstrates that same

14

assumption of a *truth* which he criticises in the
Christians, Mohamedens and other proponents of religions.
Ed.]

8. In conclusion, permit us to say that the numerous and overwhelming facts of this work render it utterly impossible that the exalted claims you put forth for your religion and its assumed author (that of a divine character) can be true. And posterity will so decide, whether you do or not.

Cherishing for you naught but feelings of kindness and brotherly love, and desiring to promote the truth, we will answer any question, or discuss any proposition embraced in this work you may desire.

Your brother,

Kersey Graves.

THE WORLD'S SIXTEEN CRUCIFIED SAVIORS.

CHAPTER I. RIVAL CLAIMS OF THE SAVIORS

IT is claimed by the disciples of Jesus Christ, that he was of supernatural and divine origin; that he had a human being for a mother, and a God for his father; that, although he was woman-conceived, he was Deity-begotten, and molded in the human form, but comprehending in essence a full measure of the infinite Godhead; thus making him half human and half divine in his sublunary origin. It is claimed that he was full and perfect God, and perfect man; and while he was God, he was also the son of God, and as such was sent down by his father to save a fallen and guilty world; and that thus his mission pertained to the whole human race; and his inspired seers are made to declare that ultimately every nation, tongue, kindred, and people under heaven will acknowledge allegiance to his government, and concede his right to reign and rule the world; that "every knee must bow, and every tongue confess that Jesus is Lord, to the glory of God the Father."

But we do not find that this prophecy has ever been or is likely to be fulfilled. We do not observe that this claim to the infinite deityship of Jesus Christ has been or is likely to be universally conceded. On the contrary, it is found that by a portion, and a large portion of the people of even those nations now called Christian, this claim has been steadily and unswervingly controverted, through the whole line of history, stretching through the nearly two thousand years which have elapsed since his advent to earth.

Even some of those who are represented to have been personally acquainted with him—aye! some of his own brethren in the flesh, children in the same household, children of the same mother—had the temerity to question the tenableness of his claim to a divine emanation. And when we extend our researches to other countries, we find this claim, so far from being conceded, is denied and contested by whole nations upon other grounds. It is met and confronted by rival claims.

Upon this ground hundreds of millions of the established believers in divine revelation—hundreds of millions of believers in the divine character and origin of religion—eject the pretentions set up for Jesus Christ. They admit both a God and a Savior, but do not accept Jesus of Nazareth as being either. They admit a Messiah, but not the Messiah; these nations contend that the title is misplaced which makes "the man Christ Jesus" the Savior of the world. They claim to have been honored with the birth of the true Savior among them, and defend this claim upon the ground of priority of date. They aver that the advent of their Messiahs were long prior to that of the Christians', and that this circumstance adjudicates for them a superiority of claim as to having had the true Messiah born upon their soil.

It is argued that, as the story of the incarnation of the Christians' Savior is of more recent date than that of these oriental and ancient religions (as is conceded by Christians themselves), the origin of the former is thus indicated and foreshadowed as being an outgrowth from, if not a plagiarism upon the latter—a borrowed copy, of which the pagan stories furnish the original. Here, then, we observe a rivalship of claims, as to which of the remarkable personages who have figured in the world as Saviors, Messiahs, and Sons of God, in different ages and different countries, can be considered the true Savior and "sent of God" or whether all should be, or the claims of all rejected.

For researches into oriental history reveal the remarkable fact that stories of incarnate Gods answering to and resembling the miraculous character of Jesus Christ have been prevalent in most if not all the principal religious heathen nations of antiquity; and the accounts and narrations of some of these deific incarnations bear such a striking resemblance to that of the Christian Savior—not only in their general features, but in some cases in the most minute details, from the legend of the immaculate conception to that of the crucifixion, and subsequent ascension into heaven—that one might almost be mistaken for the other.

More than twenty claims of this kind—claims of beings invested with divine honor (deified)—have come forward and presented themselves at the bar of the world with their credentials, to contest the verdict of Christendom, in having proclaimed Jesus Christ, "the only son, and sent of God:" twenty Messiahs, Saviors, and Sons of God, according to history or tradition, have, in past times, descended from heaven, and taken upon themselves the form of men, clothing themselves with human flesh, and furnishing incontestable evidence of a divine origin, by various miracles, marvelous works, and superlative virtues; and finally these twenty Jesus Christs (accepting their character for the name) laid the foundation for the salvation of the world, and ascended back to heaven.

1. Chrishna of Hindostan.

2. Budha Sakia of India.

3. Salivahana of Bermuda.

4. Zulis, or Zhule, also Osiris and Orus, of Egypt.

5. Odin of the Scandinavians.

6. Crite of Chaldea.

7. Zoroaster and Mithra of Persia.

8. Baal and Taut, "the only Begotten of God," of Phenicia.

9. Indra of Thibet.

10. Bali of Afghanistan.

11. Jao of Nepaul.

12. Wittoba of the Bilingonese.

13. Thammuz of Syria.

14. Atys of Phrygia.

15. Xamolxis of Thrace.

16. Zoar of the Bonzes.

17. Adad of Assyria.

18. Deva Tat, and Sammonocadam of Siam.

19. Alcides of Thebes.

20. Mikado of the Sintoos.

21. Beddru of Japan.

22 Hesus or Eros, and Bremrillah, of the Druids.

23. Thor, son of Odin, of the Gauls.

24. Cadmus of Greece.

25. Hil and Feta of the Mandaites.

26. Gentaut and Quexalcote of Mexico.

27. Universal Monarch of the Sibyls.

28. Ischy of the Island of Formosa.

29. Divine Teacher of Plato.

30. Holy One of Xaca.

31. Fohi and Tien of China.

32. Adonis, son of the virgin Io of Greece.

33. Ixion and Quirinus of Rome.

34. Prometheus of Caucasus.

35. Mohamud, or Mahomet, of Arabia.

These have all received divine honors, have nearly all been worshiped as Gods, or sons of God; were mostly incarnated as Christs, Saviors, Messiahs, or Mediators; not a few of them were reputedly born of virgins; some of them filling a character almost identical with that ascribed by the Christian's bible to Jesus Christ; many of them, like him, are reported to have been crucified; and all of them, taken together, furnish a prototype and parallel for nearly every important incident and wonder-inciting miracle, doctrine and precept recorded in the New Testament, of the Christian's Savior. Surely, with so many Saviors the world cannot, or should not, be lost.

We have now presented before us a two-fold ground for doubting and disputing the claims put forth by the Christian world in behalf of "Our Lord and Savior Jesus Christ." In the first place, allowing the question to be answered in the affirmative as to whether he was really a Savior, or supernatural being, or more than a mere man, a negative answer to which seems to have been sprung (as previously intimated) at the very hour of his birth, and that by his kindred, his own nearest relatives; as it is declared, "his own brethren did not believe on him"—a skepticism which has been growing deeper and broader from that day to this.

And now, upon the heel of this question, we find another formidable query to be met and answered, viz.: Was he (Christ) the only Savior, seeing that a multitude of similar claims are now upon our council-board to be disposed of?

We shall, however, leave the theologians of the various religious schools to adjust and settle this difficulty among themselves. We shall leave them to settle the question as best they can as to whether Jesus Christ was the only son and sent of God—"the only begotten of the Father," as John declares him to be (John i. 14)—in view of the fact that long prior to his time various personages, in different nations, were invested with the title "Son of God," and have left behind them similar proofs and credentials of the justness of their claims to such a title, if being essentially alike—as we shall prove and demonstrate them to be—can make their claims similar.

We shall present an array of facts and historical proofs, drawn from numerous histories and the Holy Scriptures and bibles appertaining to these various Saviors, and which include a history of their lives and doctrines, that will go to show that in nearly all their leading features, and mostly even in their details, they are strikingly similar.

A comparison, or parallel view, extended through their sacred histories, so as to include an exhibition presented in parallels of the teachings of their respective bibles, would make it clearly manifest that, with respect to nearly every important thought, deed, word, action, doctrine, principle, precept, tenet, ritual, ordinance or ceremony, and even the various important characters or personages, who figure in their religious dramas as Saviors, prophets, apostles, angels, devils, demons, exalted or fallen genii—in a word, nearly every miraculous or marvelous story, moral precept, or tenet of religious faith, noticed in either the Old or New Testament Scriptures of Christendom—from the Jewish cosmogony, or story of creation in Genesis, to the last legendary tale in St. John's "Arabian Nights" (alias the Apocalypse)—there is to be found an antitype for, or outline of, somewhere in the sacred records or bibles of the oriental heathen nations, making equal if not higher pretention to a divine emanation and divine inspiration, and admitted by all historians, even the most orthodox, to be of much more ancient date; for while Christians only claim, for the earthly advent of their Savior and the birth of their religion, a period less than nineteen hundred years in the past, on the contrary, most of the deific or divine incarnations of the heathen and their respective religions are, by the concurrent and united verdict of all history, assigned a date several hundred or several thousand years earlier, thus leaving the inference patent that so far as there has been any borrowing or transfer of materials from one system to another, Christianity has been the borrower.

And as nearly the whole outline and constituent parts of the Christian system are found scattered through these older systems, the query is at once sprung as to whether Christianity did not derive its materials from these sources—that is, from heathenism, instead of from high heaven—as it claims.

19

CHAPTER II. MESSIANIC PROPHECIES

NEARLY all religious history is prophetic of the coming of Saviors, Messiahs, Redeemers, and virgin-born Gods. Most religious countries, and more than a score of religious systems, had a standing prophecy that a divine deliverer would descend from heaven and relieve them from their depressed state, and ameliorate their condition. And in most cases that prophecy was believed to have been fulfilled by the birth of a being, who, as he approached the goal of moral and intellectual manhood exhibited such remarkable proof of superiority of mind as to be readily accepted as the promised Messiah.

We can only find room for a few citations and illustrations in proof of this statement. Many texts have been hunted out and marked in the Christian bible, by interested priests, as prophetic of the coming and mission of Christ. But a thorough, candid, and impartial investigation will convince any reader that *none of these texts* have the remotest allusion to Christ, nor were they intended to have. On the contrary, most of them refer to events already past. The others are the mere ebullitions of pent-up feelings hopefully prayerful in their anticipation of better times, but very indefinite as to the period and the agencies or means in which, or by which, the desired reformation was to be brought about. A divine man was prayed for and hopefully expected. But no such being as Jesus Christ is anticipated, or alluded to, or dreamed of, by the prophecies. And it requires the most unwarrantable distortion to make one text refer to him.

But this perversion has been wrought on many texts. We will cite one case in proof. In Isaiah's "famous prophecy" so-called, the phrase "Unto us a child is born" (Isa. ix. 6), the context clearly shows, refers to the prophet's own child, and the past tense, "is born," is an evidence the child was then born. And the title "Mighty God," found in the text, Dr. Beard shows should have been translated "the Mighty Hero," thus proving it has no reference to a God. And "the Everlasting Father" should have been rendered, according to this Christian writer, "the Father of the Everlasting Age." And other texts often quoted as prophecies by biased Christian writers, the doctor proves, are erroneously translated, and have no more reference to Christ than to Mahomet.

It is true the Jews, in common with other nations, cherished strong anticipations of the arrival of a Mighty Deliverer amongst them; and this august personage some of them supposed would be a God, or a God-man (a demi-God). Hence, such prophetic utterances as "Behold, a king shall reign in righteousness" (Isa. xxxii. i), "And all nations shall flow unto Zion" (Isa. ii. 2).

The Hindoo Budhists long previously indulged similar anticipations with respect to the triumph of their religion. Hence, their seers prophesied that at the end of the Cali Yug period, a divine child (Avatar, or Savior) would be born, who would understand the divine writings (the Holy Scriptures) and the sciences, without the labor of learning them. "He will supremely understand all things." "He will relieve the earth of sin, and cause justice and truth to reign everywhere. And will bring the whole earth into the acceptance of the Hindoo religion." And the Hindoo prophet Bala also predicted that a divine Savior would "become incarnate in the house of Yadu, and issue

20

forth to mortal birth from the womb of Devaci (a Holy Virgin), and relieve the oppressed earth of its load of sin and sorrow." Much more similar language may be found in their holy bible, the Vedas. Colonel Wilford tells us the advent of their Savior Chrishna occurred in exact fulfillment of prophecy found in their sacred books.

And the Chinese bible also contains a number of Messianic prophecies. In one of the five volumes a prophecy runs thus: "The Holy one, when he comes, will unite in himself all the virtues of heaven and earth. By his justice the world will be established in righteousness. He will labor and suffer much,.... and will finally offer up a sacrifice worthy of himself," i. e., worthy of a God. And a singular animal, called the Kil n (signifying the Lamb of God), was seen in the yard, with a stone in its mouth, on which was inscribed a prophecy of the event. And when the young God (Chang-ti) was born, in fulfilment of this prophecy, heavenly music, and angels and shepherds attended the scene. (See "History of China," by Martinus; also Halde's "History of China.")

We will also give place to a Messianic prophecy of Persia. Mr. Faber, an English writer, in his "History of Idolatry," tells us that Zoroaster prophetically declared, that "A virgin should conceive and bear a son, and a star would appear blazing at midday to signalize the occurrence." "When you behold the star," said he to his followers, "follow it whithersoever it leads you. Adore the mysterious child, offering him gifts with profound humility. He is indeed the Almighty Word which created the heavens. He is indeed your Lord and everlasting Ring" (Faber, vol. ii. p. 92). Abulfaragius, in his "Historia Dynastarium," and Maurice, in his "Indian Skeptics Refuted," both speak of this prophecy, fulfilled, according to Mr. Higgins, by the advent of the Persian and Chaldean God Josa. And Chalcidus (of the second century), in his "Comments on the Times of Plato," speaks of "a star which presaged neither disease nor death, but the descent of a God amongst men, and which is attested by Chaldean astronomers, who immediately hastened to adore the newborn deity, and present him gifts."

We are compelled to omit, for the want of room, the notice of numerous Messianic prophecies found in the sacred writings of Egypt, Greece, Rome, Mexico, Arabia, and other countries, all of which tend to show that the same prophetic spirit pervaded all religious countries, reliable only to the extent it might have issued from an interior spiritual vision, or have been illuminated by departed spirits. And we find as much evidence that these pagan prophecies were inspired, and also fulfilled, as those found in Jew-Christian bible, thus reducing all to a common level. The possibility of the interior vision being expanded and illuminated by spiritual beings, so as to enable the possessor to forestall the occurrence of future events, we, however, by no means deny, since we have abundant proof of it in connection with the practical history of modern spiritualism. (See Chapter XXXIV, section 2).

CHAPTER III. PROPHECIES BY THE FIGURE OF A SERPENT

The Seed of the Woman Bruising the Serpent's Head.

"AND I will put enmity between thee and the woman, and between thy seed and her seed. It shall bruise thy head, and thou shall bruise his heel." (Gen. ill. 15.) This text is often cited by Christian writers and controversialists as prefiguring the mission of the Christian Savior, viz., the destruction of the serpent, alias the devil. St. John calls "the grand adversary of souls which deceiveth the whole world," "the dragon, the serpent, the devil, and Satan." (Rev. xii. 8.) The serpent, then, is the devil; that is, the dragon, the serpent, the devil and Satan are all one. The object of this chapter is to show the origin of the singular figure set forth in the first text quoted, and to prove that those Christian writers who assume it to be a revelation from heaven were profoundly ignorant of oriental history, as the same figure is found in several heathen systems of older date, as we will now cite the facts to prove.

Some of the saviors or demigods of Egypt, India, Greece, Persia, Mexico and Etruria are represented as performing the same drama with the serpent or devil. "Osiris of Egypt (says Mr. Bryant) bruised the head of the serpent after it had bitten his heel." Descending to Greece, Mr. Faber relates that, "on the spheres Hercules is represented in the act of contending with the serpent, the head of which is placed under his foot; and this serpent guarded the tree with golden fruit in the midst of the garden Hesperides"—Eden. (Origin of Idolatry, vol. i. p. 443.) "And we may observe," says this author, "the same tradition in the Phoenician fable of Ophion or Ophiones." (Ibid.) In Genesis the serpent is the subject of two legends. But here it will be observed that they are both couched in one.

Again, it is related by more than one oriental writer that Chrishna of India is represented on some very ancient sculptures and stone monuments with his heel on the head of a serpent. Mr. Maurice, in his Indian Antiquities, vol. ii., speaks of "Chrishna crushing the head of a serpent with his foot," and pronounces the striking similarity of this story with that found in the Christian bible as "very mysterious." Another author tells us "The image of Chrishna is sculptured in the ancient temples of India, sometimes wreathed in the folds of a serpent which is biting his foot, and sometimes treading victoriously on the head of a serpent." (Prog. Rel. Ideas, vol. i.) In the Mexican Antiquities, vol. vi., we are told, "A messenger from heaven announced to the first woman created (Suchiquecul), that she should bear a son who should bruise the serpent's head, and then presented her with a rose." Here is the origin of the Genesis legend, the rose being the fruit of the tree of "the knowledge of good and evil." "The ancient Persians," says Volney, in his "Ruin of Empires," p. 169, "had the tradition of a virgin, from whom they predicted would be born, or would spring up, a shoot (a son) that would crush the serpent's head, and thus deliver the world from sin." And both the serpent and the virgin, he tells us, are represented imaginarily in the heavens, and pictured on their astronomical globes and spheres, as on those of the Romish Christian. (See Burritt's Geography of the Heavens.)

In the ancient Etrurian story, instead of "the seed of the woman" (the virgin), it is the woman herself who is represented as standing with one foot on the head of a serpent, which has the twig of an apple tree in its mouth to which an apple is suspended (the forbidden fruit), while its tail is twisted around a celestial globe, thus reminding us of St. John's dragon hauling down one-third of the stars with his tail. (See Rev. xii. 4.) In the ancient celestial diagram of the Etrurian, the head of the virgin is surmounted with a crown of stars—doubtless the same legend from which

St. John borrowed his metaphor of a "a woman with a crown of twelve stars on her head." (Rev. xiii.) "The *Regina Stellarum*" (Queen of the Stars), spoken of in some of the ancient systems appertains to the same fable. Also the tradition of Achilles of Greece being invulnerable in the heel, as related by Homer. The last clause of the first text quoted reads "*It* shall bruise thy head"—a very curious prophetic reference to the savior of the world, if the text refers to him, to represent him as being of the neuter gender, for the neuter pronoun *it* always refers to a thing without sex.

In the further exposition of the serpent tradition, we are now brought to notice, and will trace to its origin, the story of the original transgression and fall of man—two cardinal doctrines of the Christian religion. Like every other tenet of the Christian faith, we find these doctrines taught in heathen systems much older than Christianity, and whose antiquity antedates even the birth of Moses. We will first notice the Persian tradition. "According to the doctrine of the Persians," says the Rev. J. C. Pitrat, "Meshia and Meshiane, the first man and first woman, were pure, and submitted to Ormuzd, their maker. But Ahriman (the evil one) saw them, and envied them their happiness. He approached them under the form of a serpent, presented fruits to them, and persuaded them that he was the maker of man, of animals, of plants, and of the beautiful universe in which they dwelt. They believed it. Since that time Ahriman was their master. Their natures became corrupt, and this corruption infested their whole posterity." This story is taken from the Vandidatsade of the Persians, pp. 305 and 428.

The Indian or Hindoo story is furnished us by the Rev. Father Bouchat, in a letter to the bishops of Avranches, and runs thus: "Our Hindoos say the Gods tried by all means to obtain immortality. After many inquiries and trials, they conceived the idea that they would find it in the tree of life, which is the Chorcan (paradise). In fact they succeeded, and by eating once in a while of the fruits of that tree, they kept the precious treasure they so much valued. A famous snake, named Cheiden, saw that the tree of life had been found by the Gods of the second order. As probably he had been intrusted with guarding that tree, he became so angry because his vigilance had been deceived, that he immediately poured out an enormous quantity of poison, which spread over the whole earth." How much like this story is the story of St. John, "And the serpent cast out of his mouth water as a flood after the woman that he might cause her to be carried away of the flood!" (Rev. xii. 15.)

The idea of a snake or serpent inundating the earth from its mouth, as taught in both stories is so novel, and so far removed from the sphere of natural causes and possible events, that we are compelled to the conclusion that one is borrowed from the other, or both from a common original.

And as facts cited in other chapters prove beyond dispute that the Hindoo system, containing this story, extends in antiquity far beyond the time of Moses, the question is thus settled as to which system borrowed the story from the other.

Before closing the chapter, we wish to call the attention of the reader to the important fact that three out of four of the cardinal doctrines of the Christian faith are taught in the two heathen mythological stories of creation just presented, viz.:—

23

1. Original sin.

2. The fall of man caused by a serpent

3. The consequent corruption and depravity of the human race.

These doctrines, then, it must be admitted, are of heathen origin, and not, as Christians claim, "important truths revealed from heaven." For a historical exposition of the other cardinal doctrine of the Christian faith, viz., man's restoration by the atonement achieved through the crucifixion of a God, see Chapters xvi. and xxi.

CHAPTER IV. MIRACULOUS AND IMMACULATE CONCEPTION OF THE GODS

THE ancients very naturally concluded that an offspring of God (a son of God) should have a purer, higher and holier maternal origin than is incident to the lot of mortals, and this was to constitute one of the evidences of his emanation from the Deity—that is, of his supernatural or divine origin. He, as a matter of course, must not only have a different origin, but one in the highest degree superior and supernatural. He must not only be able to claim the highest *paternal* origin, but the highest *maternal* also. And on the part of the mother, a sexual connection with the great Potentate of heaven would evince for her offspring the very acme of superiority with respect to his origin, moral perfection and authority. That the Savior was born of a woman could not possibly be made a matter of concealment. But his paternal parentage was not so obvious and apparent to general observation, being cognizant alone to the mother. This circumstance furnished the most propitious opportunity to concoct the story that "The Most High" had condescended and descended to become both a father and a grandfather to a human being, or a being apparently human at least.

We say grandfather, because, if God (as the Christian bible itself frequently asserts, both directly and by implication) is father of the whole human family, then he was father to the maternal parent; so that her son, though deriving existence from him, would be his grandson as well as his son. Hence the corollary, *Jesus Christ was a grandson of God as well as a son of God*, and Jehovah both his father and grandfather.

Again, to make the origin and character of the God and Savior stand higher for purity, and partake in the highest degree of the miraculous, the impression must go abroad that he was born of a woman *while she was yet a maiden*—i. e., before she was contaminated by illicit association with the masculine sex. Hence, nearly all the saviors were reputedly born of virgins. And the process of birth, too, was out of the line of natural causes, in order to invest the character of the savior with the *ne plus ultra* of the miraculous.

24

And hence it is related of Jesus Christ (in an Apocryphal Gospel), of Chrishna of India, and other saviors, that they were born through the mother's side.

It is true our present canonical gospels are silent as to the manner of Christ's birth; but one of the Apocryphal gospels, which gives the matter in fuller detail, and whose authority in the earlier ages of the Christian church was not disputed, declares that the manner of his birth was as related above. And, besides, some of the early Christian fathers fully indorsed the story. The same is related in the pagan bibles of heathen Gods. The motives which originated the reports of the immaculate conception of the Saviors, it may be further remarked, were of a two-fold character:—

1. To establish their spotless origin (as the word immaculate means spotless.)

2. To make it appear that there was a Deific power and agency concerned in their conception.

And we may observe here that it is not the Saviors alone who are reported to have been ushered into tangible existence without a human father, but it is declared of beings known and acknowledged to be men, as Plato, Pythagoras, Alexander, Augustus and a number of others. Of Plato an author remarks, "He was born of Paretonia, and begotten of Apollo, and not Ariston, his father." Both the manner, or process, and the source of the influence by which the Gods and Saviors were generated, seem to have been different in different countries, though the idea of "overshadowing with the Holy Ghost" seems to have been most current. Mr. Higgins says that "the Supreme First Cause was generally believe to overshadow, or in some other mysterious manner to impregnate, the mother of the God, or personage" (vol. i. 378). We are told that Pythais, the mother of Pythagoras, five hundred and fifty years B. C., conceived by a spectre or ghost (of course the Holy Ghost) of the God Apollo, or God Sol.

In Malcolm's "History of Persia" (vol. i. 494) the author tells us that "Zoroaster was born of an immaculate conception by a ray from the Divine Reason." The immaculate conception of Juno of Greece is thus described by the poet:—

```
"Juno touched the flower;
Its wondrous virtues such,
She touched it, and grew pregnant at the touch;
Then entered Thrace—the Propontic shore;
When mistress of her touch,
God Mars she bore."
```

This case may certainly be set down as the *ne plus ultra* of etiquette with respect to sexual commerce or purity of conception. The sweet odor of an expanded flower, we are here taught, is adequate to the conception and production of a God. Here we have "the immaculate conception" in the superlative degree, and while much more beautiful and grand it cannot be more senseless or unreasonable than the conception by a ghost. It proves at least that the doctrine of the immaculate conception is of very ancient date. And this fastidious maiden lady and immaculate virgin, Juno, not only conceived the God Mars by the touch of a flower, but she also (so the story reads) conceived Vulcan by being overshadowed by the wind—exactly a parallel case with that of the virgin Mary, as we find that ghost, in the original, means wind. Thus we observe that

25

Vulcan, long before Jesus Christ, was "born of the Holy Ghost," i. e., both were conceived by the "Holy Wind." And the author of the "Perennial Calendar" speaks of the miraculous conception of Juno Jugulis, "the blessed virgin queen of heaven," and describes it as falling on the second of February, the very day which the early Christians celebrated with a festival, as being the date of the conception of the "ever Blessed Virgin Mary."

Of the ancient Mexicans, it is said "they had the immaculate conception, the crucifixion, and the resurrection after three days." (Mex. Antiq., vol. i.) And in an ancient work called "Codex Vaticanus," the immaculate conception is spoken of as a part of the history of Quexalcote, the Mexican Savior. "Suchiquecal," says the Mexican Antiquities, "was called the Queen of Heaven. She conceived a son without connection with a man"—a very obvious case of immaculate conception.

Alvarez Semedo, in his "History of China," page 89, speaks of a sect in that country who worshiped a Savior known as Xaca, who was reputedly conceived of his mother, Maia, by a white elephant, which she saw in her sleep, and "for greater purity, she brought him forth from one of her sides." Colonel Tod, of England, tells us in his "History of the Rajahs," page 57, that Yu, the first Chinese monarch, was conceived by his mother being struck with a star while traveling.

In the case of Christ, it will be recollected, the star did not appear till after his birth. But here the star is the author and agent of the conception.

According to Ranking's "History of the Moguls," page 178, Tamerlane's mother (of Bermuda) professedly conceived by having had sexual intercourse with "the God of Day." The mother of Ghengis Khan, of Tartary, "being too modest to claim that she was the mother of the son of God, said only that he was the *son of the sun*." (History of Mogul, page 65.)

Both Julis and Osiris of Egypt are spoken of by some authors as having been honored with a divine immaculate conception—the former being the son of the beautiful virgin Cronis Celestine, and "begotten by the Father of all Gods."

Both Budha and Chrishna, of India, are reported as having been immaculately conceived. The mother of the latter (God) was (as the Hindoo Holy Book declares) overshadowed by the Supreme God, Brahma, while the spirit-author of the conception (that is, the Holy Ghost) was Naraan. The mother of Apollonius of Cappadocia, who was cotemporary with Jesus Christ (according to his history by Philostratus)—and his (Apollonius') disciple Damis testifies to the same effect gave birth to this God and rival Savior of Jesus Christ, by having been previously "overshadowed" by the supreme God Proteus. For the corporeal existence and earthly career of Augustus Caesar, the world has ostensibly to acknowledge itself indebted to the "overshadowing" influence and generating power of Jove, by whose divine influence he was immaculously conceived in the temple of Apollo, according to the statement of Nimrod, his biographer. The virgin mother Shing-Mon of China furnishes another case of immaculate conception. Possessing a sensibility too lofty and too refined to descend to the ordinary routine of the world, she gave birth to the God Yu from previous conception by a water lily. This case, with respect to the degree of procreative delicacy and refinement evinced, may be classed with that of Juno of Greece. Here it may be noted as a curious circumstance, that several of the virgin mothers of Gods and great men are specifically represented as going ten months between conception and delivery. The mothers of Hercules, Sakia, Guatama, Scipio, Arion, Solomon and Jesus Christ may be mentioned as samples of this character. This tradition probably grew out of the established belief in the ten sacred cycles which constitute the great prospective and portentous millennial epoch, as described in Chapter XXX. Arion, mentioned above, is represented as being both miraculously and immaculously conceived by the Gods in the citadel of Byrsa.

In view of the foregoing facts, drawn from accredited histories, the reader will readily concede that the tradition of the miraculous conceptions of Gods (sons of God), Saviors and Messiahs was very prevalent in the world at a very ancient period of time, and long before the mother of Jesus was "overshadowed by the Most High." Indeed, says Mr. Higgins, "the belief in the immaculate conception extended to every nation in the world." And Grote, referring to Greece, makes the remarkable declaration, that "the furtive pregnancy of young women, often by a God, is one of the most frequently recurring incidents in the legendary narratives of the country." And we find that both the prevalency and great antiquity of the doctrine of the immaculate conception among the heathen is conceded by Christian writers themselves (of former ages) in their attempts to find arguments and commendatory precedents to justify their own belief in the doctrine. For proof of this, we need only cite the Christian writer Mr. Bailey, who remarks, "What I have said of St. Augustine is applicable also to Origen and Lactanius, who have endeavored to persuade us of the immaculate virginity of the mother of Jesus Christ by the example of similar events stored by the heathen." Here we have several Christian authorities cited by another writer, also a Christian, for placing the doctrine of the immaculate conception among the heathen legends in ages long anterior to Christ.

With respect to the degree of credence to be attached to the story of the immaculate conception of the mother of Jesus, it need only be observed that there was no other person concerned in the transaction but herself who could possess positive, absolute knowledge of the parentage. And she, let it be noted, settles the matter forever, by virtually affirming that Joseph was his father in the declaration addressed to Jesus when she found him in the temple, "*I and thy father* have sought thee sorrowing." (Luke ii. 48.) No one will dispute that the father here spoken of was Joseph, which amounts to a positive declaration by the mother, that Joseph was Jesus' father.

IMMACULATE CONCEPTION AND MIRACULOUS BIRTH OF THE CHRISTIAN SAVIOR.

The following considerations exhibit some of the numerous absurdities involved in the story of the miraculous birth of Jesus Christ.

1. The evangelical narratives show that Christ himself did not claim to have a miraculous birth. He did not once allude to such an event; while if, as Christians claim, it is the principal evidence of his deityship, he certainly would have done so.

2. His paternal genealogy, as made out by Matthew and Luke, completely disproves the story of his miraculous conception by a virgin. For they both trace his lineage through Joseph, which they

could not do only on the assumption that Joseph was his father. This, of course, disproves his sireship by the Holy Ghost, ergo, the miraculous conception. It is the lineage and parentage of Joseph, and not Mary, that is given in tracing back his ancestry to the royal household—a fact which completely overthrows the story of his miraculous birth.

3. And the fact that his *own disciple* (Philip) declared him to be the *son of Joseph*, and that several texts show that it was the current impression, is still further confirmation of the conclusion.

4. We find the story of the immaculate conception resting entirely upon the slender foundation comprised in the legends of an angel and a dream. We are told that Mary got it by an angel, and Joseph by a dream. And through these sources we have the whole groundwork and foundation of the story of the divinity of Jesus Christ.

5. It should be noticed that we have neither Joseph's nor Mary's report of these things, but only Matthew and Luke's version of the affair. And we are not informed that either of them ever saw or conversed with Joseph or Mary on the subject. It is probable they got it from Dame Rumor, with her thousand tongues.

6. If Christ were a miraculously born God, is it possible his mother would have reproved him for misconduct when she found him in the temple, as she must have known his character?

7. If Mary was miraculously conceived, why was the important secret kept so long from Joseph? Why did she keep the "wool drawn over his eyes" till an angel had to be sent from heaven to let him into the secret?

8. If she were a virtuously-minded woman, why did she thus attempt to deceive him?

9. Why did not God inform Joseph by "inspiration" instead of employing the roundabout way of sending an angel to do it?

10. We are told that "Mary was found with child of the Holy Ghost." But as we are not informed who found it out, or who made the discovery, or how it was made, is it not thus left in a very suspicious aspect?

11. As the whole affair seems to have been based on dreams, and was carried on through dreams, and has no better foundation than dreams, why should we consider it entitled to any better credit than similar stories found in works on heathen mythology?

12. And would it not prove that Christianity is rather a dreamy religion?

13. Should not the astounding and incredible report of the birth of a God be based on a better foundation than that of dreams and angels and the legends of oriental mythology, to entitle it to the belief of an intelligent and scientific age?

14. Or can any man of science entertain for a moment the superlative solecism of an Infinite God by any special act "overshadowing" a finite human female, especially as modern science teaches us that God is both male and female, and as much one as the other?

15. As history teaches us the ancient orientalists believed that sexual commerce is sinful and contaminating to the child thus begotten and born, and hence had their incarnate Gods sent into the world through human virgins, can any unbiased mind resist the conviction that this is the source of the origin of the story of Christ's immaculate conception?

16. And finally, if it were necessary for Christ to come into the world in such a way as to avoid the impure channel of human conception and parturition, why did he not descend directly from heaven in person? Why could he not "descend on the clouds" by his first advent, as the bible says he will do when he makes his second advent?

17. Would not this course have furnished a hundred fold more convincing proof and demonstration of his divine power and divine attributes than the ridiculous story and inscrutable mystery of the divine conception, which is not susceptible of either investigation or proof?

CHAPTER V. VIRGIN MOTHERS AND VIRGIN-BORN GODS

THE report in authentic history of a case of a virtuous woman giving birth to a child with the usual form, and possessing the usual characteristics of a human being, and who should testify she had no male partner in the conception, might in an age of miracles and ignorance of natural law, be believed with implicit credulity. But in an age of intelligence, when the keys of science have unlocked the sacred shrines and hallowed vaults of sacerdotal mysteries, and modern researches of history have laid bare the fact that most ancient religious countries abound in reports of this character, a profound and general skepticism must be the result, and a total rejection of their truth by all men of science and historic intelligence.

Many are the cases noted in history of young maidens claiming a paternity for their male offspring by a God.

In Greece it became so common that the reigning king issued an edict, decreeing the death of all young women who should offer such an insult to deity as to lay to him the charge of begetting their children. The virgin Alcmene furnishes a case of a young woman claiming God as the father of her offspring, when she brought forth the divine Redeemer Alcides, 1280 years B. C. And Ceres, the virgin mother of Osiris, claimed that he was begotten by the "father of all Gods." Mr. Kenrick tells us the likeness of this virgin mother, with the divine child in her arms, may now be seen represented in sculpture on some of the ancient, ruined temples of that ruined empire. And Mr. Higgins makes the broad declaration that "the worship of this virgin mother, with her God-begotten child, prevailed everywhere." This author also quotes Mr. Riquord as saying, this son of God "was exhibited in effigy, lying in a manger, in the same manner the infant Jesus was afterward laid in the cave at Bethlehem." Mr. Higgins further testifies that the worship of this virgin God-mother (that is, the God and the mother) is of very ancient date and universal prevalence in all the eastern countries, as is proved by sculptured figures bearing the marks of great age.

In corroboration of this statement we might cite many cases, if our space would permit, from the religious records of India, Egypt, Persia, Greece, Rome, Mexico, Thibet, etc. Maia, mother of Sakia and Yasoda of Chrishna; Celestine, mother of the crucified Zulis; Chimalman, mother of Quex-alcote; Semele, mother of the Egyptian Bacchus, and Minerva, mother of the Grecian Bacchus; Prudence, mother of Hercules; Alcmene, mother of Alcides; Shing-Mon, mother-of Yu, and Mayence, mother of Hesus, were all as confidently believed to be pure, holy and chaste virgins, while giving birth to these Gods, sons of God, Saviors and sin-atoning Mediators, as was Mary, mother of Jesus, and long before her time.

Mr. Higgins remarks that the mother was still held to be a virgin, even after she had given birth to other children besides the deity-begotten bantling, which furnishes another striking parallel to the history of Mary, as she was still called a virgin after she had given birth to Jesus and his brothers James and John. And it is an incident worth noticing here, that, in the case of Mayence, virgin-mother of the God-sired Hesus of the Druids, the ancient traditions of the country, more than two thousand years old, represent her body as being enveloped in light, and a crown of twelve stars upon her head, corresponding exactly to the apocalyptic figure described by the mystagogue, St. John, in the twelfth chapter of his Revelation. She is also represented with her foot on the head of a serpent, according to Davie's "Universal Etymology." (Vide the case of the seed of the woman bruising the serpent's head, Gen. iii. 15.)

Auguste Nichols tells us, in his "Philosophical Essays on Christianity," that Io is called, in Eschylus, "the Chaste Virgin," and her son "the Son of God." (For other similar cases, see Guigne's History of the Huns.) Gonzales informs us he found on an ancient temple in India the Latin inscription *Patiuro virginis*, "the virgin about to bring forth." And similar inscriptions have been found on pagan temples in the country of the ancient Gauls. (For proof, see Riquord's Theology of the Ancient Gauls, Chapter X.) "He who hath ears to hear, let him hear," and treasure up these facts. According to Chinese history there were two beings—Tien and Chang-Ti—worshiped in that country as Gods more than twenty-five hundred years ago, born of virgins "who knew no man." The mother of the mighty and the almighty God Hercules, we are told, "knew only Jove."

If history and tradition, then, are to be credited, God had many "well beloved sons," born of pious and holy virgins, besides Jesus Christ. And some of them are represented as being his "only begotten," and others his "first begotten," sons. And all these cases appear to be equally as well authenticated as the story of Jesus Christ. All stand upon a level, the same kind and the same amount of evidence being offered in each case.

Here we will note it as a curious circumstance, that several of the above-named Saviors are represented as being black, Jesus Christ included with this number.

There is as much evidence that the Christian Savior was a black man, or at least a dark man, as there is of his being the son of the Virgin Mary, or that he once lived and moved upon the earth. And that evidence is the testimony of his disciples, who had nearly as good an opportunity of knowing what his complexion was as the evangelists, who omit to say anything about it. In the pictures and portraits of Christ by the early Christians, he is uniformly represented as being black. And to make this the more certain, the red tinge is given to the lips; and the only text in the Christian bible quoted by orthodox Christians, as describing his complexion, represents it as being black. Solomon's declaration, "I am black, but comely, O ye daughters of Jerusalem" (Sol. i. 5), is often cited as referring to Christ. According to the bible itself, then, Jesus Christ was a black man.

Let us suppose that, at some future time, he makes his second advent to the earth, as some Christians anticipate he will do, and that he comes in the character of a sable Messiah, how would he be received by our negro-hating Christians, of sensitive olfactory nerves? Would they worship a negro God? Let us imagine he enters one of our fashionable churches, with his "rough and ready" linsey-woolsey, seamless garment on, made of wild sea-grass, thus presenting a very forbidding appearance, and what would be the result? Would the sexton show him to a seat? Would he not rather point to the door, and exclaim, "Get out of here; no place here for niggers?" What a ludicrous series of ideas is thus suggested by the thought that Jesus Christ was a "darkey."

And the tradition of divine Saviors being born of undefiled and undeflowered virgins has an astronomical chapter we must not omit to notice. The virgin, with her God-begotten child, was pictured imaginarily in the heavens from time immemorial. They are represented on the Hindoo zodiac, at least three thousand years old, and on the ancient Egyptian planispheres. And if you will examine "Burritt's Geography of the Heavens," you will find the infant God-son (the sun) is represented as being born into a new year on the 25th of December (the very date assigned for Christ's birth), and may be seen rising over the eastern horizon, out of Mary, Maria, or Mare (the Latin for *sea*), with the infant God in her arms, being heralded and preceded by a bright star, which rises immediately preceding the virgin and her child, thus suggesting the text, "We have seen his star in the east, and have come to worship him." (Matt. ii.8.) Such facts led the learned Alphonso to exclaim, "The adventures of Jesus Christ are all depicted among the stars."

And such facts fasten the conviction on our mind that the stories of Gods cohabiting with young maids or virgins, and begetting other Gods, is of astrological origin—the story of Jesus Christ included. A critical research shows that astronomy and religion were interblended, interwoven, and confounded together at a very early period of time, so indissolubly, that it now becomes impossible to separate them.

CHAPTER VI. STARS POINT OUT THE TIME AND THE SAVIORS' BIRTH-PLACE

PROFUSION of evidence is furnished at every step along the devious pathway of sacred history, tending to show that all the systems of worship which have existed in the past have had a dip in "the halo of the heavenly orbs," and hence shine with a light derived from that source.

We find the stars acting directly a conspicuous part at the births of several of the Saviors, besides figuring in some cases by marking important events in their subsequent history.

Mr. Higgins remarks that "Among the ancients there seems to have been a very general idea that the arrival of Gods and great personages who were expected to come, would be announced by a star." And the cases of Abraham, Caesar, Pythagoras, Yu, Chrishna, and Christ, may be cited in proof of this declaration. A star figured either before or at the birth of each, according to their respective histories.

And it is a historical fact that should be noted here that the practice of calculating nativities by the stars was in vogue in the era and country of Christ's birth, and had been for a long period previously in various countries. "We have seen his star in the east, and have come to worship him." (Matt. ii. i.) Now mark, here, it was not *the star*, nor *a star*, but "*his star*;" thus disclosing its unmistakable astrological features. Mr. Faber (in his "Origin of Idolatry," vol. ii. p. 77) reports Zoroaster (600 B. C.) as prophetically announcing to "the wise men" of that country that a Savior would be born, "attended by a star at noonday." For a fuller exposition of this case see Chapter II.

In the history of the Hindoo Savior Chrishna, we are told that "as soon as Nared, who, having heard of his fame, had examined the stars, he declared him to be from God;" i. e., the Son of God' The Roman Calcidius speaks of "a wonderful star, presaging the descent of a God amongst men." (See Maurice's "Indian Skeptics Refuted," p. 62.) Quite suggestive of the star "apprising the wise men" of Christ's descent from above. And a star is said to have foretokened the birth of the Roman Julius Cæsar. The Chinese God Yu was not only heralded by a star, but conceived and brought to mortal birth by a star.

In Numbers xxiv. 17, it is declared "There shall come a star out of Jacob," etc. This is a text often quoted by Christian writers as having a prophetic reference to the Christian Messiah. But the same text declares further, "It shall destroy the children of Seth," a prediction which no rational interpretation can make apply to Jesus Christ. And then we find this star of Jacob or Judah (the same) represented on astronomical maps as a prominent star in the constellation Virgo (the Virgin), fancifully termed by the Hebrew Ephraim.

It was known in the Syrian, Arabian and Persian systems of astronomy as Messaeil (suggestive of Messiah), and was considered the ruling genius of the constellation.

The "star of Jacob," then, was simply a figure borrowed from the ancient pagan systems of astronomy, in which they fancifully represent a virgin rising with an infant Messiah (Messaeil) in her arms. Messaeil is, when analyzed, Messaeh-el (Messiah-God), and is found in the constellation Virgo, which commences rising at midnight, on the 25th of December, with this "star in the east" in her arms—the star which piloted "the wise men." The whole thing, then, is evidently an astronomical legend.

Albert the Great, in his "Book on the Universe," tells us, "The sign of the celestial virgin rises above the horizon, at the moment we find fixed for the birth of our Lord Jesus Christ." To which we will add the declaration of Sir William Drummond, who, in his "Odipus Judaicus," p. 27, most significantly remarks, "The anointed of *El* the male infant, who rises in the arms of Virgo, was called Jesus by the Hebrews,... and was hailed as the anointed king or Messiah"—still further proof of the astrological origin of the story.

Dr. Hales, in his "Chronology," calls Christ "the star of our salvation, the true Apollo, the sun of righteousness"—all of which are astronomical terms.

And here we may recur to the fact that some of the early inhabitants of the earth regarded a star as a thing of life, because it appeared to move, and acted as though controlled by a living spirit. And this fetchic idea we observe lurking amongst the borrowed orientalisms of the Jewish Old Testament. The representation of the morning stars joining in a chorus and singing together (see Job xxxviii. 9), is an instance of this kind of fetchic conception.

And then we find a much stronger and more conclusive case in the New Testament, where Matthew represents a star as breaking loose from its orbit, and traveling some millions of miles, in order to stand over the young child Jesus, as he lay amongst the oxen and asses in a stable. (See Matt. ii. 7.) Wonderfully accommodating star indeed! How did its inhabitants feel while thus traveling with the velocity of lightning? This achievement would not only require life, but an active intelligence, on the part of the star, as it is represented as being an act of the planet itself.

"All nations," says Mr. Higgins, "once believed that the planetary bodies or their inhabitants controlled the affairs of men, and even their births." Hence the cant phrases, "My stars," "He is ill-starred," etc., in use then, and still in use at the present day. The good or ill luck of a person was attributed to the good or evil stars which it was believed ruled at the hour of his birth.

We find a counterpart to the story of Matthew's traveling star in Virgil's writings, who declares (60 B. C.) that a star guided Æneas in a journey westward from Troy. In the days of Pliny (see his "Natural History," Book II.), the people of Rome fancied they saw a God in a star or comet in the form of a man. The Apocryphal book of Seth relates that a star descended from heaven and lighted on a mountain, in the midst of which a divine child was seen bearing a cross. Christ betrays the same ignorance of astronomy, when he speaks of "the stars falling from heaven to the earth." (See Matt. xxiv. 29.) For if there could be any falling in the case, the falling would be in the other direction, and the earth would fall to the stars, as larger bodies always attract smaller ones.

As shown above, the stupendous orbs of night were represented by Jew, Pagan and Christian as breaking away from their orbits, and running hither and thither, like a fly on a ceiling, or a ball from a sky-rocket, being regarded as mere jack-a-lanterns, that could appear anywhere at any time creative fancy might dictate or require; while science teaches that the stars are stupendous orbs, some of them a thousand times larger than the planet on which we live, and that they could not depart one rod from their accustomed orbits without breaking up the whole planetary system, and destroying the universe.

33

And then observe the absurdity in Matthew's story, which teaches that the wise men followed the star in the east, when they, coming from the east, were, as a matter of course, traveling westward, which would place the star to their backs. That must be a *sui generis* pilot or guide which follows after, instead of going before. Omitting further citations from history, we will only observe further that the ancient Hindoos, Egyptians, Chaldeans, Syrians, Mexicans, etc., took great account of stars, and employed them on all important occasions, especially on long journeys and at the births of Gods and great personages—a circumstance which aids in explaining the star chapter in the gospel history of Christ.

CHAPTER VII. ANGELS, SHEPHERDS AND MAGI VISIT THE INFANT SAVIORS

IN an age when Gods and men were on the most familiar terms, and when the character of one furnished a transcript for the other, and when each consented to act a reciprocal part towards elevating, honoring and glorifying the other, the birth of a God or Messiah was, as a matter of course, regarded as an event of sufficient importance to attract the attention of the great ones of the earth, and even the denizens of heaven also.

And hence we find it related in the history of several of the God-begotten Saviors of antiquity, that as soon as they were born into the world they were visited by "wise men from a distance" (or Magi, as they were called by the Persians and Brahmins). And in some cases they were likewise waited upon and adored by the neighboring shepherds; and even celestial spirits are reported in some instances as leaving their star-gilt homes to wing their way to the humble mansion, the rude tenement, containing a new-born God, that they might honor and adore "the Savior of men, the Savior of the world."

The sacred biographies of both Confucius and Christ furnish examples of the angel host forsaking their golden pavilions in the skies to pay their devoirs to a Deity-begotten bantling, sent down by the "Father of Mercies," to save a guilt-laden world. And in both cases the Magi are reported as assembling to present their offerings to the infant God.

In the case of Confucius (born 598 B. C.), it is declared, "Five wise men from a distance came to the house, celestial music was heard in the skies, and angels attended the scene." (See the Five Volumes.) Now let us observe how strikingly similar to this ancient legend, in each of the several characteristics, is the Christian story. Matthew (ii. 1) speaks of "wise men from the east" journeying to Jerusalem to visit the infant Christ, soon after his birth, amongst the mules and oxen in a stable, though he omits to state the number of itinerant adorers who presented themselves on the occasion.

The Persian story is more specific, as it gives the number of Magi who visited the young Savior of that country as five.

Luke (ii. 13) speaks of "a multitude of the heavenly host praising God," in gratulation of the birth of the Judean Savior. Now, when we bear in mind that one method of praising God, with the orientals, was by music, as we will at once observe that this is only another mode of proclaiming, as in the case of Confucius, that "celestial music was heard in the skies."

And "angels attended the scene" of Confucius' birth. So, likewise, Luke (ii. 15) relates that the angels, after rejoicing with the shepherds on the occasion of the birth of Christ, "went away into heaven."

How complete the parallel! and, but for the digression, and monopoly of space, we might trace it much further, and show that Confucius, like Christ, had twelve chosen disciples; that he was descended from a royal house of princes, as Christ from the royal house of David; that he, in like manner, retired for a long period from the noise and bustle of society into religious contemplative seclusion; that he inculcated the same Golden Rule of doing to others as we desire them to act toward us, and other moral maxims equal in importance to anything that can be found in the Christian Scriptures, etc.

But to the line of history. Other Saviors at birth, we are told, were visited by both angels and shepherds, also "wise men," at least great men. Chrishna, the eighth avatar of India (1200 B. C.) (so it is related by the "inspired penman" of their pagan theocracy) was visited by angels, shepherds and prophets (avatars). "Immediately after his birth he was visited by a chorus of devatas (angels), and surrounded by shepherds, all of whom were impressed with the conviction of his future greatness." We are informed further that "gold, frankincense and myrrh" were presented to him as offerings.

The well-known modern traveler, Mr. Ditson, who visited India but a few years since, uses the emphatic declaration, "In fact, as soon as Chrishna was born he was saluted by a chorus of devatas, or angels." In the evangelical narrative of the Christian Savior an angel is reported to have saluted his mother thus: "Hail, thou that art highly favored; the Lord is with thee; blessed art thou among women." (Luke, i. 28.) And in the next chapter the angel is reported as joining with "the heavenly host" in praising God. A similar report is found in the Hindoo bible (the Ramayana), appertaining to the mother of the eighth Savior, of whom it is declared "Brahma and Siva, with a host of attending spirits, came to her and sang, 'In thy delivery, O favored among women, all nations shall have cause to exult.'" And when the celestial infant (Chrishna) appeared (it is related in a subsequent chapter), "a chorus of heavenly spirits saluted him with hymns; the whole room was illuminated by his light, and the countenance of his father and mother shone with brightness and glory (by reflection), their understandings were opened so that they knew him to be the Preserver of the world, and they began to worship him." The last text here quoted brings to mind Luke xxiv. 45, which declares, "Then he (Christ) opened their (his parents) understandings."

The ninth avatar of India (Sakia) furnishes to some extent a similar parallel. According to the account of an exploration made in India, and published in the New York Correspondent of 1828, "There is on a silver plate in a cave in India an inscription stating that about the time of the advent of Budha Sakia (600 B. C.), a saint in the woods learned by inspiration that another avatar (Messiah or Savior) had appeared in the house of Rajah of Lailas. Learning which, he flew through the air to the place, and when he beheld the new-born Savior he declared him to be the great avatar (Savior or prophet), and that he was destined to establish a new religion"—the New Covenant Religion.

We next draw on the history of Greece. It is authentically related of Pythagoras (600 B.), that his fame having reached Miletas and neighboring cities, men renowned for wisdom (wise men) came to visit him. (Progress of Religious Ideas, vol. i.) In the Anacalypsis we are told that "Magi came from the East to offer gifts at Socrates' birth, bringing gold, frankincense and myrrh," the same kind of offering as that presented to the two divine infants Chrishna and Christ, according to their respective "inspired" biographers. (See Matt. ii. 4, and the Ramayana).

And the legend of Mithra, of Persia, might also be included in our category of comparison, if we had space for it. All the four Saviors last named (if Socrates may be called such) are reported as having been honored and enriched with aromatic offerings at their respective births. And we have the statement from Mr. Higgins, that the same assortment of spices (with the gold) constituted the materials offered as gifts to the sun, in Persia more than three thousand years ago; and likewise in Arabia near the same era. And it may be stated here, that an ancient historic account of Zoroaster of Persia (6,000 B. C., according to Pliny and Aristotle), speaks of his having also been visited by Magi, or "Magia," at the period of his earthly advent.

And it is, perhaps, well to note in this place, that "Magi" is the term used in the Apocryphal Gospels, to designate the "wise men" who visited Christ at birth; and that Magi, Magic and Magician are but variations of the same word, at least derivations from the same root, all suggesting a wisdom correlated to the Gods. Osiris, an incarnate deity of Egypt, we may cite as another case of an infantile God receiving signal honors and eclat at birth, as he was visited while yet in the cradle by a host of admiring adorers. "People flocked from all parts of the world to behold the heaven-born infant." Such a world-wide fame must have had the effect to attract, with the numerous crowd who thronged to see and worship him, no small number of "wise men."

At this stage of our historical exposition, we will suggest it as rather a singular circumstance that the divine Father, in his infinite wisdom, should have chosen to reveal the intelligence of the birth of his son Jesus Christ to a set of nomadic heathen idolaters hundreds of miles distant (though known as "wise men" because of their skill in astrology) before he made it known to his own "chosen people" (the Jews), who had ever regarded themselves as the recipients of his special favors. And perhaps it is still more singular that these pagan pedestrians should have been denominated "wise men," while men of God's own election, according to the Christian bible, were often stigmatized and denounced as "fools," a ".generation of vipers," etc. But it so happens that "human reason" finds many Incongruities in "Divine Revelations."

CHAPTER VIII. THE TWENTY-FIFTH OF DECEMBER
THE BIRTHDAY OF THE GODS.

DIVESTED of all explanation, the announcement of the fact that the time of the birth of many of the incarnated Gods and Saviors of antiquity was fixed at the same period, and this period the twenty-fifth of December, celebrated all over Christendom as the birthday of Jesus Christ, would sound marvelously strange, especially when it is noticed that this period formerly dated the birth of a new year—the birth of King Sol. And when we find that the ancient pagans were in the habit of celebrating this venerated twenty-fifth of December as the birthday of their Gods in the same manner Christians now celebrate it as the birthday of Christ, we are driven to admit that something more than mere fortuitous accident must be adduced to account for the coincidence.

According to Dr. Lightfoot, the temple of Jerusalem was employed in celebrating the birthday of a pagan God (Adonis) on the very night Christians assign for the birth of Christ. And Robert Taylor informs us that nearly all the nations of the East were once in the habit of rising at midnight to celebrate the birthday of their Gods, on the twenty-fifth of December. And to this statement Mr. Higgins adds that, 'At the first moment after midnight of the twenty-fourth of December, the ancient nations celebrated the accouchement of the queen of heaven and celestial virgin, and the birth of the God Sol, the infant Savior, and the God of Day."

Bacchus of Egypt, Bacchus of Greece, Adonis of Greece, Chrishna of India, Chang-ti of China, Chris of Chaldea, Mithra of Persia, Sakia of India, Jao Wapaul (a crucified Savior of ancient Britain), were all born on the twenty-fifth of December, according to their respective histories. Chrishna is represented to have been born at midnight on the twenty-fifth of the month Savarana, which answers to our December, and millions of his disciples celebrated his birthday by decorating their houses with garlands and gilt paper, and the bestowment of presents to friends. The Rev. Mr. Barret tells us, "It was once common for the women in Rome to perambulate the streets on the twenty-fifth of December, singing in a loud voice, 'Unto us a child is born this day.'"

The twenty-fifth of December, then, it will be observed, was marked as the birthday of the incarnated Gods, Saviors, and Sons of God, of many of the religious systems of antiquity, long prior to the birth of Christ And why his birth was fixed at that date is not hard to account for. According to the celebrated Christian writer Mr. Goodrich, the Christian world had no chronology and recorded no dates for several centuries after the commencement of the Christian era. (See History of all Nations, p. 23.) No event of their history was marked by dates for nearly four hundred years. Hence, the time of Christ's birth is altogether a matter of conjecture, as is also every other event noticed in the Christian bible. This is proved by the fact that the ablest Christian writers and chronologists differ to the extent of thirty-five hundred years in fixing the time of every event in the bible. A Mr. Kennedy presents us with three hundred different chronological systems, by different Christian writers, all founded on the bible, and proving that the date of its various events are inextricably involved in a labyrinth of doubt, darkness and uncertainty.

Relative to the time of Christ's birth, the "Encyclopedia Britannica" says: "Christians count one hundred and thirty-three contrary opinions of different authors concerning the year the Messiah appeared on earth—many of them celebrated writers." (Art. Chron.) Mark the declaration—one hundred and thirty-three different opinions as to the year Christ was born in; one hundred and thirty-three different years fixed on by different Christian chronologists as the time of the birth of the most extraordinary and most noted being, as Christians would have us believe, that ever appeared on earth. Think of an omnipotent God descending from heaven, performing astounding miracles, and presenting other proofs of being a God, and yet not one of the three hundred writers of that era take any notice of him, or make any note of his birth or any event of his life. This circumstance is of itself sufficient to banish and dissipate all faith in his divinity.

It is evident, from the facts just presented, that all systems of Christian chronology are founded on mere conjecture, and hence should be rejected as worthless. What event of Christ's life, then, can be accepted as certain, when no record was made of it till the time was forgotten, and none for at least half a century after the dawn of the Christian era, according to Dr. Lardner, when nearly all who witnessed it must have been dead?

We think the most reasonable conclusion in the case is, that Christ, instead of performing those Munchausen prodigies attributed to him—such as casting out devils, raising the dead, controlling the elements of nature, etc.—led such an ordinary, obscure life—excelling only in healing the sick and other noble deeds of charity and philanthropy—that he attracted but little notice by the higher classes, or by anybody but those of a similar turn of mind, till he was deified by Constantine, in the year 325 A. D. Hence, the time of his birth was not recorded, and was forgotten. Consequently, the twenty-fifth of December was selected as his birthday, because it was the birthday of other Gods, and because it was regarded by the heathen, from time immemorial, as the birthday of Sol, the glorious luminary of heaven, it being the period he is born again into a new year, and "commences again his journey and his life;" and because, also, this epoch was, as Sharon Turner informs us, in his "History of the Anglo-Saxons," the commencement of a new year up to the tenth century.

These events signalized the twenty-fifth of December, and made it a period of sufficient importance to lead the early Christians to suppose it must have been the birthday of their Messiah. Mosheim, however, confesses that the day or the year in which it happened "has not been fixed with certainty, notwithstanding the profound researches of the learned." So that it is still an open question as to when Christ was born. What day of the month, what year, or what century it took place in, is still unknown. This circumstance is, as before suggested, sufficient of itself to utterly prostrate all faith in the divine claims for Jesus Christ. What would be thought of a witness who should testify in court to the truth of an occurrence of which he did not know the year, or even the century, in which it took place, or who could come no nearer than one hundred and thirty-three years in fixing or guessing at the time. Would the court accept such testimony?

CHAPTER IX. TITLES OF THE SAVIORS

THE various deific titles applied to Jesus Christ in the New Testament are regarded by some Christian writers as presumptive evidence of his divinity. But the argument proves too much for the case; as we find the proof in history that many other beings, whom Christians regard as men, were honored and addressed by the same titles, such as God, Lord, Savior, Redeemer, Mediator, Messiah, etc.

The Hindoo Chrishna, more than two thousand years ago, was prayerfully worshiped as "God the Most High." His disciple Amarca once addressed him thus: "Thou art the Lord of all things, the God of the universe, the emblem of mercy, the bestower of salvation. Be propitious O most High God," etc. Here he is addressed both as Lord and God. He is also styled "God of Gods."

Adonis of Greece was addressed as "God Supreme," and Osiris of Egypt as "the Lord of Life." In Phrygia, it was "Lord Atys," as Christians say, "Lord Jesus Christ" Narayan of Bermuda was styled the "Holy Living God." The title 'Son of God" was so common in nearly all religious countries as to excite but little awe or attention.

St. Basil says, "Every uncommonly good man was called 'the Son of God.'" The "Asiatic Researches" says, "the Tamulese adored a divine Son of God," and Thor of the Scandinavians was denominated "the first-born Son of God" and so was Chrishna of India, and other demigods.

It requires, therefore, a wide stretch of faith to believe that Jesus Christ was in any peculiar sense "the Son of God," because so denominated, or "the only begotten Son of God," when so many others are reported in history bearing that title.

The title Savior is found in the legends of every religious country. So also God, Redeemer, and Mediator. "When a Mogul or Thibetan is asked who is Chrishna," says the Christian missionary Hue, "the reply is, instantly, 'the Savior of men.'" Budha was known as "the Savior, Creator and Wisdom of God," and Mithra as both Mediator and Savior, also as "the Redeemer," and Chrishna as "the Divine Redeemer," also "the Redeemer of the World." The terms Mediator and Intercessor were also frequently applied to him by his disciples. And both he and Quexalcote were hailed as "the Messiah." In short, most ancient religious nations were honored with or expected a Messiah.

Was Jesus Christ the "Lamb of God?" (John i. 9.) So was Chrishna styled "the Holy Lamb." The Mexicans, preferring a full-grown sheep, had their "Ram of God." The Celts had their "Heifer of God," and the Egyptians their "Bull of God." All these terms are ludicrous emblems of Deity, representing him as a quadruped, as the title "Lamb of God" does Jesus Christ, a term no less ludicrous than the titles of the pagan Gods as cited above.

And was Christ "the True Light?" (John i. 9.) So was Chrishna likewise called "the True Light," also "the Giver of Light," "the Inward Light," etc. Osiris was "the Redeemer of Light," and Pythagoras was both "Light and Truth." Apollonius was styled the "True Light of the World;" while Simon Magus was called "the Light of all Men."

Several nations had also their Christs. though in many cases the word is differently spelled. Chrest, the Greek mode of spelling Christ, may be found on several of the ancient tombstones of that country. The Christian writer Elsey, in his "Annotations of the Gospels" (vol. i. p. 25), spells the word Christ in this manner, Chrest The people of Loretto had a black Savior, called Chrest, or Christ. Lucian, in his "Philopatris," admits the ancient Gentiles had the name of Christ,

39

which shows it was a heathen title. The Chaldeans had their Chris, the Hindoos their Chrishna, the Greeks their Chrest, and the Christians their Christ, all, doubtless, derived from the same original root.

As for Jesus, it was a common name among the Jews long before the advent of Christ. Josephus refers to seven or eight persons by that name, as "Jesus, brother of Onias," "Jesus, son of Phabet," etc. Joshua in the Greek form, Jesus, was in still more common use.

Again, was Jesus Christ "the Alpha and Omega, the Beginning and the End?" so, likewise, Chrishna proclaimed, "I am the Beginning, the Middle, and the End." Osiris and Chrishna were both proclaimed "Judge of the Dead," as Jesus was "Judge of quick and dead." Isaiah represents the Father as proclaiming, "I am Jehovah; besides me there is no Savior." (Isa. xliii. 11.) With what consistency, then, can Christ be called "*the Savior*," if there is but *one Savior*, and that is the Father?

And other divine titles besides those above named—in fact, all those applied to Christ—are found used also in reference to the older pagan gods, and hence prove nothing.

ORIGIN OF THE TERMS MEDIATOR, INTERCESSOR, ETC.

Several causes contributed to originate a belief in the offices imaginarily assigned to divine God-descended Mediators, Redeemers, and Intercessors.

1. In the first place, the Great Supreme God was believed to be too far off and too aristocratic to be on familiar terms with his subjects, or at all times accessible to their prayers. Hence, was gotten up a "Mediator," or middle God, to stand midway between the Great Supreme and the people, and transmit messages one from the other, and thus serve as agent for both parties. Confirmatory of this statement is the declaration of Mamoides, in his "Guide to the Erring," that "the ancient Sabeans conceived the principal God, on account of his great distance, to be inaccessible; and hence, in imitation of the people in their conduct toward their king, who had to address him through a person appointed for the purpose, they imaginarily employed a middle divinity, who was called a Mediator, to present their claims to the Supreme God." Here the whole secret is out, the whole thing is explained, and we now understand why Christ is called a Mediator, Intercessor, "Advocate with the Father," etc.

2. Again, the Supreme God was supposed to be frequently angry with the people, and threatening to punish if not to destroy them. "I will punish the multitude." (Jer. xlvi. 25.) "I will destroy the people." (Ex. xxiii. 27). Hence, this middle divinity, this second person of the trinity, stepped in to plead and intercede on their behalf, being, as we must presume, a better-natured and more merciful being than the Father. And thus interceding, he received the titles of Intercessor and "Advocate with the Father." (1 John, ii. 1.)

3. The principal circumstance, however, which led to the conception of a divine Savior was the desire to find some way to continue in sin and wrong-doing and escape its natural and legitimate consequences; in other words, to evade the penalty. Hence, it came to be believed that people might run riot in sin, and plunge into the indulgence of their passions and their lusts, till the hour

of death approached, when they would have nothing to do but to ask forgiveness, and cast the burden of their sins and sufferings on the merits of "a crucified Savior and Redeemer," who "suffered once for all, that we might escape," and thus dodge the penalty for sin. It was, as Mr. Fleurbach expresses it, "A realized wish to be free from the laws of morality, and escape the natural consequences of wrong doing."

CHAPTER X. THE SAVIORS OF ROYAL DESCENT, BUT HUMBLE BIRTH

WE have the singular coincidence presented in the histories of several of the Saviors of their lineal descent through a line of kings or princes, and yet commencing their probationary life under the most humble and adverse circumstances—being born in stables, caves, and other inauspicious situations.

The story of their royal blood was calculated to add dignity to their characters, while their humble birth in the midst of poverty, and unmarked by ostentation, would evince their humility, meekness, condescension, and absence of pride, and thus proclaim a lesson of humility and resignation to their disciples and followers.

Here, seems to be plainly indicated the motives for assigning them to such a birth, and such a character.

Christ's lineal descent, it will be remembered, is professedly traced (though in a very zig-zag, disjointed manner) from the royal house of David. And yet his royal blood did not save him from the most ignoble and ignominious birth, and obscure exordium of his earth life.

A singular story, and yet a similar story, is told of the Indian Savior Chrishna, who was, according to the Rev. Mr. Allen (India, p. 379) of the royal house of Kousa, traced back through many generations. Yet, in order to teach the world a lesson of true humility, and administer a just reprehension to pride, he submitted to be born in a cave, amid the denizens of subterranean abodes. And here let it be noted, the best and most orthodox writers concede that while Christ is said to have born in a manger, that manger was in a cave. Mr. Fleetwood (a very popular Christian writer) testifies in this matter that "the Greek fathers generally agree that the place of Christ's birth was a cave." (Life of Christ, p. 568.) Then the coincidence in this respect between Christ and Chrishna may be set down as complete.

We have no means of learning how many of the Saviors were of royal blood, as the genealogy of some of them is not given. But those whose lineal descent is furnished us are almost uniformly traced to or evinced as springing from royal parentage, and practical humility—so far as it can be taught by an unostentatious birth—is a lesson taught by nearly all. Budha Sakia of Hindostan is directly traced through a royal pedigree.

Speaking on this point, one writer remarks: "Tradition affirms that his mother was betrothed to a rajah, and of course her son belonged to the same royal caste that Chrishna did during his existence on earth." (Prog. Rel. Ideas, vol, i. 84.)

"The Great Prophet" of Arabia (Mahomet) not only commenced his earthly career in a humble situation, but resembled Christ in having "nowhere to lay his head." It is said of the Great Prophet, "A cloak spread on the ground served him for a bed, and a skin filled with date leaves was his pillow." The genealogy of the God Yu (of China) is traced through a line of princes to a very remote origin, while his whole life was a lesson of practical humility, and proclaimed at every step, "This is the way; walk ye in it."

CHAPTER XI. CHRIST'S GENEALOGY

IN order to exalt the dignity and character of the Christian Messiah still higher than a mere claim for a divine origin paternally would have the effect to do, two of his assumed to be inspired biographers have set up for him a claim to a royal lineage through the maternal line.

Hence, they tell us that he descended from and through a line of kings embracing the house of David. But in presenting the names, and the number of generations, in their attempts to make out this royal distinction, this kingly exaltation of birth, they exhibit a most egregious bungle, and the most barefaced tissue of discrepancies. For they not only differ widely with each other in this matter, but differ with the Old Testament genealogy, and differ with those texts which give the maternal ancestry of Jesus.

Indeed, though varying as wide as the poles from each other, they both miss Jesus and arrive at Joseph in tracing down the generations from Abraham (unless we assume they intended to represent Joseph as being his father).

Luke, in his gospel, names and counts off forty-one generations from David to Joseph, though he had previously represented it as being forty-two; but Matthew says that "from Abraham to David are fourteen generations," but according to his own showing, and according to his own list of names, there are but thirteen. And then he tells us there are but fourteen generations from David to the carrying away into Babylon. BUt according to the Old Testament genealogy (see i Chron. iii.) there were eighteen.

And then the names comprised in the two genealogies of Matthew and Luke are so widely different from that found in Chronicles, as to set all analogy and agreement at defiance.

In fact, in their whole list of names, from David down to Joseph, they only come together twice. Their names are all different but two, that of Salathiel and Zorobabel, which names alone are found in both lists.

Matthew tells us that the son of David, through whom Joseph descended, was Solomon, but Luke says it was Nathan. The next name in Matthew's list is that of Roboam, but the corresponding name in Luke's list is Mattatha. Matthew's next name is Abia, which Luke gives as Menan, while Chronicles differs from both, and gives it as Abijah. Matthew says Joram begat Ozias, but Chronicles virtually declares Joram had no such son, although he had a great-great-grandson Uzziah. But Luke says, in effect, there was no such person in the genealogical tree, or family line, as either Joram, Ozias or Uzziah. Matthew says again, "Josias begat Jechonias and his brethren, about the time they were carried away to Babylon." (Matt. i. ii.)

But Chronicles declares that Jechonias was Jehoiakim's son, and not Josiah's, and that Josiah had no such son. And, besides, we learn, from 2 Kings xiii., that Josiah was killed eleven years before the exile to Babylon, and could not well beget a son after he had been defunct a tenth of a century.

Matthew, after naming twenty-four generations as filling out the line, and making it complete between David and Jacob, concludes by saying, "and Jacob begat Joseph, the husband of Mary."

But Luke, antecedent to spinning out his list to fourteen generations more than Matthew, i. e., making it fourteen generations longer, declares that "Joseph was the son of Heli." So that Joseph either had two fathers, Jacob and Heli, or Matthew or Luke, or both, were most egregiously mistaken, with all their "inspiration."

Again, Luke says that Salathiel was the son of Neri; but Chronicles says he was the son of Jechonias. And after Chronicles had registered Zorobabel as the son of Penniah, Matthew and Luke, assuming to become "wise above what was written," both declare that he was the son of Salathiel. They agree here in contradicting Chronicles, which is the only instance but one of their agreement in the whole list of progenitors from David to Joseph.

With this exception they contradict each other all the way through, and in many instances that of Chronicles, too.

This is a strange way, indeed, of proving Jesus Christ to have had two fathers!—to be both the son of God and son of David! And it is still stranger that they should trace his genealogy to Joseph, if they did not consider him Joseph's son. Otherwise, the genealogy of "Sinbad the Sailor," or "Harry Haulaway," would have been as apropos.

Such are the beautiful harmony and agreement in the words of "divine inspiration" which Christians prate so much about.

And all this appears to be the result of an attempt to elevate the man Christ Jesus to a level with the demigods of antiquity, nearly all of whom claimed to be of royal or princely descent. Such continual blundering, guessing, cross-firing, and clashing of names as is exhibited in the foregoing exposition, reminds us of the Hibernian's reply when asked for the number and names of his brothers:

"Well, sir, I have fourteen brothers, and they are all named Bill but Bob—his name is Tom."

43

Matthew and Luke's attempt to exalt and dignify the character of Christ by making out for him a pure, holy and royal lineage we find, upon a critical examination not only proved a very signal but a very singular and ludicrous failure, for all his female anchors who are brought to notice were persons of libidinous or licentious tendencies, according to their own biblical history.

"It is remarkable," says Dr. Alexander Walker, (a Christian writer, in his work on Woman, p. 330), "that in the genealogy of Christ only four women are named: Thamar, who seduced the father of her late husband, and Rachel, a common prostitute, and Ruth, who, instead of marrying one of her cousins, went to bed with another of them, and Bathsheba, an adulteress, who espoused David, the murderer of her first husband."

What a pedigree for an incarnate God—a being ostensibly of spotless origin! though his impure ancestral origin does not detract from the high moral character and distinguished moral life which marks the history of "the man Christ Jesus," many incidents of whose life show him to have been what is now known as a spiritual medium.

CHAPTER XII. THE WORLD'S SAVIORS SAVED FROM DESTRUCTION IN INFANCY

OF course such an extraordinary circumstance as the birth of a God into the world must be marked with unusual incidents and great eclat. This was first exhibited by angels, shepherds, prophets, magi or "wise men," flocking around their cradles. In the second place we observe an unusual display of divine power and providential care on the part of the great Father God, who was still left in heaven to save the young saviors through their infancy.

It is certainly a remarkable circumstance that so many of the infant Saviors should have been threatened with the most imminent danger of destruction, and yet in every case miraculously preserved, and thus were the *Saviors saved.*

A jealousy seems to have existed in several instances in the mind of the tyrant king or ruler of the country that the young Saviors and prospective spiritual rulers (who were mostly of royal descent) would ultimately acquire such favor with the people, by such a display of superior power and greatness of mind, as to endanger his retaining peaceable possession of the secular throne; to express it in brief, he feared the young God would prove a rival king, and hence took measures to destroy him.

In the case of the Christian Savior we are told that an angel, or "the angel," warned Joseph (the assumed father) to take the young Savior and God and flee with him into Egypt, because "Herod the king sought to destroy the young child's life," and had, in order to effect this end, decreed the destruction of all the children under two years old. And Joseph heeded the divine warning, and fled as directed. An angel and a dream, then, it will be observed, were the instrumentalities used to save the young Judean Savior from massacre.

And strange as it may seem, we find the same agencies had been previously employed to effect the rescue of other Saviors likewise and similarly threatened.

In the case of Chrishna of India, in particular, the similitude is very striking in nearly every feature of the whole story.

In the first place there is the angel warning. In the Christian story we are not specifically informed how the tyrant Herod first became apprised of the birth of the Judean Savior. The Hindoo story is fuller, and indicates that the angel was not only sufficiently thoughtful to warn the parents to flee from a danger which threatened to dispossess them of a divine child, and the world of a Savior, but was condescending enough to apprise the tyrant ruler (Cansa) of his danger likewise—as we are told he heard an angel voice announcing that a rival ruler was born in his kingdom.

And hence, like Herod, he set about concocting measures to destroy him without a direct attack. Why either of them should have taken such a circuitous or roundabout way of killing an infant, when the life of the strongest man, and every man in their kingdoms, was at their instant disposal, "divine inspiration" does not inform us.

But so it was. And we must not seek to "become wise above what is written" in their bibles. Herod's decree required the destruction of all infants under two years of age (see Matt. ii. 16)— first ordering, however, "Go, and search diligently for the young child." (Matt. ii. 8.) Cansa's decree ran thus: "Let active search be made for whatever young children there may be upon earth, and let every boy in whom there may be found signs of unusual greatness be slain without remorse."

Now, let it be specially noticed that there is to this day in the cave temple at Elephanta, in India, the sculptured likeness of a king represented with a drawn sword, and surrounded with slaughtered infants—admitted by all writers to be much older than Christianity. Mr Forbes, in his "Oriental Memories," vol. iii. p. 447, says, "The figures of the slaughtered infants in the cave of Elephanta represent them as being all boys, who are surrounded by groups of figures of men and women in the act, apparently, of supplicating for those children." And Mr. Higgins testifies relative to the case, that Chrishna was carried away by night, and concealed in a region remote from his natal place, for fear of a tyrant whose destroyer it had been foretold he would become, who, for that reason, had ordered all the male children born at that time to be slain. Sculptures in Elephanta attest the story where the tyrant is represented as destroying the children. The date of this sculpture is of the most remote antiquity. "He who hath ears to hear, let him hear," and deduce the pregnant inference. Joseph and Mary fled with the young Judean God into Egypt; Chrishna's parents likewise fled with the young Hindoo Savior to Gokul.

Now, let us observe for a moment the chain or category or resemblance.

1. There was an angel warning in each case relative to the impending danger.

45

2. The governor or ruler was hostile in each case to the mission of the young Savior.

3. A bloody decree was issued in both cases, having for its object the destruction of these infant Messiahs.

4. The hurried flight of the parents takes place in each case.

5. And it may be remarked further, that the "Gospel of the Infancy of Jesus," once believed by the Christian world to be "inspired," and which for hundreds of years passed current as divine authority, relates that Christ and his parents sojourned for a time at a place called Matarea, or Mathura, as Sir William Jones spells it, who says it was the birth place of Chrishna.

It is further related in the case of Chrishna, that as he and his parents approached the River Jumna in their flight, the waters "parted hither and thither," so that they passed over "dry shod," like Moses and the Israelites in crossing the Red Sea. And here let it be noted that the representation of this flight, which is said to have occurred at midnight, is like that of the massacre perpetuated and attested by imperishable monuments of stone bearing evidence of being now several thousand years old.

Sir William Jones says:—

"The Indian incarnate God Chrishna, the Hindoos believe, had a virgin mother of the royal race, who was sought to be destroyed in his infancy about nine hundred years before Christ. It appears that he passed his life in working miracles, and preaching, and was so humble as to wash his friends' feet; at length, dying, but rising from the dead, he ascended into heaven in the presence of a multitude." The Cingalese relate nearly the same things of their "Budha." And several authors of Egyptian history refer to a story perpetuated in the Egyptian legends concerning the God Osiris, who was threatened with destruction by the tyrant Amulius, to save whom his parents fled and concealed him in an arm of the River Nile, as Christ was concealed in the same country, and, for aught that appears to the contrary, in the same locality. The mother of another and older Savior of Egypt fled by a timely warning to Epidamis before the birth of the divine child, and was there delivered of "our Lord and Savior," Horus. And the earthly or adopted father of the Grecian Savior, and God, Alcides, had to flee with him and his mother to Galem for protection from threatening danger.

In the ninth and tenth volumes of the "Asiatic Researches," we find the story of the "only begotten" or "first begotten son of God," Salvahana, of Cape Comorin, son of a virgin mother (as were all the other Saviors referred to), and a carpenter by the name of Taishnea. (It will be remembered that Joseph, "foster-father of Jesus," was a carpenter.) The story of this "Son of God" presents several features very similar to that relating to Jesus. Sir William Jones, Colonel Wilford, and the Rev. Mr. Maurice all confess to the antiquity of this story, as originating before the birth of Christ. Speaking of Zoroaster of Persia (another case), 600 B. C., an author remarks, "Tradition reports that his mother had alarming dreams of evil spirits seeking to destroy the child to whom she was about to give birth. But a good spirit came to rescue him, and consoled her by saying, 'Fear not; God Ormuzd will protect the infant, who has sent him as a prophet to the people and the world who are waiting for him."

China, too, presents us with a case of the threatened destruction of a Savior in infancy, evidently recorded more than two thousand five hundred years ago. It is the case of the God Yu, who was concealed in a manner similar to that of Moses—a commemoration of the story of which is perpetuated by an image or picture of the virgin mother with a babe upon her knee—sometimes in her arms. Now, let it be noted that these virgin-born Gods, who, we are told, came "to save the world," could not save themselves, but had to be protected and saved by other Gods.

Without pursuing the subject further in detail, we may mention by way of recapitulation, that Chrishna, Alcides, Zoraster, Salvahana, Yu, to which list we may add Bacchus, Romulus, Moses and Cyrus, according to their reputed history, were threatened with death and destruction, but were providentially and miraculously preserved. The case of Augustus is related by Suetonius, that of Romulus by Livy, and that of Cyrus by Herodotus. It will be recollected that Pharaoh, like Herod, in order to reach the infant Moses, ordered the massacre of all the male infants (Herod making no distinction of sex), in order that he might, by this singular and circuitous method, reach the object of his jealousy and malignity without passing a direct sentence of death upon him.

The whole story of Herod's slaughter edict, with the familiar history of its execution, like nearly every other miraculous incident related in "The Holy Scriptures," which detail their histories, are traceable in the skies. Herod, we are told, literally means hero of the skin—a term applied also to Hercules, a personification of the sun—because the sun, on entering the constellation of the Zodiac in July, was supposed or assumed to invest himself with the skin of the lion, and this became "the hero of the skin," or a hero with a new skin. Now this solar Herod, passing through the astronomical twins and young infants of May, was said to destroy them, though the word destroy is in the Greek anairean, which any person, on turning to the Greek lexicon, will observe means also to take away, pass through, or withdraw from, so that Pharaoh more properly passed through the infants than destroyed them

The text, "In Rama there was a voice heard," "Rachel weeping for her children," etc., is quoted by a writer (Strauss) as referring to the children slaughtered by Pharaoh. Let two things be noticed here: 1. Rama is the Indian and Phoenician name for the zodiac. 2. Rachel had but two children to weep for—Joseph and Benjamin—just the number found in the fifth sign, or May sign, of the zodiac. And Venus, among the ancient Assyrians and Phoenicians, was in tears when the sun, in his annual cross through the heavens, passed through or over the astronomical Twins (Gemini), doubtless fearfully apprehending their destruction.

The case of the massacre is an illustration and example of the manner in which all the miraculous stories related in the Christian Scriptures, as having been practically exemplified in the life of Jesus Christ, are traceable to older sources, frequently terminating among the stars.

SECTION II.—INCREDIBILITY OF THE STORY OF THE MASSACRE OF THE HEBREW INFANTS.

1. It is a cogent and potent fact, calculated to render the story of the murder of the Hebrew children by Herod wholly incredible, that not one writer of that age, or that nation, or any other nation, makes any mention of the circumstance.

2. Even the Rabbinical writers who detail his wicked life so minutely, and who bring to his charge so many flagitious acts, fail to record any notice of this horrible and atrocious deed, which must have been published far and wide, and known to all the writers of that age and country, had it occurred.

3. And still more logically ruinous to the credit of the story is the omission of Josephus to throw out one hint that such a wholesale slaughter ever took place in Judea. And yet he not only lived in that country, but was related to Herod's wife, and regarded him as his most implacable enemy, and professes to write out the whole history of his wicked life in the most minute detail, devoting thirty-seven chapters of his large work to this subject, and apparently enumerates every evil act of his life. And yet Josephus says not a word about his inhuman and infamous butchery of the babes which Matthew charges him with (about fourteen thousand in number)—a bloody deed, unmatched in the annals of tyranny. Such facts prove the story not only incredible, but impossible. Josephus could not and would not have omitted to notice this the most notorious and nefarious act of his life, had it occurred. It, therefore, could not have occurred. And it is almost equally incredible that Roman historians, who furnish us with a particular account of Herod's character, should pass over in silence such a villainous and bloody deed.

4. And then some of our ablest and most reliable chronologists have shown that Herod was not living at the time this bloody decree should have been issued by him; that he died about three years prior to that period, and hence could have been guilty of no such villainy, and highhanded murder, and cruel infanticide.

5. And even if living, he would have been an old man (not less than sixty-eight according to Josephus). Hence, he could not have calculated on surviving long enough for the son of a village carpenter, then a babe, to oust him from his throne.

6. It is wholly incredible, also, that Herod should have adopted such a roundabout method of destroying the object of his fear and envy when he could have singled him out, and put him to death at once, and thus avoid the felonious act of breaking the hearts of thousands of parents, and his most loyal subjects, too.

7. From the foregoing considerations, we endorse the sentiment of the Rev. Edward Evanson, that it is "an incredible, borrowed fiction."

48

CHAPTER XIII. THE SAVIORS EXHIBIT EARLY PROOFS OF DIVINITY.

OF course, all Gods must be heroes—physically or intellectually, or both. The more danger they encounter, and the earlier they manifest a precocious or preternatural smartness, the more like Gods.

And hence we find several of the Saviors in very early childhood displaying great physical prowess in meeting and conquering danger, while others exhibit their superiority mentally by vanquishing their opponents in argument. Christ first began to exhibit proof of his divine character and greatness by meeting and silencing the doctors in the temple when only about twelve years of age.

And similar proofs of divinity at or near this age is found in the history of some of the pagan Saviors.

Of Christ it is declared, "There went out a fame of him through all the region round about." (Luke iv. 14.) And of the Grecian Esculapius it is likewise declared, "The voice of fame soon published the birth of a miraculous child," and "the people flocked from all quarters to behold him." Of Confucius of China it is declared, "His extensive knowledge and great wisdom soon made him known, and kings were governed by his counsels, and the people adored him wherever he went." And it is further declared of this "Divine Man," that he seemed to arrive at reason and the perfect use of his faculties almost from infancy. It is reported of the God Chang-ti, that when questioned on the subject of government and the duties of princes and rulers while yet a child, his answers were such as to astonish the whole empire by his knowledge and wisdom.

It is related of a Grecian God that he demolished the serpents which attempted to bite or destroy him while in his cradle. "The proof of Osiris's divinity was a blaze of light shining around his cradle soon after he was born. Relative to Pythagoras of the same country, we have it upon the authority of a Christian writer, that he exhibited such a remarkable character, even in youth, as to attract the attention of all who saw and heard him speak." And the author further testifies of him that he "never was at any time overcome with anger, laughter, or perturbation of mind or precipitation of conduct." "His fame having reached Miletus and neighboring cities," it is said by another writer, "the people flocked to see and hear him, and he was reverenced by multitudes."

Luke declares of Christ, that the people "were astonished at his understanding and answers." (Luke ii. 47.) And the "Gospel of the Infancy" tells us that his tutor Zacheas was astonished at his learning, which reminds us of the statement found in "The Divine Word" of the Hindoos (The Mahabarat), that the parents of the Savior Chrishna, in making arrangements to give him an education, sent him to a learned Brahmin as tutor, whom he instantly astonished with his vast learning, and under whose tuition he mastered the whole circle of sciences in a day and a night. "Men, seeing the wonders performed by this child, told Nanda (his adopted father) that this could not possibly be his son."

It is told of Budha Sakia of India that, "as soon as he was born, a light shone around his cradle, when he stood up and proclaimed his mission, and that the River Ganges daring this time rose in a miraculous manner, which was stilled by his divine power, as Christ stilled the tempest on the sea." "He was born," says the New American Cyclopedia (vol. iv. p. 61), "amidst great miracles, and soon as born, most solemnly proclaims his mission."

Of Narayan, "the Holy," it is declared that "mysterious words dropped from his lips on various occasions, giving hints of his divine nature and the purposes for which he had come down to the earth." (Prog. Rel. Ideas, vol. i. p. 128.) The divine power and mission of Yu of China was very early evinced by the display of great miracles.

And here let us observe that some of the Old Testament or Jewish heroes—as Moses, Solomon and Samuel—are reported as exhibiting great superiority of mind in very early life; thus proving (it was thought) that if they were not Gods, they were at least from God—that is, endowed by him with divine power while yet mere children. Thus the histories of all Gods and divine personages run in parallel grooves.

CHAPTER XIV. THE SAVIORS; KINGDOMS NOT OF THIS WORLD

Retirement and Forty Days' Fasting.

CHRIST taught, "My kingdom is not of this world."

And we find that most of the other Saviors virtually and practically taught the same doctrine.

The first practical evincement of it was exhibited by retiring from the world; that is, they retired from the noise and commotion, from the busy scenes of life, into some sequestered spot excluded from human observation. Christ is reported to have withdrawn from society, and to have spent some forty days in the wilderness fasting and being tempted by Satan—a man of straw conjured up in order to furnish the hero God something to combat with, that he might thereby exhibit practical proof of his divine power and prowess. It was simply the two kings or rulers of two hostile kingdoms (heaven and hell) contending for the mastery.

Lord Kingsborough tells us, "The ancient Mexicans had a forty days' fast in honor and memory of one of their demigods or Saviors, who was tempted forty days on a mountain. He is called 'the Morning Star'." Mr. Kingsborough (being a Christian) remarks, "These things are very curious and mysterious."

It is said of "the Son of God" and Savior Chrishna that "he imparted his doctrines and precepts in the silent depths of the forest." Of the Egyptian God Osiris, we are informed in his sacred legends, that "he observed both fasting and penance," while Pythagoras of Greece spent several years in meditation and retirement in a cave, and was much given to fasting, and often inculcated the doctrine of "forsaking the world" and "the things thereof." He taught these things both by precept and example, even to "the forsaking of relations." Both Confucius and the Divine Savior Chang-ti of China, "in order to attain to a more perfect state of holiness," spent several years in retirement and "divine meditation," the former in a wilderness, the latter on a mountain, and fasted, and their disciples after them often fasted in a very devout manner. The Persian Zoroaster also spent several years in retirement and "contemplation on true holiness"—partly in a wilderness and partly on a "holy mountain," "holy mountains" being the favorite places of resort of most of the holy Saviors, holy Gods, and holy men of antiquity. One of the most ancient Saviors, Thammuz, is reported to have spent "twelve years in devout and contemplative retirement from the busy world." According to the Christian bible, Moses, Elijah, and Christ, each fasted forty days, and a Mexican Savior, too (Quexalcote), spent forty days in a similar manner, and other cases are so reported.

We may institute the inquiry here, "How happens this coincidence?"

The answer is indicated by "the Hierophant," which says, "Jesus in his baptism and forty days' fast imitated the passage of the sun through the constellation Aquarius, where John, Joannes, or Janus the baptizer had his domicile, and baptized the earth with his yearly rains." Having been baptized in Jordan, he fasted forty days in the wilderness, in imitation of the passage of the sun from the constellation Aquarius through the Fishes to the Lamb or Ram of March. During the forty days when the sun is among the Fishes (in the sign of the Fish) the faithful Catholics, Episcopalians and Mahommedans abstain from meat and live upon the fishes during the season of Lent, as did the Jews and pagans, and did also Jesus, "to fulfill all righteousness."

CHAPTER XV. THE SAVIORS WERE REAL PERSONAGES

IT is unwarrantably assumed by Christian writers that the incarnated Gods and crucified Saviors of the pagan religions were all either mere fabulous characters, or ordinary human beings invested with divine titles, and divine attributes; while, on the other hand, the assumption is put forth with equal boldness that Jesus Christ was a real divine personage, "seen and believed on in the world, and finally crucified on Mount Calvary."

But we do not find the facts in history to warrant any such assumptions or any such distinctions. They all stand in these respects upon the same ground and on equal footing.

And their respective disciples point to the same kind of evidence to prove their real existence and their divine character, and to prove that they once walked and talked amongst men, as well as now sit on the eternal throne in heaven "at the right hand of the father." And we find even

Christian writers admitting the once *bona fide* or personal existence on earth of most of the pagan Saviors.

As to the two chief incarnated Gods of India—Chrishna and Sakia—there is scarcely "a peg left to hang a doubt upon" as to the fact of their having descended to the earth, taken upon themselves the form of men, and having been worshiped as veritable Gods.

Indeed, we believe but few of the missionaries who have visited that country question the statement and general belief prevalent there of their once personal reality. Col. Todd, in his "History of the Rajahs" (p. 44), says: "We must discard the idea that the Mahabaret, the history of Rama, of Chrishna, and the five Padua brothers are mere allegories; colossal figures, ancient temples, and caves inscribed with characters yet unknown, confirm the reality, and their race, their cities, and their coins yet exist." To argue further the personal reality of this crucified God would be a waste of words, as it is generally admitted, both by historical writers and missionaries.

Mr. Higgins declares, "Chrishna lived at the conclusion of the brazen age, which is calculated to have been eleven hundred or twelve hundred years before Christ." Here is a very positive and specific declaration as to his tangible actuality. Col. Dow, Mr. Robinson, and others use similar language.

Relative to Bacchus, of whose history many writers have spoken as being wholly fabulous or fictitious, Diodorus Siculus says (lib. iii. p. 137), "the Libyans claim Bacchus, and say that he was the son of Ammon, a king of Libya; that he built a temple to his father, Ammon." And that world-wide famous historian (Mr. Goodrich) is still more explicit, if possible, as to his material entity. After giving it directly as his opinion that there was such a being, he says, "He planted vine-yards and fig-trees, and erected many noble cities." He moreover tells us, "His skill in legislation and agriculture is much praised" (p. 499).

With respect to Osiris of Egypt, another God-Savior, Mr. Hittle declares unqualifiedly that "Herodotus saw the tomb of Osiris, at Sais nearly five centuries before Christ" (vol. i. p. 246). Rather a strong evidence of his previous personality certainly, but not more so than that furnished by the *New York Journal of Commerce* a few years since, relative to the Egyptian Apis or Thulis, whose theophany was annually celebrated, at the rising of the Nile, with great festivities and devotion, several thousand years ago. The Paris correspondent of that journal, after speaking of Mr. Auguste Marietta's travels, "a distinguished scientific gentleman who for four years past had been employed by the French Government in making Egyptian researches," having returned home, says, "The most important of Mr. Marietta's discoveries was the tomb of Apis (Thulis), a monument excavated entirely in lime-rock." "There are (he says in conclusion) epitaphs, forming a chronological record of each of the Apis buried in the common tomb. The sculpture is of the date of the Pyramids, and the statues are in the best state of preservation; the colors are perfectly bright The execution is admirable, and they convey an exact idea of the physical character of the primitive population."

The New American Cyclopedia (art. Apis) in speaking of this Egyptian God, tells us his lifetime was twenty-five years; in harmony with one of the theologico-astronomical cycles of the

Egyptians. The same work and volume (p. 132), in speaking of the real existence of Adonis of Greece, tells us, upon the authority of the poet Panyasis, that he was a veritable son of Theias, king of Syria.

But of all the characters who figured in the mythological works or lawless rhapsodies of the ancients, and worshiped by them as crucified Gods and sin-atoning Saviors, none has, perhaps, been so indubitably, so positively, and so universally set down as mythological or fabulous as that of Prometheus of Caucasus.

And yet Mr. Lempriere, D. D., tells us in his Classical Dictionary that he was the son of Japetus. Sir Isaac Newton says he was a descendant of the famous African Sesostris; while that erudite and masterly historian (Mr. Higgins) seems to have entertained no doubt of his personal esse; nor, indeed, of many, if any, of the pagan Saviors, as the following declaration will show. He says, "Finding men in India and other countries of the same name of the inferior Gods (as it is quite common to name men for them) has led some to conclude that those deified men never existed, but are merely mythological names of the sun. True, the first supreme God of every nation (not excepting the Jews) was the sun. But more modernly the names were transferred to men." Again, he says, "Inasmuch as some of them are found to have been real bona fide human beings, there is nothing unreasonable in concluding that all were" And if we take into consideration the true and indisputable fact that the priests had everything at their disposal, and the strongest motives for concealing and suppressing, not to say garbling and destroying evidence, it is not to be wondered at that the histories of some of these Gods should be somewhat obscure and ambiguous. Further on he declares, "In every case the Savior was incarnate, and in nearly every case the place in which he was actually born was exhibited to the people." And upon the authority of the Hierophant, we will add, the memories of many of them have been consecrated and perpetuated by tombs placed beside their temples, which is perhaps the most convincing species of evidence that could be offered.

The evidence, then, is precisely of the same character as that offered in the case of Jesus Christ to prove that the pagan Saviors did really possess a substantial, earthly and bodily existence. Though it is true that it never has been universally conceded or believed by Christian themselves that Jesus Christ ever had a personal or corporeal existence on earth.

Cotilenius, in a note on Ignatius, Epistle to the Trallians, written in the third century of the Christian era, declares that "it is as absurd to deny the doctrine which taught that Jesus Christ's body was a phantom as to deny that the sun shone at midday." His physical body of course was meant, for it appears he believed in his eternal existence as a spirit in heaven.

And we find whole sects advocating similar views in the early ages of the Christian church. "One of the most primitive and learned sects," says a writer, "were the Manicheans, who denied that Jesus Christ ever existed in flesh and blood, but believed him to be a God in spirit only;" others denied him to be a God, but believed him to have been a prophet, or inspired character, like the Unitarians of the present day. Some denied his crucifixion, others asserted it. It is more than probable that this was the cause of dispute between Paul and Barnabas, mentioned in the Acts of the Apostles, seeing that Paul had laid such peculiar emphasis on "Jesus Christ and him crucified."

And this conclusion is corroborated by its being expressly stated in the Gospel of Barnabas that "Jesus Christ was not crucified, but was carried to heaven by four angels." "There was a long list," says the same writer, "from the earliest times, of sincere Christians who denied that Jesus Christ rose from the dead;" while, as we may remark here, there could not have been at that early date any grounds for denying these things, had he really figured in the world in the miraculous and extraordinary and public manner as that related in the Gospels.

CHAPTER XVI. SIXTEEN SAVIORS CRUCIFIED

"For I determined not to know anything among you, save Jesus Christ and him crucified." (i Cor. ii. 2.) There must have existed a very considerable amount of skepticism in the community as to the truth of the report of the crucifixion of Jesus Christ in the country and era of its occurrence to make it necessary thus to erect it into an important dogma, and make it imperative to believe it There must have been a large margin for distrusting its truth.

The determination not to know anything but the crucifixion of Jesus Christ was narrowing down his knowledge to rather a small compass.

And such a resolution would necessarily preclude him from acquainting himself with the history of any other cases of crucifixion that might have occurred before that of his own favorite Messiah. "What! Was there ever a case of crucifixion beside that of Jesus Christ?" a good Christian brother or sister sometimes exclaims, when the world's sixteen crucified Saviors are spoken of.

We meet the question with the reply, You seem to be a disciple of Paul, whose position would not allow him to know of any other cases of crucifixion but that of Jesus Christ. Hence, he may have considered it meritorious to perpetuate his ignorance on the subject And you, perhaps, are ignorant from the same cause.

It is the nature of all religions based on fear and unchangeable dogmas, to deter and thus exclude its disciples from all knowledge adverse to their own creeds. And sometimes their own religious systems are magnified to such an exalted appreciation above all others as to lead them to destroy the evidence of the existence of the latter for fear of their ultimate rivalry.

Mr. Taylor informs us that some of the early disciples of the Christian faith demolished accessible monuments representing and memorializing the crucifixion of the ancient oriental sin-atoning Gods, so that they are now unknown in the annals of Christian history. Hence, the surprise excited in the minds of Christian professors when other cases are mentioned.

Such influences as referred to above have shut out from the minds of the disciples of several religious systems a knowledge of all crucified Gods but their own. Hence, the Hindoo rejoices in knowing only "Chrishna and him crucified." The Persian entwines around his heart the remembrance only of the atoning sufferings on the cross of Mithra the Mediator. The Mexican daily sends up his earnest, soul-breathing prayer for the return of the spirit of his crucified Savior—Quexalcote. While the Caucasian, with equal devotion, chants daily praises to his slain "Divine Intercessor" for voluntarily offering himself upon the cross for the sins of a fallen race. And the Christian disciple hugs to his bosom the bloody cross of the murdered Jesus, unhaunted by the suspicion that other Gods died for the sins of man long anterior to the advent of the immaculate Nazarene.

We will now lay before the reader a brief account of the crucifixion of more than a dozen virgin-born Gods and sin-atoning Saviors, predicated upon facts which have escaped the hands of the Christian iconoclasts determined to know only Jesus Christ crucified. We will first notice the case of the Indian God—Chrishna.

I.—CRUCIFIXION OF CHRISHNA OF INDIA, 1200 B. C.

Among the sin-atoning Gods who condescended in ancient times to forsake the throne of heaven, and descend upon the plains of India, through human birth, to suffer and die for the sins and transgressions of the human race, the eighth Avatar, or Savior, may be considered the most important and the most exalted character, as he led the most conspicuous life, and commanded the most devout and the most universal homage. And while some of the other incarnate demigods were invested with only a limited measure of the infinite deityship, Chrishna, according to the teachings of their New Testament (the Ramazand), comprehended in himself "a full measure of the God-head bodily." The evidence of his having been crucified is as conclusive as any other sacrificial or sin-atoning God, whose name has been memorialized in history, or embalmed as a sacred idol in the memories of his devout worshipers.

Mr. Moore, an English traveler and writer, in a large collection of drawings taken from Hindoo sculptures and monuments, which he has arranged together in a work entitled "The Hindoo Pantheon," has one representing, suspended on the cross, the Hindoo crucified God and Son of God, "our Lord and Savior" Chrishna, with holes pierced in his feet, evidently intended to represent the nail-holes made by the act of crucifixion. Mr. Higgins, who examined this work, which he found in the British Museum, makes a report of a number of the transcript drawings intended to represent the crucifixion of this oriental and mediatorial God, which we will here condense. In plate ninety-eight this Savior is represented with a hole in the top of one foot, just above the toes, where the nail was inserted in the act of crucifixion.

In another drawing he is represented exactly in the form of a Romish Christian crucifix, but not fixed or fastened to a tree, though the legs and feet are arranged in the usual way, with nail-holes in the latter. There is a halo of glory over it, emanating from the heavens above, just as we have seen Jesus Christ represented in a work by a Christian writer, entitled "Quarles' Emblems," also in other Christian books. In several of the icons (drawings) there are marks of holes in both feet, and in others of holes in the hands only. In the first drawing which he consulted the marks are very faint, so as to be scarcely visible. In figures four and five of plate eleven the figures have nail-holes in both feet, while the hands are not represented. Figure six has on it the representation of a round hole in the side. To his collar or shirt hangs an emblem of a heart, represented in the same manner as those attached to the imaginary likenesses of Jesus Christ, which may now be found in some Christian countries Figure ninety-one has a hole in one foot and a nail through the other, and a round nail or pin mark in one hand only, while the other is ornamented with a dove and a serpent (both emblems of deity in the Christian's bible).

Now, we raise the query here, and drive it into the innermost temple of the Christian's conscience, with the overwhelming force of the unconquerable logic of history—*What does all this mean?*

And if they will only let conviction have its perfect work while answering this question unhampered by the inherited prejudices of a thousand years, they can henceforth rejoice in the discovery of a glorious historical truth, calculated to disenthrall their minds from the soul-cramping superstitions of crosses, crucifixions and bloody atonements on which they have been accustomed to hang the salvation of the world.

If the credibility of the relation of these incidents going to prove an astonishing coincidence in the sacred histories of the Hindoo and Christian Saviors, and demonstrating the doctrine of the crucifixion as having been practically realized, and preached to the world long anterior to the offering of a God "once for all" on Mount Calvary; if its credibility rested on mere *ex parte* testimony, mere pagan tradition, or even upon the best digested and most authentic annals of the past that have escaped the ravages of time, there might still be a forlorn hope for the stickler for the Christian faith now struggling in the agonies of a credal skepticism, that the whole thing has been plagiarized from the Christian Gospels. For paper and parchment history can be—and has been—mutilated. But the verity of this account rests upon no such a precarious basis. Its antiquity, reaching far beyond the Christian era, is corroborated and demonstrated by imperishable monuments, deep-chiseled indentures burrowed into the granite rock, which bid defiance to the fingers of time, and even the hands of the frenzied iconoclast, to destroy or deface, though impelled and spurred on to the effort by the long-cherished conviction burning in his soul, that the salvation of the human race depends upon believing that "there is no other name given under heaven whereby men can be saved" than his own crucified God, and that all others are but thieves, robbers and antichrists. Some of the disciples of the oriental systems cherished this conviction, and Christians and Mahommedans seem to have inherited it in magnified proportions.

Hence, we are credibly informed that some of the earlier Christian saints, having determined, like Paul, "to know only Jesus Christ and him crucified," made repeated efforts to obliterate these sacred facts (so fatally damaging to their one-sided creeds) from the page of history. Mr. Higgins suggests that if we could have persons less under the influence of sectarian prejudice to visit, examine, and report on the sculptures and monuments of India, covered over as they are with antiquated and significant figures appertaining to and illustrating their religious history, we might accumulate still more light bearing upon the history of the crucifixion of the Savior and sin-atoning Chrishna. "Most of our reports," he declares, "are fragmentary, if not one-sided, having come through the hands of Christian missionaries, bishops and priests."

He informs us that a report on the Hindoo religion, made out by a deputation from the British Parliament, sent to India for the purpose of examining their sacred books and monuments, being left in the hands of a Christian bishop at Calcutta, and with instructions to forward it to England, was found, on its arrival in London, to be so horribly mutilated and eviscerated as to be scarcely cognizable. The account of the crucifixion was gone—-cancelled out. The inference is patent.

And we have it upon the authority of this same reliable and truthful writer (Sir Godfrey Higgins) that the author of the Hindoo Pantheon (Mr. Moor), after having announced his intention to publish it to the world, was visited and labored with by some of his devout Christian neighbors zealous "for the faith once delivered to the saints," who endeavored to dissuade him from publishing such facts to the world as he represented his book to contain, for fear it would have the effect to unsettle the faith of some of the weak brethren (some of the weak-kneed church members) in the soul-saving religion of Jesus Christ, by raising doubts in their minds as to the originality of the gospel story of the crucifixion of Christ, or at least of his having been crucified as a God for a sin-offering. His crucifixion is a possible event. It may be thus far a true narrative, but the adjunct of the atonement, with its efficacy to obliterate the effects of sin, connected with the idea that an infinite, omnipotent and self-existent God was put to death, when a human form was slain upon the cross—never, no, never. It is a thought too monstrous to find lodgment in an enlightened human mind.

Another case evincing the same spirit as that narrated above is found in the circumstance of a Christian missionary (a Mr. Maurice) publishing a historical account of this man-god or demigod of the Hindoos, and omitting any allusion to his crucifixion; this was entirely left out, apparently from design. His death, resurrection and ascension were spoken of, but the crucifixion skipped over. He could not have been ignorant of this chapter in his history as the writers preceding him, from whom he copied, had related it.

Among this number may be mentioned the learned French writer Monsieur Guigniant, who, in his "Religion of the Ancients," speaks so specifically of the crucifixion of this God, as to name the circumstance of his being nailed to a tree. He also states, that before his exit he made some remarkable prophecies appertaining to the crimes and miseries of the world in the approaching future, reminding us of the wars and rumors of wars predicted by the Christian Messiah. Mr. Higgins names the same circumstance.

We have it upon the authority of more than one writer on Hindoo or Indian antiquities that there is a rock temple at Mathura in the form of a cross, and facing the four cardinal points of the compass, which is admitted by all beholders as presenting the proof in bold relief of extreme age, and inside of this temple stands a statue of "the Savior of men," Chrishna of India, presenting the proof of being coeval in construction with the temple itself by the circumstance of its being cut out of the same rock and constituting a part of the temple. (Further citations of this character will be found under the head of Parallels, Chapter XXXII.)

Thus we have the proof deeply and indelibly carved in the old, time-chiseled rocks of India—that their "Lord and Savior Chrishna" atoned for the sins of a grief-stricken world by "pouring out his blood as a propitiatory offering" while stretched upon the cross. No wonder, in view of such historic bulwarks, Col. Wiseman, for ten years a Christian missionary should have exclaimed, "Can we be surprised that the enemies of our holy religion should seize upon this legend (the crucifixion of Chrishna) as containing the original of our gospel history?"

Christian reader, please ponder over the facts of this chapter, and let conviction have its perfect work.

LIFE, CHARACTER, RELIGION, AND MIRACLES OF CHRISHNA.

The history of Chrishna Zeus (or Jeseus, as some writers spell it) is contained principally in the Baghavat Gita, the episode portion of the Mahabaret bible. The book is believed to be divinely inspired, like all other bibles; and the Hindoos claim for it an antiquity of six thousand years. Like Christ, he was of humble origin, and like him had to encounter opposition and persecution.

But he seems to have been more successful in the propagation of his doctrines; for it is declared, "he soon became surrounded by many earnest followers, and the people in vast multitudes followed him, crying aloud, 'This is indeed the Redeemer promised to our fathers.'" His pathway was thickly strewn with miracles, which consisted in healing the sick, curing lepers, restoring the dumb, deaf and the blind, raising the dead, aiding the weak, comforting the sorrow-stricken, relieving the oppressed, casting out devils, etc. He come not ostensibly to destroy the previous relgion, but to purify it of its impurities, and to preach a better doctrine. He came, as he declared, "to reject evil and restore the reign of good, and redeem man from the consequences of the fall, and deliver the oppressed earth from its load of sin and suffering." His disciples believed him to be God himself, and millions worshiped him as such in the time of Alexander the Great, 330 B. C.

The hundreds of counterparts to the history of Christ, proving their histories to be almost identical, will be found enumerated in Chapter XXXII., such as—1. His miraculous birth by a virgin. 2. The mother and child being visited by shepherds, wise men and the angelic host, who joyously sang, "In thy delivery, O favored among women, all nations shall have cause to exult." 3. The edict of the tyrant ruler Cansa, ordering all the first born to be put to death. 4. The miraculous escape of the mother and child from his bloody decree by the parting of the waves of the River Jumna to permit them to pass through on dry ground. 5. The early retirement of Chrishna to a desert. 6. His baptism or ablution in the River Ganges, corresponding to Christ's baptism in Jordan. 7. His transfiguration at Madura, where he assured his disciples that "present or absent, I will always be with you." 8. He had a favorite disciple (Arjoon), who was his bosom friend, as John was Christ's. 9. He was anointed with oil by women, like Christ. 10. A somewhat similar fish story is told of him—his disciples being enabled by him to catch large draughts of the finny prey in their nets. (For three hundred other similar parallels, see Chapter XXXII.)

Like Christ, he taught much by parables and precepts. A notable sermon preached by him is also reported, which we have not space for here.

On one occasion, having returned from a ministerial journey, as he entered Madura, the people came out in crowds to meet him, strewing the ground with the branches of cocoa-nut trees, and desiring to hear him. He addressed them in parables—the conclusion and moral of one of which, called the parable of the fishes, runs thus: "And thus it is, O people of Madura, that you ought to protect the weak and each other, and not retaliate upon an enemy the wrongs he may have done you." Here we see the peace doctrine preached in its purity. "And thus it was," says a writer, "that Chrishna spread among the people the holy doctrines of purest morality, and initiated his hearers into the exalted principles of charity, of self-denial, and self-respect at a time when the desert countries of the west were inhabited only by savage tribes;" and we will add, long before Christianity was thought of. Purity of life and spiritual insight, we are told, were distinguishing traits in the character of this oriental sin-atoning Savior, and that "he was often moved with compassion for the downtrodden and the suffering."

A Budhist in Ceylon, who sent his son to a Christian school, once remarked to a missionary, "I respect Christianity as a help to Budhism.' Thus is disclosed the fact that the motives of some of "the heathen" in sending to Christian schools is the promotion of their own religion, which they consider superior, and in many respects most of them are. (For proof, see Chapter on Bibles.)

We have the remarkable admission of the *Christian Examiner* that "the best precepts of the (Christian) bible are contained in the Hindoo Baghavat." Then it is not true that "Christ spake as man never spake." And if his "best precepts" were previously recorded in an old heathen bible, then they afford no proof of his divinity. This suicidal concession of the *Examiner* pulls up the claims of orthodox Christianity by the roots.

And many of the precepts uttered by Chrishna display a profound wisdom and depth of thought equal to any of those attributed to Jesus Christ. In proof of the statement, we will cite a few examples out of the hundreds in our possession:—

1. Those who do not control their passions cannot act properly toward others.

2. The evils we inflict upon others follow us as our shadows follow our bodies.

3. Only the humble are beloved of God.

4. Virtue sustains the soul as the muscles sustain the body.

5. When the poor man knocks at your door, take him and administer to his wants, for the poor are the chosen of God. (Christ said, "God hath chosen the poor.")

6. Let your hand be always open to the unfortunate.

7. Look not upon a woman with unchaste desires.

8. Avoid envy, covetousness, falsehood imposture and slander, and sexual desires.

9. Above all things, cultivate love for your neighbor.

10. When you die you leave your worldly wealth behind you, but your virtues and vices follow you.

11. Contemn riches and worldly honor.

12. Seek the company of the wicked in order to reform them.

13. Do good for its own sake, and expect not your reward for it on earth.

14. The soul is immortal, but must be pure and free from all sin and stain before it can return to Him who gave it.

15. The soul is inclined to good when it follows the inward light.

16. The soul is responsible to God for its actions, who has established rewards and punishments.

17. Cultivate that inward knowledge which teaches what is right and wrong.

18. Never take delight in another's misfortunes.

19. It is better to forgive an injury than to avenge it

20. You can accomplish by kindness what you cannot by force.

21. A noble spirit finds a cure for injustice by forgetting it.

22. Pardon the offense of others, but not your own.

23. What you blame in others do not practice yourself.

24. By forgiving an enemy you make many friends.

25. Do right from hatred of evil, and not from fear of punishment.

26. A wise man corrects his own errors by observing those of others.

27. He who rules his temper conquers his greatest enemy.

28. The wise man governs his passions, but the fool obeys them.

29. Be at war with men's vices, but at peace with their persons.

30. There should be no disagreement between your lives and your doctrine.

31. Spend every day as though it were the last.

32. Lead not one life in public and another in private.

33. Anger in trying to torture others punishes itself.

34. A disgraceful death is honorable when you die in a good cause.

35. By growing familiar with vices, we learn to tolerate them easily.

36. We must master our evil propensities, or they will master us.

37. He who has conquered his propensities rules over a kingdom.

38. Protect, love and assist others, if you would serve God.

39. From thought springs the will, and from the will action, true or false, just or unjust.

40. As the sandal tree perfumes the axe which fells it, so the good man sheds fragrance on his enemies.

41. Spend a portion of each day in pious devotion.

42. To love the virtues of others is to brighten your own.

43. He who gives to the needy loses nothing himself.

44. A good, wise and benevolent man cannot be rich.

45. Much riches is a curse to the possessor.

46. The wounds of the soul are more important than those of the body.

47. The virtuous man is like the banyan tree, which shelters and protects all around it.

48. Money does not satisfy the love of gain, but only stimulates it.

49. Your greatest enemy is in your own bosom.

50. To flee when charged is to confess your guilt.

51. The wounds of conscience leave a scar.

Compare these fifty-one precepts of Chrishna with the forty-two precepts of Christ, and you must confess they suffer nothing by the comparison. If we had space we would like to quote also from the Vedas. We will merely cite a few examples relative to woman.

1. He who is cursed by woman is cursed by God.

2. God will punish him who laughs at woman's sufferings.

3. When woman is honored, God is honored.

4. The virtuous woman will have but one husband, and the right-minded man but one wife.

5. It is the highest crime to take advantage of the weakness of woman.

6. Woman should be loved, respected and protected by husbands, fathers and brothers, etc. (For more, see Chapter on Bibles.)

Before we close this chapter we must anticipate and answer an objection. It will be said that the reported amours of Chrishna and his reencounter with Cansa constitute a criticism on his character. If so, we will point to Christ's fight or angry combat with the money-changers in the temple as an offset to it And then it should be remembered that Chrishna's disciples claim that these stories are mere fable, or allegorical, and are not found in the most approved or canonical writings.

II.—CRUCIFIXION OF THE HINDOO SAKIA, 600 B. C.

How many Gods who figured in Hindoo history suffered death upon the cross as atoning offerings for the sins of mankind is a point not clearly established by their sacred books. But the death of the God above named, known as Sakia, Budha Sakia, or Sakia Muni, is distinctly referred to by several writers, both oriental and Christian, though there appears to be in Budhist countries different accounts of the death of the famous and extensively worshiped sin-atoning Saviors.

In some countries, the story runs, a God was crucified by an arrow being driven through his body, which fastened him to a tree; the tree, with the arrow thus projecting at right angles, formed the cross, emblematical of the atoning sacrifice.

Sakia, an account states, was crucified by his enemies for the humble act of plucking a flower in a garden—doubtless seized on as a mere pretext, rather than as being considered a crime.

One of the accusations brought against Christ, it will be remembered, was that of plucking the ripened ears of corn on the Sabbath. And it is a remarkable circumstance, that in the pictures of Christian countries representing the virgin Mary with the infant Jesus in her arms, either the child or the mother is frequently represented with a bunch of flowers in the hand.

Here, let it be noted, the association of flowers with divinely born Saviors, in India, is indicated in the religious books of that country to have originated from the conception of the virgin parting with the flowers of her virginity by giving birth to a divine child, whereby she lost the immortality of her physical nature, it being transferred by that act to her Deity-begotten son. And from this circumstance, Sakia is represented as having been crucified for abstracting a flower from a garden. That his crucifixion was designed as a sin-atoning offering, is evident from the following declaration found in his sacred biography, viz.: "He in mercy left Paradise, and came down to earth because he was filled with compassion for the sins and miseries of mankind. He sought to lead them into better paths, and took their sufferings upon himself that he might expiate their crimes and mitigate the punishment they must otherwise inevitably undergo." (Prog. Rel. Ideas, vol. i. p. 86.)

He believed and taught his followers that all sin is inevitably punished, either in this or the future life; and so great were his sympathy and tenderness, that he condescended to suffer that punishment himself, by an ignominious death upon the cross, after which he descended into

Hades (Hell), to suffer for a time (three days) for the inmates of that dreadful and horrible prison, that he might show he sympathized with them. After his resurrection, and before his ascension to heaven, as well as during his earthly sojourn, he imparted to the world some beautiful, lofty, and soul-elevating precepts.

"The object of his mission," says a writer, "was to instruct those who were straying from the right path, and expiate the sins of mortals by his own suffering, and procure for them a happy entrance into Paradise by obedience to his precepts and prayers to his name." (Ibid.) "His followers always speak of him as one with God from all eternity." (Ibid.) His most common title was "the Savior of the World." He was also called "the Benevolent One," "the Dispenser of Grace," "the Source of Life," "the Light of the World," "the True Light," etc.

His mother was a very pure, refined, pious and devout woman; never indulged in any impure thoughts, words or actions. She was so much esteemed for her virtues and for being the mother of a God, that an escort of ladies attended her wherever she went. The trees bowed before her as she passed through the forest, and flowers sprang up wherever her foot pressed the ground. She was saluted as "the Holy Virgin, Queen of Heaven."

It is said that when her divine child was born, he stood upright and proclaimed, "I will put an end to the sufferings and sorrows of the world." And immediately a light shone around about the young Messiah. He spent much time in retirement, and like Christ in another respect, was once tempted by a demon who offered him all the honors and wealth of the world. But he rebuked the devil, saying, "Be gone; hinder me not."

He began, like Christ, to preach his gospel and heal the sick when about twenty-eight years of age. And it is declared, "the blind saw, the deaf heard, the dumb spoke, the lame danced and the crooked became straight." Hence, the people declared, "He is no mortal child, but an incarnation of the Deity." His religion was of a very superior character. He proclaimed, "My law is a law of grace for all." His religion knew no race, no sex, no caste, and no aristocratic priesthood.

"It taught," says Max Muller, "the equality of all men, and the brotherhood of the human race." "All men, without regard to rank, birth or nation," says Dunckar, "form, according to Budha's view, one great suffering association in this earthly vale of tears; therefore, the commandments of love, forbearance, patience, compassion, pity, brotherliness of all men." Klaproth (a German professor of oriental languages) says this religion is calculated to ennoble the human race. "It is difficult to comprehend," says a French writer (M. Leboulay), "how men, not assisted by revelation, could have soared so high, and approached so near the truth."

Dunckar says this oriental God "taught self-denial, chastity, temperance, the control of the passions, to bear injustice from others, to suffer death quietly, and without hate of your persecutor, to grieve not for one's own misfortunes, but for those of others." An investigation of their history will show that that they lived up to these moral injunctions. "Besides the five great commandments," says a Wesleyan missionary (Spense Hardy) in his Dahmma Padam, "every shade of vice, hypocrisy, anger, pride, suspicion, greediness, gossiping, and cruelty to animals is guarded against by special precepts. Among the virtues, recommended, we find not only reverence for parents, care for children, submission to authority, gratitude, moderation in all things, submission in time of trial, equanimity at all times, but virtues, unknown in some systems of morality, such as the duty of forgiving injuries, and not rewarding evil for evil." And we will add, both charity and love are specially recommended.

We have it also upon the authority of Dunckar that "Budha proclaimed that salvation and redemption have come for all, even the lowest and most abject classes." For he broke down the iron caste of the Brahminical code which had so long ruled India, and aimed to place all mankind upon a level. His followers have been stigmatize! by Christian professors as "idolaters." But Sir John Bowling, in his "Kingdom and People of Siam," denies that they are idolaters—"because," says he, "no Budhist believes his image to be God, or anything more than an outward representation of Deity." Their deific images are looked upon with the same views and feelings as a Christian venerates the photograph of his deceased friend. Hence, if one is an idolater, the other is also. With respect to the charge of polytheism, Missionary Hue says, "that although their religion embraces many inferior deities, who fill the same offices that angels do under the Christian system, yet,"—adds M. Hue—"monotheism is the real character of Buddhism;" and confirms the statement by the testimony of a Thibetan.

It should be noted here that although Budhism succeeded in converting about three hundred millions, or one-third of the inhabitants of the globe, it was never propagated by the sword, and never persecuted the disciples of other religions. Its conquests were made by a rational appeal to the human mind. Mr. Hodgson says, "It recognizes the infinite capacity of the human intellect." And St. Hilaire declares, "Love for all beings is its nucleus; and to love our enemies, and not prosecute, are the virtues of this people." Max Muller says, "Its moral code, taken by itself, is one of the most perfect the world has ever known."

Its five commandments are:—

1. Thou shalt not kill.

2. Thou shalt not steal.

3. Thou shalt not commit adultery or any impurity.

4. Thou shall not lie.

5. Thou shalt not intoxicate thyself.

To establish the above cited doctrines and precepts, Budha sent forth his disciples into the world to preach his gospel to every creature. And if any convert had committed a sin in word, thought or deed, he was to confess and repent. One of the tracts which they distributed declares, "There is undoubtedly a life after this, in which the virtuous may expect the reward of their good deeds.... Judgment takes place immediately after death."

Budha and his followers set an example to the world of enduring opposition and persecution with great patience and non-resistance. And some of them suffered martyrdom rather than abandon their principles, and gloried in thus sealing their doctrines with their lives.

A story is told of a rich merchant by the name of Purna, forsaking all to follow his lord and master; and also of his encountering and talking with a woman of low caste at a well, which reminds us of similar incidents in the history of Christ. But his enemies, becoming jealous and fearful of his growing power, finally crucified him near the foot of the Nepaul mountains, about 600 B. C. But after his death, burial and resurrection, we are told he ascended back to heaven, where millions of his followers believed he had existed with Brahma from all eternity.

[Note.—In the cases of crucifixion which follow, nothing like accuracy can be expected with respect to the dates of their occurrence, as all history covering the period beyond the modern era, or prior to the time of Alexander the Great (330 B. C.) is involved in a labyrinth of uncertainty with respect to dates. Hence, bible chronologists differ to the extent of three thousand years with respect to the time of every event recorded in the Old Testament. Compare the Hebrew and Septuagint versions of the bible: The former makes the world three thousand nine hundred and forty four, and the latter five thousand two hundred and seventy years old at the birth of Christ— a difference of thirteen hundred and twenty-six years. And other translations differ still more widely. All the cases of crucifixion which follow occurred before the time of Christ, but the exact time of many of them cannot be fixed with certainty.]

III.—THAMMUZ OF SYRIA CRUCIFIED, 1160 B. C.

The history of this God is furnished us in fragments by several writers, portions of which will be found in other chapters of this work. The fullest history extant of this God-Savior is probably that of Ctesias (400 B. C.), author of "Persika." The poet has perpetuated his memory in rhyme.

```
"Trust, ye saints, your Lord restored,
Trust ye in your risen Lord,
For the pains which Thammuz endured
Our salvation have procured "
```

Mr. Higgins informs us (Anac. vol. i. p. 246) that this God was crucified at the period above named, as a sin-atoning offering The stanza just quoted is predicated upon the following Greek text, translated by Godwin: "Trust ye in God, for out of his loins salvation has come unto us." Julius Firmicus speaks of this God "rising from the dead for the salvation of the world." The Christian writer Parkhurst alludes to this Savior as preceding the advent of Christ, and as filling to some extent the same chapter in sacred history.

IV.—CRUCIFIXION OF WITTOBA OF THE TELINGONESS, 552 B. C.

We have a very conclusive historical proof of the crucifixion of this heathen God. Mr. Higgins tells us, "He is represented in his history with nail-holes in his hands and the soles of his feet." Nails, hammers and pincers are constantly seen represented on his crucifixes, and are objects of adoration among his followers. And the iron crown of Lombardy has within it a nail of what is claimed as his true original cross, and is much admired and venerated on that account. The worship of this crucified God, according to our author, prevails chiefly in the Travancore and other southern countries in the region of Madura.

V.—IAO OF NEPAUL CRUCIFIED, 622 B. C.

With respect to the crucifixion of this ancient Savior, we have this very definite and specific testimony that "he was crucified on a tree in Nepaul." (See Georgius, p. 202.) The name of this incarnate God and oriental Savior occurs frequently in the holy bibles and sacred books of other countries. Some suppose that Iao (often spelt Jao) is the root of the name of the Jewish God Jehovah.

VI.—HESUS OF THE CELTIC DRUIDS CRUCIFIED, 834 B. C.

Mr. Higgins informs us that the Celtic Druids represent their God Hesus as having been crucified with a lamb on one side and an elephant on the other, and that this occurred long before the Christian era. Also that a representation of it may now be seen upon "the fire-tower of Brechin."

In this symbolical representation of the crucifixion, the elephant, being the largest animal known, was chosen to represent the magnitude of the sins of the world, while the lamb, from its proverbial innocent nature, was chosen to represent the innocency of the victim (the God offered as a propitiatory sacrifice). And thus we have "the Lamb of God taking away the sins of the world"—symbolical language used with respect to the offering of Jesus Christ. And here is indicated very clearly the origin of the figure. It is evidently borrowed from the Druids. We have the statement of the above writer that this legend was found amongst the Canutes of Gaul long before Jesus Christ was known to history. (See Anac. vol. ii. p. 130.)

VII.—QUEXALCOTE OF MEXICO CRUCIFIED, 587 B. C.

Historical authority, relative to the crucifixion of this Mexican God, and to his execution upon the cross as a propitiatory sacrifice for the sins of mankind, is explicit, unequivocal and ineffaceable. The evidence is tangible, and indelibly engraven upon steel and metal plates. One of these plates represents him as having been crucified on a mountain; another represents him as having been crucified in the heavens, as St. Justin tells us Christ was. According to another writer, he is sometimes represented as having been nailed to a cross, and by other accounts as hanging with a cross in his hand. The "Mexican Antiquities" (vol. vi. p. 166) says, "Quexalcote is represented in the paintings of 'Codex Borgianus' as nailed to the cross." Sometimes two thieves are represented as having been crucified with him.

That the advent of this crucified Savior and Mexican God was long anterior to the era of Christ, is admitted by Christian writers, as we have shown elsewhere. In the work above named "Codex Borgianus," may be found the account, not only of his crucifixion, but of his death, burial, descent into hell, and resurrection on the third day. And another work, entitled "Codex Vaticanus," contains the story of his immaculate birth by a virgin mother by the name of Chimalman.

Many other incidences are found related of him in his sacred biography, in which we find the most striking counterparts to the more modern gospel story of Jesus Christ, such as his forty days' temptation and fasting, his riding on an ass, his purification in the temple, his baptism and regeneration by water, his forgiving of sins, being anointed with oil, etc. "All these things, and many more, found related of this Mexican God in their sacred books," says Lord Kingsborough (a Christian writer), "are curious and mysterious." (See the books above cited.)

VIII.—QUIRINUS OF ROME CRUCIFIED, 506 B. C.

The crucifixion of this Roman Savior is briefly noticed by Mr. Higgins, and is remarkable for presenting (like other crucified Gods) several parallel features to that of the Judean Savior, not only in the circumstances related as attending his crucifixion, but also in a considerable portion of his antecedent life.

He is represented, like Christ:—

1. As having been conceived and brought forth by a virgin.

2. His life was sought by the reigning king (Amulius),

3. He was of royal blood, his mother being of kingly descent.

4. He was "put to death by wicked hands"—i. e., crucified.

5. At his mortal exit the whole earth is said to have been enveloped in darkness, as in the case of Christ, Chrishna, and Prometheus.

6. And finally he is resurrected, and ascends back to heaven.

IX.—(ÆSCHYLUS) PROMETHEUS CRUCIFIED, 547 B. C.

In the account of the crucifixion of Prometheus of Caucasus, as furnished by Seneca, Hesiod, and other writers, it is stated that he was nailed to an upright beam of timber, to which were affixed extended arms of wood, and that this cross was situated near the Caspian Straits. The modern story of this crucified God, which represents him as having been bound to a rock for thirty years, while vultures preyed upon his vitals, Mr. Higgins pronounces an impious Christian fraud. "For," says this learned historical writer, "I have seen the account which declares he was nailed to a cross with hammer and nails." (Anac. vol. i. 327.) Confirmatory of this statement is the declaration of Mr. Southwell, that "he exposed himself to the wrath of God in his zeal to save mankind."

The poet, in portraying his propitiatory offering, says

```
"Lo! streaming from the fatal tree
His all atoning blood,
Is this the Infinite?—
Yes, 'tis he,
Prometheus, and a God!

"Well might the sun in darkness hide,
And veil his glories in,
When God, the great Prometheus, died
For man the creature's sin."
```

The "New American Cyclopedia" (vol. i. p. 157) contains the following significant declaration relative to this sin-atoning oriental Savior: "It is doubtful whether there is to be found in the whole range of Greek letters deeper pathos than that of the divine woe of the beneficent demigod Prometheus, crucified on his Scythian crags for his love to mortals." Here we have first-class authority for the crucifixion of this oriental God.

In Lempriere's "Classical Dictionary," Higgins' "Anacalypsis," and other works, may be found the following particulars relative to the final exit of the God above named, viz.:—

1. That the whole frame of nature became convulsed.

2. The earth shook, the rocks were rent, the graves were opened, and in a storm, which seemed to threaten the dissolution of the universe, the solemn scene forever closed, and "Our Lord and Savior" Prometheus gave up the ghost.

"The cause for which he suffered," says Mr. Southwell, "was his love for the human race." Mr. Taylor makes the statement in his Syntagma (p. 95), that the whole story of Prometheus' crucifixion, burial and resurrection was acted in pantomime in Athens five hundred years before Christ, which proves its great antiquity. Minutius Felix, one of the most popular Christian writers of the second century (in his "Octavius," sect. 29), thus addresses the people of Rome: "Your victorious trophies not only represent a simple cross, but a cross with a man on it," and this man St. Jerome calls a God.

These coincidences furnish still further proof that the tradition of the crucifixion of Gods has been very long prevalent among the heathen.

X.—CRUCIFIXION OF THULIS OF EGYPT, 1700 B. C.

Thulis of Egypt, whence comes "Ultima Thule," died the death of the cross about thirty-five hundred years ago.

Ultima Thule was the island which marked the ultimate bounds of the extensive empire of this legitimate descendant of the Gods.

This Egyptian Savior appears also to have been known as Zulis, and with this name—Mr. Wilkison tells us—"his history is curiously illustrated in the sculptures, made seventeen hundred years B. C., of a small, retired chamber lying nearly over the western adytum of the temple-" We are told twenty-eight lotus plants near his grave indicate the number of years he lived on the earth. After suffering a violent death, he was buried, but rose again, ascended into heaven, and there became "the judge of the dead," or of souls in a future state. Wilkison says he came down from heaven to benefit mankind, and that he was said to be "full of grace and truth."

XI.—CRUCIFIXION OF INDRA OF THIBET, 725 B. C.

The account of the crucifixion of the God and Savior Indra may be found in Georgius, Thibetinum Alphabetum, p. 230. A brief notice of the case is all we have space for here. In the work just referred to may be found plates representing this Thibetan Savior as having been nailed to the cross. There are five wounds, representing the nailholes and the piercing of the side. The antiquity of the story is beyond dispute.

Marvelous stories are told of the birth of the Divine Redeemer. His mother was a virgin of black complexion, and hence his complexion was of the ebony hue, as in the case of Christ and some other sin-atoning Saviors. He descended from heaven on a mission of benevolence, and ascended back to the heavenly mansion after his crucifixion. He led a life of strict celibacy, which, he taught, was essential to true holiness. He inculcated great tenderness toward all living beings. He could walk upon the water or upon the air; he could foretell future events with great accuracy. He practiced the most devout contemplation, severe discipline of the body and mind, and acquired the most complete subjection of his passions. He was worshiped as a God who had existed as a spirit from all eternity, and his followers were called "Heavenly Teachers."

XII.—ALCESTOS OF EURIPIDES CRUCIFIED, 600 B. C.

The "English Classical Journal" (vol. xxxvii.) furnishes us with the story of another crucified God, known as Alcestos—a female God or Goddess; and in this respect, it is a novelty in sacred history, being the first, if not the only example of a feminine God atoning for the sins of the world upon the cross. The doctrine of the trinity and atoning offering for sin was inculcated as a part of her religion.

XIII.—ATYS OF PHRYGIA CRUCIFIED, 1170 B. C.

Speaking of this crucified Messiah, the Anacalypsis informs us that several histories are given of him, but all concur in representing him as having been an atoning offering for sin. And the Latin phrase "suspensus lingo," found in his history, indicates the manner of his death. He was suspended on a tree, crucified, buried and rose again.

XIV.—CRITE OF CHALDEA CRUCIFIED, 1200 B. C.

The Chaldeans, as Mr. Higgins informs us, have noted in their sacred books the account of the crucifixion of a God with the above name. He was also known as "the Redeemer," and was styled "the Ever Blessed Son of God," "the Savior of the Race," "the Atoning Offering for an Angry God." And when he was offered up, both heaven and earth were shaken to their foundations.

XV.—BALI OF ORISSA CRUCIFIED, 725 B. C.

We learn by the oriental books, that in the district of country known as Orissa, in Asia, they have the story of a crucified God, known by several names, including the above, all of which, we are told, signify "Lord Second," having reference to him as the second person or second member of the trinity, as most of the crucified Gods occupied that position in the trial of deities constituting the trinity, as indicated by the language "Father, Son, and Holy Ghost," the Son, in all cases, being the atoning offering, "the crucified Redeemer," and the second person of the trinity. This God Bali was also called Baliu, and sometimes Bel. The Anacalypsis informs us (vol. i. 257) that monuments of this crucified God, bearing great age, may be found amid the ruins of the magnificent city of Mahabalipore, partially buried amongst the figures of the temple.

XVI.—MITHRA OF PERSIA CRUCIFIED, 600 B. C.

This Persian God, according to Mr. Higgins, was "slain upon the cross to make atonement for mankind, and to take away the sins of the world." He was reputedly born on the twenty-fifth day of December, and crucified on a tree. It is a remarkable circumstance that two Christian writers (Mr. Faber and Mr. Bryant) both speak of his "being slain," and yet both omit to speak of the manner in which he was put to death. And the same policy has been pursued with respect to other crucified Gods of the pagans, as we have shown elsewhere.

Our list is full, or we might note other cases of crucifixion. Devatat of Siam, Ixion of Rome, Apollonius of Tyana in Cappadocia, are all reported in history as having "died the death of the cross."

Ixion, 400 B. C., according to Nimrod, was crucified on a wheel, the rim representing the world, and the spokes constituting the cross. It is declared, "He bore the burden of the world" (that is, "the sins of the world") on his back while suspended on the cross. Hence, he was sometimes called "the crucified spirit of the world."

With respect to Apollonius, it is a remarkable, if not a suspicious circumstance that should not be passed unnoticed, that several Christian writers, while they recount a long list of miracles and remarkable incidents in the life of this Cappadocian Savior, extending through his whole life, and forming a parallel to similar incidents of the Christian Savior, not a word is said about his crucifixion.

And a similar policy has been pursued with respect to Mithra and other sin-atoning Gods, including Chrishna and Prometheus, as before noticed.

This important chapter in their history has been omitted by Christian writers for fear the relation of it would damage the credibility of the crucifixion of Christ, or lessen its spiritual force. For, like Paul, they were "determined to know nothing but Jesus Christ and him crucified" (i Cor. ii. 2) i. e., to *know* no other God had been crucified but *Jesus Christ*. They thus exalted the tradition of the crucifixion into the most important dogma of the Christian faith. Hence, their efforts to conceal from the public a knowledge of the fact that it is of pagan origin.

By reference to Mackey's "Lexicon of Freemasonry" (p. 35) we learn that Freemasons secretly taught the doctrine of the crucifixion, atonement and resurrection long anterior to the Christian era, and that similar doctrines were taught in "all the ancient mysteries," thus proving that the conception of these tenets of faith existed at a very early period of time.

And it may be noted here, that the doctrine of salvation by crucifixion had likewise, with most of the ancient forms of religious faith, an astronomical representation—i. e., a representation in astronomical symbols. According to the emblematical figures comprised in their astral worship, people were saved by the sun's crucifixion or crossification, realized by *crossing* over the

70

equinoctial line into the season of spring, and thereby gave out a saving heat and light to the world and stimulated the generative organs of animal and vegetable life. It was from this conception that the ancients were in the habit of carving or painting the organs of generation upon the walls of their holy temples. The blood of the grape, which was ripened by the heat of the sun, as he crossed over by resurrection into spring, (i. e., was crucified), was symbolically "the blood of the cross," or "the blood of the Lamb."

If we should be met here with the statement, that the stories of the ancient crucifixions of Gods were mere myths or fables, unwarrantably saddled on to their histories as mere romance, and have no foundation in fact, we reply—there is as much ground for suspecting the same thing as being true of Jesus Christ.

One of the most celebrated and most frequently quoted Christian writers of the ancient bishops (Irenæus) declares upon the authority of the martyr Polycarp, who claimed to have got it from St. John and all the elders of Asia, that Jesus Christ was not crucified, but lived to be about fifty years old.

We find there has always been a margin for doubt amongst his own followers as to the fact of his crucifixion.

Many of the early Christians and cotemporary Jews and Gentiles doubted it, and some openly disputed its ever having taken place. Others bestowed upon it a mere spiritual signification, and not a few considered it symbolical of a "holy life." One circumstance, calculated to lead to the entire discredit of the story of the crucifixion of Christ, is the relation, in connection with it, of a violent convulsion of nature, and the resurrection of the long-buried saints—events not supported by any authentic cotemporaneous history, sacred or profane. (See Chap. XVII., Aphanasia).

And as these events must be set down as fabulous, they leave the mind in doubt with respect to the fact of the crucifixion itself, especially when the many absurdities involved in the doctrine of the crucifixion are brought to view, in connection with it, some of them so palpably erroneous that an unlettered savage could see and point them out.

The Indian chief Red Jacket is reported to have replied to the Christian missionaries, when they urged upon his attention the benefits of Christ's death by crucifixion, "Brethren, if you white men murdered the son of the Great Spirit, we Indians have nothing to do with it, and it is none of our affair. If he had come among us, we would not have killed him. We would have treated him well. You must make amends for that crime yourselves."

This view of the crucifixion suggested to the mind of an illiterate heathen we deem more sensible and rational than that of the orthodox Christians, which makes it a meritorious act and a moral necessity. For this would not only exonerate Judas from any criminality or guilt for the part he took in the affair, but would entitle him as well as Christ to the honorable title of a "Savior" for performing an act without which the crucifixion and consequent salvation of the world could not have been effected. If it was necessary for Christ to suffer death upon the cross as an atonement for sin, then the act of crucifixion was right, and a monument should be erected to the memory of Judas for bringing it about. We challenge Christian logic to find a flaw in this argument.

71

And another important consideration arises here. If the inhabitants of this planet required the murderous death of a God as an atonement, we must presume that the eighty-five millions of inhabited worlds recently discovered by astronomers are, or have been, in equal need of a divine atonement. And this would require the crucifixion of eighty-five millions of Gods. Assuming one of these Gods to be crucified every minute, the whole would occupy a period of nearly twenty years. This would be killing off Gods at rather a rapid rate, and would make the work of the atonement and salvation a very murderous and bloody affair—a conception which brings to the mind a series of very revolting reflections.

The conception of Gods coming down from heaven, and being born of virgins, and dying a violent death for the moral blunders of the people, originated in an age of the world when man was a savage, and dwelt exclusively upon the animal plane, and blood was the requisition for every offense. And it was an age when no world was known to exist but the one we inhabit. The stars were then supposed to be mere blazing tapers set in the azure vault to light this pygmy planet, or peep-holes for Gods to look out of heaven, to see and learn what is going on below. Such conceptions are in perfect keeping with the doctrine of the atoning crucifixion of Gods, which could never have originated or been entertained for a moment by an astronomer, with a knowledge of the existence of innumerable inhabited worlds. For as there is to the monotheistic Christian but one God, or Son of God, to be offered, he must be incarnated and crucified every day for a thousand years to make a sin-offering for each of these worlds—a conception too monstrous and preposterous to find a lodgment in a rational mind.

ORIGIN OF THE BELIEF OF THE CRUCIFIXION OF GODS.

It has always been presumed that death, and especially death by crucifixion, involved the highest state of suffering possible to be endured by mortals. Hence, the Gods must suffer in this way as an example of courage and fortitude, and to show themselves willing to undergo all the affliction and misery incident to the lot, and unavoidable to the lives, of their devoted worshipers. They must not only be equal, but superior to their subjects in this respect Hence, they would not merely die, but choose, or at least uncomplainingly submit to the most ignoble and ignominious mode of suffering death that could be devised, and that was crucifixion. This gave the highest finishing touch to the drama.

And thus the legend of the crucifixion became the crowning chapter, the aggrandizing episode in the history of their lives. It was presumed that nothing less than a God could endure such excruciating tortures without complaining.

Hence, when the victim was reported to have submitted with such fortitude that no murmur was heard to issue from his lips, this circumstance of itself was deemed sufficient evidence of his Godship. The story of the crucifixion, therefore, whether true or false, deified or helped deify many great men and exalt them to the rank of Gods. Though some of the disciples of Budhism, and some of the primitive professors of Christianity also (including, according to Christian history, Peter and his brother Andrew), voluntarily chose this mode of dying in imitation of their crucified Lord, without experiencing, however, the desired promotion to divine honors. They failed of an exaltation to the deityship, and hence are not now worshiped as Gods.

72

Christian reader, what can you now make of the story of the crucifixion of Jesus Christ but a borrowed legend—at least the story of his being crucified *as a God!*

Note.—The author desires it to be understood with respect to the cases of crucifixion here briefly narrated, that they are not vouched foras actual occurrences, of which there is much ground to doubt. It has neither been his aim or desire to prove them to be real historical events, nor to establish any certain number of cases. Indeed, he deems it unimportant to know, if it could be determined, whether they are fact or fiction, or whether one God was crucified, or many. The moral lesson designed to be taught by this chapter is, simply, that the belief in the crucifixion of Gods was prevalent in various oriental or heathen countries long prior to the reported crucifixion of Christ. If this point is established—which he feels certain no reader will dispute—then he is not concerned to know whether he has made out sixteen cases of crucifixion or not. Six will prove it as well as sixteen. In fact, one case is sufficient to establish the important proposition in view. The reader is, therefore, left to decide each case for himself, according as he may value the evidence presented. More authorities could have been adduced, and a more extended history presented of each God brought to notice. But this would have operated to exclude other matter, which the author considers of more importance.

CHAPTER XVII. THE APHANASIA, OR DARKNESS AT THE CRUCIFIXION.

MATTHEW tells us (xxvii. 31) that when Christ was crucified, there was darkness all over the land for three hours, and "the earth did quake, and the rocks were rent, and many of the saints came out of their graves."

Here we have a series of events spoken of so strange, so unusual and so extraordinary that, had they occurred, they must have attracted the attention of the whole world—especially the amazing scene of the sun's withdrawing his light and ceasing to shine, and thereby causing an almost total darkness near the middle of the day. And yet no writer of that age or country, or any other age or country, mentions the circumstance but Matthew. A phenomenon so terrible and so serious in its effects as literally to unhinge the planets and partially disorganize the universe must have excited the alarm and amazement of the whole world, and caused a serious disturbance in the affairs of nations. And yet strange, superlatively strange, not one of the numerous historians of that age makes the slightest allusion to such an astounding event.

Even Seneca and the elder Pliny, who so particularly and minutely chronicle the events of those times, are as silent as the grave relative to this greatest event in the history of the world. Nor do Mark, Luke or John, who all furnish us with a history of the crucifixion, make the slightest hint at any of these wonder-exciting events, except Mark's incidental allusion to the darkness.

Gibbon says, "It happened during the life of Seneca and the elder Pliny, who must have experienced its immediate effects, or received the earliest intelligence of the prodigy. Each of these philosophers, in a labored work, has recorded all the phenomena of Nature's earthquakes, meteors and eclipses, which his indefatigable curiosity could collect. Both the one and the other have omitted to mention the greatest phenomenon, to which the mortal eye has been witness since the creation of the world." (Gibbon, p. 451.)

2. With reference to the "bodies" of the dead saints coming out of their tombs (for it is declared their "bodies arose," see Matt, xxvii. 52), many rather curious and puzzling questions might be started, which would at once disclose its utter absurdity.

We might ask, for example

1. Who were those "many saints" who came out of their graves, seeing there were as yet but few Christians to occupy graves, if they had been all dead, as the enumeration at Antioch made out only one hundred and twenty? (See Acts.) 2. How long had they lain in their graves?

3. How long since their bodies had turned to dust, and been food for worms? 4. And would not those worms have to be hunted up and required to disgorge the contents of their stomachs in order to furnish the saints with the materials for their bodies again? 5. And were the shrouds or grave clothes of those saints also resurrected? or did they travel about in a state of nudity? 6. For what purpose were they re-animated? 7. And should not Matthew have furnished us, by way of proof, with the names of some of these ghostly visitors? 8. How long did they live the second time? 9. Did they die again, or did they ascend to heaven with their new-made bodies? 10. What business did they engage in? 11. Why have we not some account of what they said and did? 12. And what finally became of them?

Until these questions are rationally answered, the story must be regarded as too incredible and too ludicrous to merit serious notice.

3. Nearly all the phenomena represented as occurring at the crucifixion of Christ are reported to have been witnessed also at the final exit of Senerus, an ancient pagan demigod, who figured in history at a still more remote period of time. And similar incidents are related likewise in the legendary histories of several other heathen demigods and great men partially promoted to the honor of Gods. In the time-honored records of the oldest religion in the world, it is declared, "A cloud surrounded the moon; and the sun was darkened at noonday, and the sky rained fire and ashes during the crucifixion of the Indian God Chrishna." In the case of Osiris of Egypt, Mr. Southwell says, "As his birth had been attended by an eclipse of the sun, so his death was attended by a still greater darkness of the solar orb." At the critical juncture of the crucifixion of Prometheus, it is declared, "The whole frame of nature became convulsed, the earth shook, the rocks were rent, the graves opened, and in a storm which threatened the dissolution of the universe, the scene closed" (Higgins). According to Livy, the last hours of the mortal demise of Romulus were marked by a storm and by a solar eclipse.

And similar stories are furnished us by several writers of Cæsar and Alexander the Great. With respect to the latter, Mr. Nimrod says, "Six hours of darkness formed his aphanasia, and his soul, like Polycarp's, was seen to fly away in the form of a dove." (Nimrod, vol. iii. p. 458.) "It is remarkable," says a writer, "what a host of respectable authorities vouch for an acknowledged fable—the preternatural darkness which followed Cæsar's death." Gibbon alludes to this event when he speaks of "the singular defect of light which followed the murder of Caesar." He likewise says, "This season of darkness had already been celebrated by most of the poets and historians of that memorable age." (Gibbon, p. 452.) It is very remarkable that Pliny speaks of a darkness attending Cæsar's death, but omits to mention such a scene as attending the crucifixion of Christ. Virgil also seeks to exalt this royal personage by relating this prodigy. (See his Georgius, p. 465.) Another writer says, "Similar prodigies were supposed or said to accompany the great men of former days."

Let the reader make a note of this fact—that the same story was told of the graves opening, and the dead rising at the final mortal exit of several heathen Gods and several great men long before it was penned as a chapter in the history of Christ.

Shakespeare, in his Hamlet says:—

```
"In the most high and palmy days of Rome,
A little ere the mighty Julius fell—
The graves stood tenantless, and the sheeted dead
Did squeak and gibber in the Roman streets."
```

These historical citations strongly press the conclusion that this portion of the history of Christ was borrowed from old pagan legends.

4. Many cases are recorded in history of the light of the sun being obscured at midday so as to result in almost total darkness, when it was known not to be produced by an eclipse. And it is probable that these natural events furnish the basis in part for those wild legends we have brought to notice. Humboldt relates in his Cosmos, that, "in the year 358, before the earthquake of Numidia, the darkness was very dense for two or three hours." Another obscuration of the sun took place in the year 360, which lasted five or six hours, and was so dense that the stars were visible at midday. Another circumstance of this kind was witnessed on the nineteenth of May, 1730, which lasted eight hours. And so great was the darkness, that candles and lamps had to be lighted at midday to dine by. Similar events are chronicled for the years 1094, 1206, 1241, 1547, and 1730. And if any such solar obscurations occurred near the mortal exit of any of the Gods above named, of course they would be seized on as a part of their practical history wrought up into hyperbole, and interwoven in their narratives, to give eclat to the pageantry of their biographies—a fact which helps to solve the mystery.

ORIGIN OF THE STORY OF THE APHANASIA AT THE CRUCIFIXION.

There is but little ground to doubt but that the various stories of a similar character then current in different countries, as shown above, first suggested the thought to Christ's biographers of investing history with the incredible events reported as being connected with the crucifixion. The principal motive, however, seems to have grown out of a desire to fulfill a prophecy of the Jewish prophet Joel, as we may find many of the important miraculous events ingrafted into

75

Christ's history were recorded by way of fulfilling some prophecy. "That the prophecy might be fulfilled" is the very language his evangelical biographers use.

Joel's prediction runs thus: "And I will show wonders in the heavens, and in the earth, flood and fire, and pillars of smoke. The sun shall be turned into darkness, and the moon into blood, before the great and terrible day of the Lord come." (Joel ii. 30.) A little impartial investigation will satisfy any unprejudiced mind that this poetic rhapsody has not the most remote allusion to the closing events in the life of Christ, and was not intended to have.

But his biographers, writing a long time after his death, supposing and assuming that this and various other texts, which they quote from the prophets, had reference to him, and had been fulfilled, incorporated it into his history as a part of his practical life. The conviction that the prophecy *must have been fulfilled*, without knowing that it had, added to similar stories of other Gods, with which Christ's history became confounded, misled them into the conclusion that they were warranted in assuming that the incredible events they name were really witnessed at the mortal termination of Christ's earthly career, when they did not know it, and could not have known it.

This view of the case becomes very rational and very forcible when we observe various texts quoted from the prophets by the gospel writers, or, rather, most butcheringly misquoted, tortured or distorted into Messianic prophecies, when the context shows they have no reference to Christ whatever.

CHAPTER XVIII. DESCENT OF THE SAVIORS INTO HELL.

THE next most important event in the histories of the Saviors after their crucifixion, and the act of giving up the ghost, is that of their descent into the infernal regions. That Jesus Christ descended into hell after his crucifixion is not expressly taught in the Christian bible, but it is a matter of such obvious inference from several passages of scripture, the early Christians taught it as a scriptural doctrine. Mr. Sears, a Christian writer, tells us that "on the doctrine of Christ's underground mission the early Christians were united.... It was a point too well settled to admit of dispute." (See Foregleams of Immortality, p. 262).

And besides this testimony, the "Apostles' Creed" teaches the doctrine explicitly, which was once as good authority throughout Christendom as the bible itself; indeed, it may be considered as constituting a part of the bible prior to the council of Nice (A. D. 325), being supposed to have been written by the apostles themselves. It declares that "Jesus Christ suffered under Pontius Pilate, was crucified (dead) and buried. He descended into hell; the third day he rose again from the dead," etc. This testimony is very explicit.

76

And Peter is supposed to refer to the same event when he says, "being put to death in the flesh, but quickened by the spirit, by which also he went and preached unto the spirits in prison." (i Peter iii. 18.) The word prison, which occurs in this text, has undoubted reference to the Christian fabled hell. For no possible sense can be attached to the word prison in this connection without such a construction. Where have spirits ever been supposed to be imprisoned but in hell? And then we find a text in the Acts of the Apostles, which seems to remove all doubt in the case, and banishes at once all ground for dispute. It is explicitly stated that "his soul was not left in hell, neither did his flesh see corruption.' (Adis ii. 31.) Why talk about his soul not being left in hell if it had never been there? Language could hardly be plainer. The most positive declaration that Christ did descend into hell could not make it more certainly a scriptural Christian doctrine.

We, then, rest the case here, and proceed to enumerate other cases of Gods and Saviors descending into Pandemonium (the realms of Pluto) long before Jesus Christ walked on the water or on the earth. It is unquestionably stated in the Hindoo bible, written more than three thousand years ago, that the Savior Chrishna "went down to hell to preach to the inmates of that dark and dreary prison, with the view of reforming them, and getting them back to heaven, and was willing himself to suffer to abridge the period of their torment." And certainly, in the midst of the fire and smoke of brimstone, it could not have been hard to effect their conversion or repentance. One writer tells us that "so great was his (Chrishna's) tenderness, that he even descended into hell to teach souls in bondage." Now observe how much "teaching souls in bondage" sounds like "preaching to souls in prison," as Peter represents Christ as doing. And can any reader doubt that the meaning in the two cases is the same? And must we not confess that we are greatly indebted to the Hindoo bible for an explanation of the two occult and mysterious texts which I have quoted from the Christian bible, and which have puzzled so many learned critics to explain, or find a meaning for?

We have another case of a God descending into hell in the person or spirit of the Savior Quexalcote of Mexico, (300 B. C.) The story will be found in the Codex Borgianus, wherein is related the account of his death, and burial after crucifixion, his descent into hell, and subsequent resurrection. Of Adonis of Greece it is declared, that "after his descent into hell, he rose again to life and immortality." Prometheus of Caucasus (600 B. C.) likewise is represented as "suffering and descending into hell, rising again from the dead, and ascending to heaven." Horus of Greece is described as "first reigning a thousand years, then dying, and being buried for three days, at the end of which time he triumphed over Typhon, the evil principle, and rose again to life evermore." And Osiris of Egypt also is represented as making a descent into hell, and after a period of three days rose again.

Homer and Virgil speak of several cases of descent into Pluto's dominions. Hercules, Ulysses and Æneas are represented as performing the hellward journey on, as we infer, benevolent missions. Higgins remarks, "The Gods became incarnate, and descended into hell to teach humility and set an example of suffering."

The story of their descent into hell was doubtless invented to find employment for them during their three days of hibernation or conservation in the tomb, that they might not appear to be really dead nor idle in the time, and as a still further proof of their matchless and unrivalled capacity and fortitude for suffering.

77

And the story of the three days' entombment is likewise clearly traceable in appearance to the astronomical incident of the sun's lying apparently dead, and buried, and motionless for nearly three days at the period of the vernal epoch, from the twenty-first to the twenty-fifth of March. It was a matter of belief or fancy that the sun remained stationary for about three days, when he gradually rose again "into newness of life." And hence, this period or era was chosen to figuratively represent the three days' descent of the Gods into hell. We are told that the Persians have an ancient astronomical figure representing the descent of a God, divine, into hell, and returning at the time that Orsus, the goddess of spring, had conquered the God or genus of winter, after the manner St. John describes the Lamb of God (see Rev. xii) as conquering the dragon, which may be interpreted as the Scorpion or Dragon of the first month of winter (October) being conquered by the Lamb of March or spring.

CHAPTER XIX. RESURRECTION OF THE SAVIORS

WE find presented in the canonized histories of several of the demigod Saviors the following remarkable coincidences appertaining to their death:—

1. Their resurrection from the dead.

2. Their lying in the tomb just three days.

3. The resurrection of several of them about the time of the vernal equinox. The twenty-fifth of March is the period assigned by the Christian world generally for the resurrection of Christ, though some Christian writers have assigned other dates for this event. They all agree, however, that Christ rose from the dead, and that this occurred three days after the entombment. Bishop Theophilus of Cesarea remarks, relative to this event, "Since the birth of Christ is celebrated on the twenty-fifth of December,.... so also should the resurrection of Jesus be celebrated on the twenty-fifth of March, on whatever day of the week it may fall, the Lord having risen again on that day." (Cent. ii. Call, p. 118.) "All the ancient Christians," says a writer, "were persuaded that Christ was crucified on the twenty-third of March, and rose from the dead on the twenty-fifth." And accordingly Constantine and cotemporary Christians celebrated the twenty-fifth of March with great eclat as the date of the resurrection. The twenty-third and twenty-fifth, including the twenty-fourth, would comprise a period of three days, the time of the entombment.

Now mark, Quexalcote of Mexico, Chris of Chaldea, Quirinus of Rome, Prometheus of Caucasus, Osiris of Egypt, Atys of Phrygia, and "Mithra the Mediator" of Persia did, according to their respective histories, rise from the dead after three days' burial, and the time of their resurrection is in several cases fixed for the twenty-fifth of March. And there is an account more than three thousand years old of the Hindoo crucified Savior Chrishna, three days after his interment, forsaking "the silent bourn, whence (as we are told) no traveler ever returns," and laying aside the moldy cerements of the dead, again walking forth to mortal life, to be again seen, recognized, admired, and adored by his pious, devout and awe-stricken followers, and thus present to the gaze of a hoping yet doubting world "the first fruits of the resurrection."

At the annual celebration of the resurrection of the Persian Savior "Mithra the Mediator," more than three thousand years ago, the priests were in the habit of exclaiming in a solemn and loud voice, "Cheer up, holy mourners; your God has come again to life; his sorrows and his sufferings will save you." (See Pitrat, p. 105.) The twenty-fifth of March was with the ancient Persians the commencement of a new year, and on that day was celebrated "the feast of the Neurone," and by the ancient Romans "the festival of the Hilaria." And we find the ancients had both the crucifixion and resurrection of a God symbolically and astronomically represented among the plants. "Their foundation," says Clement of Alexandria, "was the fictitious death and resurrection of the sun, the soul of the world, the principle of life and motion." The inauguration of spring (the twenty-fifth of March), and the summer solstice (the twenty-fifth of June), were both important periods with the ancients.

Hence, the latter period was fixed on as the birthday of John the Baptist (as marked in the almanacs), when the sun begins to decline southward—that is, decrease. How appropriately, therefore, John is made to say, "I shall decrease, but he shall increase." And the consecrated twenty-fifth of March is also the day marked in our calendars as the date of the conception and annunciation of the Blessed Virgin Mary. And it was likewise the period of the conception of the ancient Roman Virgin Asteria, and of the ever-chaste and holy virgin Iris, as well as the time of the conjugal embrace of the solar and lunar potentates of the visible universe. May we not, then, very appropriately exclaim of religion and astronomy, "what God hath joined together, let no man put asunder."

Resurrection of Jesus Christ.

With respect to the physical resurrection of the Christian Savior, it may be observed that, aside from the physical impossibility of such an occurrence, the account, as reported to us by his four "inspired" Gospel biographers, are so palpably at variance with each other, so entirely contradictory in their reports, as to render their testimony as infallible writers utterly unworthy of credence, and impels us to the conclusion that the event is both physically and historically incredible. There is scarcely one incident or particular in which they all agree. They are at loggerheads,—

1. With respect to the time of its discovery.

2. The persons who made the discovery (for no witness claims to have seen it).

3. With respect to what took place at the sepulchre.

4. What Peter saw and did there.

5. And as to what occurred afterward, having a relation to that event.

1. Relative to the time the witness or witnesses visited the sepulchre and learned of the resurrection, Matthew (chap. xxviii.) tells us, "It was at the end of the Sabbath, as it began to dawn;" but according to Mark (xvi.), the "Sabbath was past, and the sun was rising;" while John (chap. xx) declares "it was yet dark." Now there is certainly some difference between the three periods, "the dawning of the day," "the rising of the sun," and "the darkness of night." If the writers were *divinely* inspired, there would be a perfect agreement.

2. With respect to the persons who first visited the sepulchre, Matthew states that it was Mary Magdalene and another Mary; but Luke says it was "Mary Magdalene and Joanna, and Mary the mother of James, and other women;" while, according to John (and he virtually reiterates it), Mary Magdalene went alone. It will be observed, then, that the first "inspired" and "infallible" witness testifies there were two women; the second that there were four; and the third witness declares there was but one. What beautiful harmony! No court in the civilized world would accept such discordant testimony!

3. And in relation to what took place at the tomb, Matthew testifies that "the angel of the Lord" sat upon a stone at the door of the sepulchre, and told the women their Lord was risen. But Luke steps forward here, and avers that instead of an angel they found two men there, not outside, but inside, and not sitting, but standing. But Mark sets the testimony of both these "inspired" witnesses aside by affirming there was but one man there, and he was sitting. While Matthew says "they," St. John says "she" (speaking of the person or persons who left the sepulchre). According to Matthew the angel who rolled away the stone from the sepulchre sent a message to the disciples. But Mark affirms that it was not an "angel" outside, but a "young man" inside, who did this. And here the question naturally arises: Why was it necessary for a being who could say, "I have power to lay down my life and take it up again" (John), to have an angel to roll away the stone from the sepulchre. Certainly, if he possessed such omnipotent power, he needed no aid from any being to perform such an act.

4. And relative to Peter's visit to the tomb, there is a total disparity in the testimony of the witnesses. According to Luke, he did not go into the sepulchre, but only stooped down and looked in. But Mark affirms he did go in, and that it was the disciple who went with him who stooped down.

5. And with respect to the events which occurred immediately subsequent to the resurrection, there is no less discrepancy, no nearer agreement, in the testimony of the evangelical witnesses. Matthew says that when Christ's disciples first met him after the resurrection, they worshiped him, and held him by the feet. (Matt. xxviii. 9) Strange, indeed, and wholly incredible, if John is a reliable witness, for he affirms he did not allow even his best and dearest friend (Mary) to touch him. And then John combats this testimony of his by declaring he invited the skeptical Thomas, not only to touch him, but to thrust his hand into his side for tangible proof of his identity.

6. And why, let us ask here, was not the skeptical Thomas damned for his doubting, when we, who live thousands of miles from the place, and nearly two thousand years from the time, are often told by the priesthood we must "believe or be damned?"

80

7. And if Thomas was really convinced by this occurrence, or if it ever took place, why have we no account of his subsequent life? What good was effected by his convincement if he never said or did anything afterward?

8. John tells us Mary first saw Christ, after his resurrection, at the tomb, but Matthew says it was on her way home she first saw him.

9. We are told by Luke (xxiv. 36) that when Christ appeared to his disciples on a certain occasion, they were frightened, supposing it to be a spirit. But John (xx. 20) says they were glad. Which must we believe?

10. According to Matthew, the disciples were all present on this occasion; but according to John, Thomas was not there.

11. Here let it be noted that none of the narrators claim to have seen Christ rise from the tomb, nor to have got it from anybody who did see it The only proof in this case is their declaration, "It came to pass."

12. And we are prompted to ask here, how "it came to pass" that the chief priests and pharisees cherished sufficient faith in Christ's resurrection to set a watch for it, as Matthew reports, when his own disciples were too faithless in such an event to be present, or to believe he had risen after the report reached their ears; for we are told some doubted. (See Matt, xxiii.)

13. And how came Matthew to know the soldiers were bribed to say Christ's body was stolen away by his disciples, when the disclosures of such a secret would have been death under the Roman government.

14. And their confession of being asleep, as related by Matthew, would have subjected them to the same fatal penalty by the civil rulers of Rome.

15. And if the soldiers were all asleep, can we not suggest several ways the body may have disappeared without being restored to life?

16. And here we would ask if Christ rose from the dead in order to convince the world of his divine power, why did not the event take place in public? Why was it seen only by a few credulous and interested disciples?

17. And if such an astonishing and miraculous event did occur, why does not one of the numerous cotemporary writers of those times make any allusion to it? Neither Pliny, Tacitus, nor Josephus, who detail the events very minutely, not only of those times, but of that very country, says a word about such a wonder-exciting occurrence. This fact of itself entirely overthrows the credibility of the story.

18. And the fact that several Christian sects, which flourished near those times, as the Corinthians and Carpocratians, etc., rejected the story in toto, furnishes another powerful argument for discrediting it.

81

19. And then add to this fact that his own chosen followers were upbraided for their unbelief in the matter.

20. And what was Christ doing during the forty days between his resurrection and ascension, that he should only be seen a few times, and but a few minutes at a time, and by but a few persons, and those interested?

21. And we would ask, likewise,—What more can be proved by Christ's physical resurrection than that of the resurrection of Lazarus, the widow's son, and several cases related in the Old Testament, or the numerous cases reported in oriental history?

22. And what analogy is there in the resurrection of the dead body of a perfect and self-existent God and that of vile man?

23. And why should Christ be called "the first fruits of the resurrection," when so many cases are reported as occurring before his?

24. And why do Christians build their hopes of immortality almost entirely upon Christ's alleged resurrection, in view of the numerous facts we have cited showing it to be a mere sandy foundation?

25. Of course no person who believes in modern spiritualism will discredit the story of Christ being visually recognized after his death *as a spirit*—for they have ocular proof that many such cases have occurred within the last decade of years. But it is the story of his physical resurrection we are combating—the reanimation of his flesh and bones after having been subjected three days to the laws of decomposition. Neither science nor sense can indorse such a story.

26. It was a very easy matter, and very natural to mistake Christ's spiritual body for his physical body; for such mistakes have been made a thousand times in the world's history.

27. Is it not strange, in view of the countless defects in the story of Christ's physical resurrection as enumerated above, that the orthodox Christian world should rely upon it as the great sheet anchor of their faith, and as their chief and almost their only hope of immortal life?

CHAPTER XX. REAPPEARANCE AND ASCENSION OF THE SAVIORS.

MANY cases are related by their respective sacred narratives of the ancient Saviors, and other beings possessing the form of man, and previously recognized as men, reappearing to their disciples and friends, after having been consigned to the tomb for three days, or a longer or shorter period of time, and of their final ascension to the house of many mansions.

It is related of the Indian or Hindoo Sav or Chrishna, that after having risen from the dead, he appeared again to his disciples. "He ascended to Voiacantha (heaven), to Brahma," the first person of the trinity (he himself being the second), and that as he ascended, "all men saw him, and exclaimed, 'Lo! Chrishna's soul ascends to his native skies.'" And it is further related that, "attended by celestial spirits,.... he pursued by his own light the journey between earth and heaven, to the bright paradise whence he had descended."

Of the ninth incarnation of India, the Savior Sakia, it is declared, that he "ascended to the celestial regions", and his pious and devout disciples point the skeptic to indelible impressions and ineffaceable footprints on the rocks of a high mountain as an imperishable proof of the declaration that he took his last leave of earth and made his ascent from that point.

It is related of the crucified Prometheus, likewise, that after having given up the ghost on the cross, "descended to hell", Christ's soul was "not left in hell," see Acts ii. 31), "he rose again from the dead, and ascended into heaven "

And then it is declared of the Egyptian Savior Alcides, that "after having been seen a number of times, he ascended to a higher life," going up, like Elijah, in "a chariot of fire."

The story of the crucifixion of Quexalcote of Mexico, followed by his burial, resurrection and ascension, is distinctly related in the "holy" and inspired "gospels" of that country, which Lord Kingsborough admitted to be more than two thousand years old.

Of Laotsi of China, it is said that when "he had completed his mission of benevolence, he ascended bodily alive into the paradise above." (Prog, of Rel. Ideas, vol. 214.) And it is related of Fo of the same country, that having completed his glorious mission on earth, he "ascended back to paradise, where he had previously existed from all eternity."

It is related also in the ancient legends, that the Savior or God Xamalxis of Thrace, having died, and descended beneath the earth, and remained there three years, made his appearance again in the fourth year after his death, as he had previously foretold, and eventually ascended to heaven about 600 B. C. Even some of the Hindoo saints are reported in their "holy" and time-honored books to have been seen ascending to heaven. "And impressions on the rocks are shown," says an author, "said to be of footprints they had left when they ascended."

It is related both by the Grecian biographer Plutarch, in his life of Romulus, and by a Roman historian, that the great founder of Rome (Romulus) suddenly ascended in a tempest during a solar eclipse, about 713 B. C. And Julius Proculis, a Roman senator of great fame and high reputation, declared, under solemn oath, that he saw him, and talked with him after his death.

ASTRONOMICAL VERSION OF THE STORY.

Before dismissing this chapter, we may state that, in common with most other religious conceptions, the doctrine of the ascension has in the ancient legends an astronomical representation.

Having said that a planet was buried because it sunk below the horizon, when it returned to light and gained its state of eminence, they spoke of it as dead, risen again, and ascended into heaven. (Volney, p. 143.) What is the story of the ascension of Christ worth in view of these ancient pagan traditions of earlier origin?

ASCENSION OF THE CHRISTIAN SAVIOR.

1. The different scriptural accounts of the ascension of Christ are, like the different stories of the resurrection, quite contradictory, and, hence, entitled to as little credit. In Luke (xxiv.), he is represented as ascending on the evening of the third day after the crucifixion. But the writer of Acts (i. 3) says he did not ascend till forty days after his resurrection; while, according to his own declaration to the thief on the cross, "This day shalt thou be with me in paradise," he must have ascended on the same day of his crucifixion. Which statement must we accept as inspired, or what is proved by such contradictory testimony?

2. Which must we believe, Paul's declaration that he was seen by above *five hundred of the brethren* at once (1 Cor. xv. 6), or the statement of the author of the Acts (i. 15), that there were *but one hundred and twenty brethren in all after that period?*

3. How would his ascension do anything toward proving his divinity, unless it also proves the divinity of Enoch and Elijah, who are reported to have ascended long prior to that era?

4. As these stories of the ascension of Christ, according to Lardner, were written many years after his crucifixion. Is it not hence probable they grew out of similar stories relative to the heathen Gods long previously prevalent in oriental countries?

5. As these gospel writers could not have been present to witness the ascension, as it must have occurred before their time of active life, does not this fact of itself seriously damage the credibility of the accounts, and more especially as neither Mark nor Luke, who are the only reporters of the occurrence, were not disciples of Christ at the time, while Matthew and John, who were, say nothing about it?—another fact which casts a shade on the credibility of the story.

CHAPTER XXI. THE ATONEMENT—ITS ORIENTAL OR HEATHEN ORIGIN.

THERE were various practices in vogue amongst the orientalists, which originated with the design of appeasing the anger, and propitiating the favor of a presumed to be irascible deity. Most of these practices consisted in some kind of sacrifice or destructive offering called the "atonement." But here let it be observed, that the doctrine of atonement for sin, by sacrifice, was unfolded by degrees, and that the crucifixion of a God was not the first practical exhibition of it. On the contrary, it appears to have commenced with the most valueless or cheapest species of property then known. And from this starting-point ascended gradually, so as finally to embody the most costly commodities; and did not stop here, but reached forward till it laid its murderous hands on human beings, and immolated them upon its bloody altars. And finally, to cap the climax, it assumed the effrontery to drag a God off the throne of heaven, to stanch its blood-thirsty spirit, as evinced by Paul's declaration, "Without the shedding of blood there can be no remission of sin." Rather a bloody doctrine, and one which our humanity rejects with instinctive horror.

We will trace the doctrine of the atonement briefly through its successive stages of growth and development.

The idea seems to have started very early in the practical history of the human race, that the sacrifice and consequent deprivation of earthly goods, or some terrestial enjoyment, would have the effect to mitigate the anger, propitiate the favor, and obtain the mercy of an imaginary and vengeful God. This idea obviously was suggested by observing that their earthly rulers always smiled, and became less rigorous in their laws, and milder in their treatment of their subjects, when they made them presents of some valuable or desirable commodity. They soon learned that such offerings had the effect to check their cruel and bloody mode of governing the people; so that when their houses were shaken down, or swallowed up by earthquakes, the trees riven by lightning, and prostrated by storms, and their cattle swept away by floods, supposing it to be the work of an angry God, the thought arose in their minds at once, that perhaps his wrath could be abated by the same expedient as that which had served in the case of their mundane lords—that of making presents of property. But as this property could not be carried up to the celestial throne, the expedient was adopted of burning it, so that the substance or quintessence of it would be conveyed up to the heavenly Potentate in the shape of steam and smoke, which would make for him, as the Jews express it, "a sweet-smelling savor." Abundant and conspicuous is the evidence in history to show that the custom of burnt-offerings and atonements for sin originated in this way.

The first species of property made use of for burnt-offerings appears to have been the fruits of the earth—vegetables, fruits, roots, etc.,—the lowest kind of property in point of value. But the thought soon naturally sprang up in the mind of the devotee, that a more valuable offering would sooner and more effectually secure the divine favor. Hence, levies were made on living herds of cattle, sheep, goats and other domestic animals. This was the second step in the ascending scale toward Gods.

And here we find the key to open and solve the mystery of Jehovah's preferring Abel's offering to Cain's. While the latter consisted in mere inanimate substances, the former embraced the firstlings of the flock—a higher and more valuable species of property, and quite sufficient to induce the selfish Jehovah to prefer Abel's offering to Cain's, or rather for the selfish Jews to cherish this conception. In all nations where offerings were made, the conclusion became established in the minds of the people that the amount of God's favor procured in this way must be proportionate to the value of the commodity or victim offered up—a conviction which ultimately led to the seizure of human beings for the atoning offerings, which brings us to the third stage of growth in the atonement doctrine. Children frequently constituted the victims in this case. The sacrifice of Jephthah's daughter, as related in Judges xi. 30, and other cases cited by bible writers, (Isaiah xxxii. 25), and modern Christian authors, prove that this practice was in vogue among "God's holy people."

One step more (constituting the *fourth* stage of development) brings us to the sacrifice of Gods. The climax is now reached; the conception can go no higher. The ancient Birmese taught that while common property in burnt-offerings would procure the temporary favor of the ruling God, the sacrifice of human beings would secure his good pleasure for a thousand years, and cancel out all the sins committed in that period. And when one of the three Gods on the throne of heaven was dragged down, or *voluntarily came down* (as some of the sects taught), and was put to death on the cross as an atonement for sin, such was the value of the victim, such the magnitude of the offering, that it "atoned for *all* sin, past, present and future, for all the human race."

The Hindoos, cherishing this conception, taught that the crucifixion of their sin-atoning Savior Chrishna (1200 B. C.) put an end to both animal and human sacrifices, and accordingly such offerings ceased in most Hindoo countries centuries ago. Thus far back in the mire and midnight of human ignorance, and amid the clouds of mental darkness, while man dwelt upon the animal plane, and was governed by his brutal feelings, and "blood for blood" was the requisition for human offenses, originated the bloody, savage and revolting doctrine of the atonement.

Another mode of adjudicating the sins of the people in vogue in some countries anterior to the custom of shedding blood as an expiation, was that of packing them on the back, head, or horns of some animal by a formal hocus-pocus process, and then driving the animal into a wilderness, or some other place so remote that the brute could not find its way back amongst the people with its cargo of sins. The cloth or fabric used for inclosing the sins and iniquities of the people was usually of a red or scarlet color—of the semblance of blood. In fact, it was generally dipped in blood. This, being lashed to the animal, would of course be exposed to the weather and the drenching rains, would consequently, in the course of time, fade and become white. Hence, we have the key to Isaiah's declaration, "Though your sins be (red) as scarlet, they shall become (white) as wool." (See Isaiah, i. 18.) And thus the meaning of this obscure text is clearly explained by tracing its origin to its oriental source.

And there are many other texts in the Christian bible which might be elucidated in a similar manner by using oriental tradition, or oriental sacred books, as a key to unlock and explain their meaning. We have stated above that some animal was made use of by different nations to convey the imaginary load of the people's sins out of the country. For this purpose the Jews had their "scapegoat," the Egyptians their "scape-ox," the Hindoos their "scape-horse," the Chaldeans their "scape-ram," the Britons their "scape-bull," the Mexicans their "scape-lamb" and "scape-mouse," the Tamalese their "scape-hen," and the Christians at a later period their *scape-God.* Jesus Christ may properly be termed the scape-God of orthodox Christians, as he stands in the same relation to his disciples, who believe in the atonement, as the goat did to the Jews, and performs the same end and office. The goat and the other sin-offering animals took away the sin of the nation in each case respectively. In like manner Jesus Christ takes away the sin of the world, being called "the Lamb of God that taketh away the sin of the world." (John i. 29.) And more than two thousand years ago the Mexicans sacrificed a lamb as an atonement, which they called "the

Lamb of God"—the same title scripturally applied to Jesus Christ. The conception in each case is, then, the same—that of the atonement for sin by the sacrifice of an innocent victim.

The above citations show that the present custom of orthodox Christendom, in packing their sins upon the back of a God, is just the same substantially as that of various heathen nations, who were anciently in the habit of packing them upon the backs of various dumb animals. If some of our Christian brethren should protest against our speaking of the church's idea of atonement as that of packing their sins upon the back of a God, we will here prove the appropriateness of the term upon the authority of the bible. Peter expressly declares Christ bore our sins upon his own body on a tree (see 1 Peter ii. 24), just as the Jews declared the *goat bore their* sins on his body, and the ancient Brahmins taught that the bulls and the heifers bore theirs away, etc., which shows that the whole conception is of purely heathen origin. And hereafter, when they laugh at the Jewish superstition of a scape-goat, let them bear in mind that more sensible and intelligent people may laugh in turn at their superstitious doctrine of a scape-God.

These superstitious customs were simply expedients of different nations to evade the punishment of their sins—an attempt to shift their retributive consequences on to other beings. The divine atonement more especially possessed this character. This system teaches that the son of God and Savior of the world was sent down and incarnated, in order to die for the people, and thus suffer by proxy the punishment meted out by divine wrath for the sins of the whole world. The blood of a God must atone for the sins of the whole human family, as rams, goats, bullocks and other animals had atoned for the sins of families and nations under older systems. Thus taught Brahminism, Budhism, Persianism, and other religious systems, before the dawn of Christianity. The nucleus of the atoning system is founded in the doctrine, "Without the shedding of blood there is no remission for sin" (Rom. v. 9)—a monstrous and morally revolting doctrine—a doctrine which teaches us that *somebodys* blood must be shed, somebody's veins and arteries depleted, for every trivial offense committed against the moral law. Somebody must pay the penalty in blood, somebody must be slaughtered for every little foible or peccadillo or moral blunder into which erring man may chance to stumble while upon the pilgrimage of life, while journeying through the wilderness of time, even if a God has to be dragged from his throne in heaven, and murdered to accomplish it Nothing less will mitigate the divine wrath.

Whose soul—possessing the slightest moral sensibility—does not inwardly and instinctively revolt at such a doctrine? We would not teach it to the world, for it is founded in butchery and bloodshed, and is an old pagan superstition, which originated far back in the midnight of mental darkness and heathen ignorance, when the whole human race were under the lawless sway of their brutal propensities, and when the ennobling attributes of love, mercy and forgiveness had as yet found no place, no abiding home, in the human bosom. The bloody soul of the savage first gave it birth. We hold the doctrine to be a a high-handed insult to the All-loving Father, who, we are told, is "long-suffering in mercy," and "plentiful in forgiveness," to charge *Him* with sanctioning such a doctrine, much less with originating it.

There is no "mercy or forgiveness" in putting an innocent being to death for any pretext whatever. And for the Father to consent to the brutal assassination of His own innocent Son upon the cross to gratify an implacable revenge toward his own children, the workmanship of his own hands, rather than forgive a moral weakness implanted in their natures by a voluntary act of his

87

own, and for which consequently he alone ought to be responsible, would be nothing short of murder in the first degree.

We cherish no such conception. We cannot for a moment harbor a blasphemous doctrine, which represents the Universal Father as being a bloody-minded and murderous being, instead of a being of infinite love, infinite wisdom, and infinite in all the moral virtues. Such a character would be a deep-dyed stigma upon any human being. And no person actuated by a strict sense of justice would accept salvation upon any such terms as that prescribed by the Christian atonement.

It is manifestly too unjust, too devoid of moral principle, besides being a flagrant violation of the first principles of civil and criminal jurisprudence. It is a double wrong to punish the innocent for the guilty. It is the infliction of injustice on the one hand, and the omission of justice on the other. It inflicts the highest penalty of the law upon an innocent being, whom that law ought to shield from punishment, while it exculpates and liberates the guilty party, whose punishment the moral law demands. It robs society of a useful man on the one hand, and turns a moral pest upon community on the other, thus committing a twofold wrong, or act of injustice. No court in any civilized country would be allowed to act upon such a principle; and the judge who should indorse it, or favor a law, or principle, which punishes the innocent for the guilty, would be ruled off the bench at once.

Here, however, we are sometimes met with the plea, that the offering of Jesus Christ was a voluntary act, that it was made with his own free will. But the plea don't do away with either the injustice or criminality of the act.

No innocent person has a right to suffer for the guilty, and the courts have no right to accept the offer or admit the substitute. An illustration will show this. If Jefferson Davis had been convicted of the crime of treason, and sentenced to be hung, and Abraham Lincoln had come forward and offered to be stretched upon the gallows in his place, is there a court in the civilized world which would have accepted the substitute, and hung Lincoln, and liberated Davis? To ask the question is but to answer it. It is an insult to reason, law and justice to entertain the proposition.

The doctrine of the atonement also involves the infinite absurdity of God punishing himself to appease his own wrath. For if "the fullness of the Godhead dwelt in Christ bodily" (as taught in Col. ii. 9), then his death was the death of God—that is, a divine suicide, prompted and committed by a feeling of anger and revenge, which terminated the life of the Infinite Ruler—a doctrine utterly devoid of reason, science or sense. We are sometimes told man owes a debt to his Maker, and the atonement pays that debt. To be sure! And to whom is the debt owing, and who pays it? Why, the debt is owing to God, and God (in the person of Jesus Christ) pays it— pays it to himself. We will illustrate. A man approaches his neighbor, and says, "Sir, I owe you a thousand dollars, but can never pay it." "Very well, it makes no difference," replies the claimant, "I will pay it myself;" and forthwith thrusts his hand into his right pocket and extracts the money, transfers it to the left pocket and exclaims—"There, the debt is paid!" A curious way of paying debts, and one utterly devoid of sense. And yet the orthodox world have adopted it for their God. We find, however, that they carefully avoid practicing this principle themselves in their dealings with each other. When they have a claim against a neighbor, we do not find them ever thrusting their hands into their own pockets to pay it off, but sue him, and compel him to pay—if he refuses to do it without compulsion—thus proving they do not consider it a correct principle of trade.

But we find, upon further investigation, that the assumed debt is not paid—after all.

When a debt is paid, it is canceled, and dismissed from memory, and nothing more said about it. But in this case the sinner is told he must still suffer the penalty for every sin he commits, notwithstanding Christ died to atone for and cancel that sin.

Where, then, is the virtue of the atonement? Like other doctrines of the orthodox creed, it is at war with reason and common sense, and every principle of sound morality, and will be marked by coming ages as a relic of barbarism.

CHAPTER XXII. THE HOLY GHOST OF ORIENTAL ORIGIN

OF all the weird, fanciful, and fabulous stories appertaining to the Gods and other spiritual entities of the olden times, whose capricious adventures we find so profusely narrated in oriental mythology—of all the strange, mythical and mystical feats, and ever-varying and ever-diverging changes in the shape, appearance, sex, and modes of manifestation which characterize the hobgoblins or ghostly beings which comprise the esoteric stock of the ancient mysteries, that appertaining to the third member of "the hypostatic union," the Holy Ghost, seems to stand pre-eminent. And I propose here to submit the facts to show that the Holy Ghost story of the Christian Gospels, like the more ancient pagan versions of the same story, is marked by the same wild, discordant and legendary characteristics which abound in all the accounts of gods and ghosts found recorded in the religious books of various nations.

The following brief exposition of the history and exploits of this anomalous, nondescript, chameleon-like being will clearly evince that the same fanciful, metaphorical and fabulous changes in the size, shape, sex and appearance of this third limb of the triune God are found in the Christian Scriptures which are disclosed in the more ancient oriental traditions.

We will first exhibit a classification of the names and characteristics of this imaginary being drawn from the gospels and epistles of the Christian bible, by which it will be observed that scarcely any two references to it agree in assigning it the same character or attributes.

1. In John xiv. 26, the Holy Ghost is spoken of as a person or personal God.

2. In Luke iii. 22, the Holy Ghost changes, and assumes the form of a dove.

3. In Matt. xiii. 16, the Holy Ghost becomes a spirit

4. In John i. 32, the Holy Ghost is presented as an inanimate, senseless object.

5. In John v. 7, the Holy Ghost becomes a God—the third member of the Trinity.'

6. In Acts ii. 1, the Holy Ghost is averred to be "a mighty, rushing wind."

7. In Acts x. 38, the Holy Ghost, we infer, from its mode of application, is an ointment.

8. In John xx. 22, the Holy Ghost is the breath, as we legitimately infer by its being breathed into the mouth of the recipient after the ancient oriental custom.

9. In Adis ii. 3, we learn the Holy Ghost "sat upon each of them," probably in the form of a bird, as at Jesus' baptism.

10. In Adis ii. 1, the Holy Ghost appears as "cloven tongues of fire."

11. In Luke ii. 26, the Holy Ghost is the author of a revelation or inspiration.

12. In Adis viii. 17, the Holy Ghost is a magnetic aura imparted by the "laying on of hands."

13. In Mark i. 8, the Holy Ghost is a medium or element for baptism.

14. In Adis xxviii. 25, the Holy Ghost appears with vocal organs, and speaks.

15. In Heb. vi. 4, the Holy Ghost is dealt out or imparted by measure.

16. In Luke iii. 22, the Holy Ghost appears with a tangible body.

17. In Luke i. 5, and many other texts, we are taught people are filled with the Holy Ghost.

18. In Matt. xi. 15, the Holy Ghost falls upon the people as a ponderable substance.

19. In Luke iv. 1, the Holy Ghost is a God within a God—"Jesus being full of the Holy Ghost."

20. In Acts xxi. 11, the Holy Ghost is a being of the masculine or feminine gender—"Thus saith the Holy Ghost," etc.

21. In John i. 32, the Holy Ghost is of the neuter gender—"It (the Holy Ghost) abode upon him."

22. In Matt. i. 18, the Holy Ghost becomes a vicarious agent in the procreation of another God; that is, this third member of the Trinity aids the first member (the Father) in the creation or generation of the second member of the triad of bachelor Gods—the Word, or Savior, or Son of God.

Such are the ever-shifting scenes presented in the Scripture panorama of the Holy Ghost. Surpassing the fabulous changes of some of the more ancient demigods, the Christian Holy Ghost undergoes (as is shown by the above-quoted texts) a perpetual metathesis or metamorphosis—being variously presented on different occasions as a personal and rational being, a dove, a spirit, an inanimate object, a God, the wind or a wind, an ointment, the breath or a breath, cloven tongue of fire, a bird, or some other flying recumbent animal, a revelator or divine messenger, a medium or element for baptism, an intelligent, speaking being, a lifeless, bodiless, sexless being, a measurable fluid substance, a being possessing a body, ponderable, unconscious substance, a God dwelling within a God, and, finally—though really first in order—the author or agent of the incarnation of the second God in the Trinity (Jesus Christ).

That many of these fabulous conceptions were drawn from mythological sources will be made manifest by the following facts of history:—

1. *The Holy Ghost in the shape of a bird, a dove or a pigeon.* This is proven to be a very ancient pagan tradition, as it is found incorporated in several of the oriental religious systems. In ancient India, whose prolific spiritual fancies constitute the primary parentage of nearly all the doctrines, dogmas and superstitions found incorporated in the Christian Scriptures, a dove was uniformly the emblem of the Holy Spirit, or Spirit of God. Confirmatory of this statement, we find the declaration in the Anacalypsis, that a "dove stood for or represented a third member of the Trinity, and was the regenerator or regeneratory power." This meets the Christian idea of "regeneration and renewing of the Holy Ghost." (Titus iii. 5.) A person being baptized under the Brahminical theocracy was said to be "regenerated and born again," or, as the above-quoted writer expresses it, "They were born into the spirit, or the spirit into them"—that is, the "dove into or upon them," (As vide the case of the Christian's "Holy Ghost descending in bodily shape like a dove," and alighting on Christ's head at baptism, as related in Luke iii. 22.) In ancient Rome a dove or pigeon was the emblem of the female procreative energy, and frequently a legendary spirit, the accompaniment of Venus. And hence, as a writer remarks, "It is very appropriately represented as descending at baptism in the character of the third member of the Trinity." The same writer tells us, "The dove fills the Grecian oracles with their spirit and power." We find the dove, also, in the romantic eclogues of ancient Syria. In the time-chiseled Syrian temple of Hierapolis, Semiramis is represented with a dove on her head, thus constituting the prototype of the dove on the head of the Christian Messiah at baptism. And a dove was in more than one of the ancient religious systems—"The Spirit of God (Holy Ghost) moving on the face of the waters" at creation, as implied in Gen. i. 2, though a pigeon, was often indiscriminately substituted. In Howe's "Ancient Mysteries" it is related that "in St. Paul's Cathedral, at the feast of Whitsuntide, the descent of the Holy Ghost was performed by a white pigeon being let fly out of a hole in the midst of the roof of the great aisle." The dove and the pigeon, being but slight variations of the same species of the feathered tribe, were used indiscriminately.

2. As evinced above, the Holy Ghost was the third member of the Trinity in several of the oriental systems. Father, Son and Holy Ghost, or Father, Word and Holy Ghost (1 John v. 7), are familiar Christian terms to express the divine triad, which shows the Holy Ghost to be the acknowledged third member of the Christian Trinity. And, as already suggested, the same is true of the more ancient systems. "The Holy Spirit and the Evil Spirit were, each in their turn (says

Mr. Higgins), third member of the Trinity." We might, if space would allow, draw largely upon the ancient defunct systems in proof of this statement. "In these triads (says Mr. Hillell) the third member, as might be supposed, was not of equal rank with the other two." And hence, in the Theban Trinity, Khonso was inferior to Arion and Mant. In the Hindoo triad, Siva was subordinate to Brahma and Vishnu. And a score of similar examples might be adduced from the fancy-constructed trinities of other and older oriental religious systems (but for the inflexible rule of brevity which forbids their presentation here), with all of which the more modern Holy Ghost conception of the Christian world is an exact correspondence, as this imaginary, fabulous being is less conspicuous than and has always stood third in rank with the Father and second to the Son, alias the Word, and is now seldom addressed in practical Christian devotion; and thus the analogy is complete. Mr. Maurice says, "This notion of a third person in the Deity (the Holy Ghost) was diffused among all the nations of the earth." (See Ind. Antiq. vol. iv. p. 75a) And Mr. Worseley, in his "Voyage" (vol. i. p. 259), avers this doctrine to be "of very great antiquity, and generally received by all the Gothic and Celtic nations."

3. The Holy Ghost was the Holy Breath which, in the Hindoo traditions, moved on the face of the waters at creation, and imparted life and vitality into everything created. A similar conception is recognized in the Christian Scriptures. In Psalms xxxiii. 6, we read, "By the Word of the Lord were the heavens made, and all the host of them by the breath of his mouth." Here is the Brahminical conception, square out, of the act of creation by the Divine Breath, which is the Holy Ghost, the same, also, which was breathed into Adam, by which he became "a living soul." M. Dubois observes, "The Prana, or principle of life, of the Hindoos is the breath of life by which the Creator (Brahma) animates the clay, and man became a living soul." (Page 293.)

4. Holy Ghost, Holy Breath and Holy Wind appear to have been synonymous and convertible terms for the living vocal emanations from the mouth of the Supreme God, as memorialized in several of the pagan traditions. The last term (Holy Wind) is suggested by "the mighty rushing wind from heaven" which filled the house, or church, on the day of Pentecost. (See Acts ii. 2.) Several of the old religious systems recognize "the Holy Wind" as a term for the Holy Ghost. The doxology (reported by a missionary) in the religious service of the Syrian worship runs thus:—

```
"Praise to the Holy Spiritual Wind, which is the Holy Ghost;
Praise to the three persons which are one true God."
```

Some writers maintain that the Hebrew *Ruk Aliem.* translated "Spirit of God" (Gen. i. 2) in our version, should read, "Wind of the Gods." And we find that the word *pneuma* of our Greek New Testament, is sometimes translated "Ghost" and sometimes "Wind," as best suited the fancy of the translators. In John iii. 5, we find the word Spirit, and in verse eight both Wind and Spirit are found; and in Luke i. 35, we observe the term Holy Ghost—all translated from the same word. Let it be specially noted that in the Greek Testament the word *pneuma* is used in all these cases, thus proving that Spirit, Holy Ghost and Wind are used in the Christian Scriptures as synonymous terms; and proving, also, that an unwarranted license has been assumed by translators in rendering the same word three different ways. M. Auvaroff, in his "Essays on the Eleusinian Mysteries," speaks of "the torch being ignited at the command of Hermes of Egypt, the spiritual agent in the workshop of creation," relative to which statement a writer remarks, "Hermes appears in this instance as a personification of Wind or Spirit, as in the bible (meaning the Christian bible), God, Wind and Spirit are often interchangeable terms, and the Word appears to be from the same windy source."

5. *The Holy Ghost as "a tongue of fire, which sat upon each of them" (the apostles)*. (See Acts. ii. 3.) Even this conception is an orientalism. Mr. Higgins tells us that "Budha, an incarnate God of the Hindoos (three thousand years ago), is often seen with a glory or tongue of fire upon his head." And the tradition of the visible manifestation of the Holy Ghost by fire was prevalent among the ancient Budhists, Celts, Druids and Etrurians. In fact, as our author truly remarks, "The Holy Ghost, or Holy Spirit, when visible, was always in the form of fire (or a bird), and was always accompanied with wisdom and power." Hence, is disclosed the origin of the ancient custom amongst the Hindoos, Persians and Chaldeans, of making offerings to the solar fire, emblem of the Holy Ghost or Holy Spirit.

6. *Inspiration by the Holy Ghost* (Luke ii. 26.) "Holy men of God," including some of the prophets, are claimed to have been inspired by the Holy Ghost (See 2 Peter i. 21; Acts xxviii. 25.) In like manner, as we are informed by Mr. Cleland in his "Specimens" (see Appendix), the ancient Celts were not only "moved by the Holy Ghost" in their divine decrees and prophetic utterances, but they claimed that their Salic laws (seventy-two in number) were inspired by the "Salo Ghost" (Holy Ghost), known also as "the Wisdom of the Spirit, or the Voice of the Spirit." This author several times alludes to the fact, and exhibits the proof, that the doctrine of the Holy Ghost was known to this ancient people.

7. *The Holy Ghost imparted by "the laying on of hands."* This, too, is an ancient oriental custom. "And by the imposition of hands on the head of the candidate," says Mr. Cleland, speaking of the Celts, "the Holy Ghost, or Holy Spirit. was conveyed." And thus was the Holy Spirit, Ghost, Gas, Wind, Electrical Fire or Spirit of Authority imparted to the hierophant or gospel novitiate. "And their public assemblies," continues our author, "were always opened by an invocation to the Holy Ghost."

8. *Baptism by or into the Holy Ghost accompanied with fire*. (Matt. iii. 11.) This rite, too, is traceable to a very ancient period, and was practiced by several of the old symbolical and mythological systems. The Tuscans, or Etrurians, baptized with fire, wind (ghost) and water. Baptism into the first member of the Trinity (the Father) was with fire; baptism into the second member of the Trinity (the Word) was with water; while baptism into the third member of the Trinity (the Holy Ghost, or Holy Spirit) consisted of the initiatory spiritual or symbolical application of gas, gust, ghost, wind. or spirit. It appears from "Herbert's Travels," that, in "ancient countries", the child was taken to the priest, who named him (christened him) before the sacred fire after which ceremony he was sprinkled with "holy water" from a vessel made of the sacred tree known as "The Holme."

9. *The Holy Ghost imparted by breathing*. (See John xx. 22). "Sometimes," says Mr. Higgins, relative to this custom among the ancient heathen, "the priest blew his breath upon the child, which was then considered baptized by *air, spiritus sanctus,* or ghost—i. e., baptism by the Holy Ghost." In case of baptism, a portion of the Holy Ghost was supposed to be transferred from the priest to the candidate. "The practice of breathing in or upon," says our author, "was quite common among the ancient heathen."

10. *The Holy Ghost as the agent in divine conception, or the procreation of other Gods.* Jesus is said to have been conceived by the Holy Ghost (see Matt. i. 18), and we find similar claims instituted still more anciently for other incarnate demigods. In the Mexican Trinity, Y, Zona was the father, Bacal the Word, and Eckvah the Holy Ghost, by the last of whom Chimalman conceived and brought forth the enfleshed God Quexalcote. (See Mex. Ant., vol. vi. p. 1650.) In the Hindoo mythos, Sakia was conceived by the Holy Ghost Nara-an.

Other cases might be cited, proving the same point.

Thus, we observe that the various heterogeneous conceptions, discordant traditions, and contradictory superstitions appertaining to that anomalous nondescript being known as the Holy Ghost, are traceable to various oriental countries, and to a very remote antiquity.

We will only occupy space with one or two more historical citations of a general nature, tending to prove the prevalence of this ghostly myth in other countries, not yet cited. "Tell me, O thou strong in fire!" ejaculated Sesostris of Egypt, to the oracle, as reported by Manetho, "who before me could subjugate all things, and who shall after me?" But the oracle rebuked him, saying, "First God, then the Word, and with them the Spirit." (See Nimrod, vol. i. p. 119.) "And Plutarch, in his 'Life of Numa,'" says our oft-quoted author, "shows that the incarnation of the Holy Spirit was known both to the ancient Romans and Egyptians."

The doctrine is thus shown to have been nearly universal.

ORIGIN OF THE HOLY GHOST SUPERSTITION.

The origin of the tradition respecting this fabulous and mythical being is easily traced to the ancient Brahminical trifold conception of the Deity, in which stands, in Trinity order, first, the God of power or might—Brahma or Brahm (the Father); second, the God of creation—the Word—answering to John's creative Word (see John i. 3); and third, the God of generation and regeneration—the Holy Spirit or Holy Ghost. The last member of the triune conception of the Deity was considered, under the Brahminical theocracy, the *living, vital, active, life-imparting agent* in both the first and second births of men and the gods.

It will be borne in mind by the reader that the Holy Ghost is represented in the Christian Scripture as being the active generating agent of Christ's conception, he being, as Matthew declares, "conceived by the Holy Ghost." The Holy Ghost was also the regenerating agent at his baptism. Although the specific object of the descent of the Holy Ghost on that occasion is not stated by Luke, who relates it; although it is not stated for what purpose the Holy Spirit, after assuming the form of a bird, alighted and sat upon his head, yet the motive is fully disclosed in the older mythical religions, where we find the matter in fuller detail.

Baptism itself is claimed by all its Christian votaries as regenerating or imparting a new spiritual life; and this new spiritual life was believed by several nations, as before stated, to make its appearance in the character and shape of a bird—sometimes a pigeon, sometimes a dove; and thus the origin of this tradition is most clearly and unmistakably exposed.

As the foregoing historical exposition exhibits the Holy Ghost as performing several distinct and discordant offices, so we likewise find it possessing at least two distinct genders, the masculine and neuter, i. e., no gender—changing, ghost-like, from one to the other, as occasion seemed to require.

From all these metamorphoses it is shown and demonstrated that the sexual and other changes of this "mysterious" being equal many of the demigods of mythology. The primary windy conception of the Holy Ghost is traceable to that early period of society when the rude and untutored denizens of the earth, in their profound ignorance of natural causes, were very easily and naturally led into the belief that wherever there was motion there was a God, or the active manifestation of a God, whether it was in the wind, breath, water, fire, or the sun.

Hence, the Buddhists had their god *Vasus* who manifested himself variously in the shape or character of fire, wind, storms, gas, ghosts, gusts, and the breath, thus constituting a very nearly-allied counterpart to the Christian Holy Ghost, which Mr. Parkhurst tells us originally meant "air in motion." This god was believed to have sprung from the supreme, primordial God, which the ancient Brahmins and Buddhists generally believed was constituted of a fine, spiritual substance,—aura, anima, wind, ether, igneous fluid, or electrical fire, i. e., fire from the sun, giving rise to "baptism by fire" and hence, the third God, or third member of the Trinity, subsequently arising out of this compound being, was also necessarily composed of or consisted of the same properties—all of which were believed to be correlated, if not identical.

Such is a complete, though brief, historical elucidation of that mysterious, imaginary being so corporally intangible that Faustus, of the third century, declared respecting it, "The Holy Spirit, the third majesty, has the air for his residence." And it is a fabulous God whose scriptural biography is invested with so many ludicrous and abstruse incidents as to incite several hundred Christian writers to labor hard with a "godly zeal," by a reconstruction of "God's Word" and a rehabiliment of the ghostly texts, to effect some kind of a reconciliation of the story with reason and common sense—with what success the reader is left to judge.

THE UNPARDONABLE SIN AGAINST THE HOLY GHOST.

Before dismissing our ghostly narrative, it may effect something in the way of mitigating the anxious fears of some of our Christian brothers and sisters to explain the nature of "the sin against the Holy Ghost," and assign the reason for its being unpardonable. The sin against the Holy Ghost consisted, according to the ancient Mexican traditions, in resisting its operations in the second birth—that is, the regeneration of the heart or soul by the Holy Ghost. And as the rectification of the heart or soul was a prominent idea with Christ, there is scarcely any ground to doubt but that this was the notion he cherished of the nature of the sin against the Holy Ghost. And it was considered unpardonable, simply because as the pardoning and cleansing process consisted in, or was at least always accompanied with baptism by water, in which operation the Holy Ghost was the agent in effecting a "new birth," therefore, when the ministrations or operations of this indispensable agent were resisted or rejected, there was no channel, no means, no possible mode left for the sinner to find a renewed acceptance with God. When a person sinned against the Father or the Word (the Son), he could find a door of forgiveness through the baptizing processes spiritual or elementary, of the Holy Ghost. But an offense committed against this third limb of the Godhead had the effect to close and bar the door so that there could be "no forgiveness, either in this life or that which is to come." To sin against the Holy Ghost was to tear down the scaffold by which the door of heaven was to be reached.

And thus it is explained the great "*mystery of godliness*," the "unpardonable sin against the Holy Ghost," which, on account of the frightful penalty annexed to it, while it is impossible to learn what it consists in—it being undefined and undefinable—has caused thousands, and probably millions, of the disciples of the Christian faith the most agonizing hours of alarm and despair.

CHAPTER XXIII. THE DIVINE "WORD" OF ORIENTAL ORIGIN.

The Word as Creator, as Second Person of the Trinity, and its Pre-Existence.

THE WORD OF ORIENTAL ORIGIN.

"In the beginning was the Word, and the Word was with God, and the Word was God." (John i. i.) The doctrine of the divine creative word (from the Greek Logos) appears to have been coeval in its origin with that of the Trinity, if not inseparably connected with it, as it constitutes the second member of the Trinity of "Father, Word, and Holy Ghost" in most of the ancient systems of religion. Works on heathen mythology show that it was anciently a very prevalent custom to personify ideas, thoughts and words into angels and Gods. Words were first personated, and transformed into men, then into angels, and finally into Gods.

And here is foreshadowed the origin of John's personification of "the Word made flesh." It was simply the word of the supreme God as it escaped from his mouth, assuming the form and characteristics of a divine being like himself, and taking position as a secondary God and second member of the Trinity. This was the orient conception, and it appears to have been John's. He evidently had no thought of Christ experiencing human birth, at first, or being born of a woman, but believed, like some of the orientalists, that he came out of the mouth of the Father, and was thus "made flesh." (John i. 2.) Not a word of Christ being born is found in John's Gospel, till after his existence as the Word is spoken of. (See first note in back of book.)

THE WORD AS CREATOR.

John also represents the Word as having been the Creator. "All things were made by him." (John i. 3.) And Peter declares, "By the word of God the heavens were of old." (2 iii. 5.) Now, let it be observed here, as a notable circumstance, that the Chinese bible, much older than the Christian's New Testament, likewise declares, "God pronounced the primeval Word, and his own eternal and glorious abode sprang into existence." Mr. Guizot, in a note on Gibbon's work, says,

"According to the Zend-Avesta (the Persian bible, more than three thousand years old), it is by the Word, more ancient than the world, that Ormuzd created the universe."

In like manner the sacred writings of the ancient Thibetans speak of "the Word which produced the world"—an exact counterpart to John's declaration, "All things were made by him." And the ancient Greek writer Amelias, speaking of the God Mercury, says, "And this plainly was the Logos (the Word), by whom all things were made, he being himself eternal," as Heraclitus would say,.... He assumed to be with God, and to be God, and in him everything that was made, has its life and being, who, descending into body, and putting on flesh, took the appearance of a man, though still retaining the majesty of his nature. Here is "the Word made flesh" set forth in most explicit terms. The Psalmist exclaims, "By the Word of God were the heavens made, and all the host of them by the Breath of his mouth." (Ps. xxxiii. 6.) Here is disclosed not only the conception of the Word as Creator, but also the Word and the Breath as synonymous terms, both of which conceptions oriental history amply proves to be of heathen derivation.

It was anciently believed that the Word and Breath of God were the same, and possessed a vitalizing power, which, as they issued from his mouth, might be transformed into another being known as a secondary God. Both the Jews and the Christians seem to have inherited this belief, as evinced by the foregoing quotations from their bible. The most ancient tradition taught that the Word emanated from the mouth of the principal God, and "became flesh," that is, took form, as the ancient Brahmins expressed it, for the special purpose of serving as agent in the work of creation, that is, to become the creator of the external universe. St. John evidently borrowed this idea. Read his first chapter.

PRE-EXISTENCE OF THE WORD.

The pre-existence or previous existence of the Word, antecedent to the date of its metamorphosis into the human form, we find taught in several of the ancient systems of religion, as well as the more modern Christian system. Several texts in the Christian New Testament set forth the doctrine quite explicitly. Christ, as the Divine Word, declared, "Before Abraham was I am," and that he had an existence with the Father before the foundation of the world, etc., which is a distinct avowal of the doctrine of pre-existence.

But oriental history proves the doctrine is much older than Christianity.

The Hindoo very anciently taught that "the Word had existed with God from all eternity, and when spoken it became a glorious form, the aggregate embodiment of all the divine ideas, and performed the work of creation." And of Chrishna, it is affirmed that "while upon the earth he existed also in heaven." (See Baghavat Gita.)

In like manner it is declared of an Egyptian God, that "though he was born into the world, he existed with his father God before the world was made." And parallel to this is the statement of the Chinese bible, that "though the Holy Word (Chang-si) will be born upon the earth, yet he existed before anything was made." Even for Pythagoras it was claimed he existed in heaven before he was born upon the earth. Mr. Higgins, in summing up the matter, declares, "All the old religions believed the world was created by the Word, and that this Word existed before creation" (Ana., vol. ii. p. 77), which clearly indicates the source of St John's creative Word.

THE DUAL OR TWO-FOLD NAME OF THE WORD.

In most cases the living Divine Word was known by different names and titles, prior to the era of its assuming the mortal form, from that by which it was known after its fleshly investment.

Among the ancient Persians, the name for the divine spiritual Word was Honover. After its human birth, it was called "Mithra the Mediator." The Hindoo oriental term for the primeval Word was Om, or Aum. After assuming its most important incarnate form, it was known as Chrishna. The Chinese Holy Interior Word was Om-i-to, and its principal incarnation was Chang-ti or Ti-en-ti. The Japanese also proclaimed their belief in a Divine Word before the Christian era, which, in their language, was Amina. They taught, like John, that it came forth from the mouth of the Supreme God (Brahm) to perform the work of creation, after which, it was known as Sakia. And that popular Christian writer, Mr. Milman, informs us that the Jewish founders of Christianity believed in an original Divine Word, which they call Memra. When it descended to the earth, and "became flesh, and dwelt amongst us" (John i. 4.) according to the evangelist John, it was known as Jesus Christ. Mr. Milman states also, that "the appellation to the Word is found in the Indian (Hindoo), Persian, the Platonic, and the Alexandrian systems." (Hist, of Chr., Book I., Chap. 2.)

Thus, the question is settled by Christian testimony—that the various conceptions of the Divine Word are of heathen origin.

THE WORD AS A SECOND MEMBER OF THE TRINITY.

"There are three that bear record in heaven, the Father, the Word, and the Holy Ghost." (1 John v. 7.) Observe, the Word is the second person in the Trinity. And this was its post in the Brahman, Hindoo, Persian, and other systems. "All religions," says a writer, "which taught the existence of the Word as a great primeval spirit, represent him as secondary to the supreme." (P. R. 3, vol. ii. p. 336.) "The Hindoos reverenced it next to Brahm." Mr. Higgins cuts the matter short by declaring "The Logos, or Word, was the second person of the Trinity in all the ancient systems, as in the Christian system," which again indicates its heathen origin.

THE WORD AS A BIBLICAL TITLE.

"The Word," "the Holy Word," "the Divine Word," etc., are terms now frequently applied to the Christian bible, without any suspicion of their heathen origin. The Zend-Avesta, the Persian bible, was always called "The Living Word of God," for that is the meaning of the term Zend-Avesta, and the oldest bible in the world is the Vedas, and it means both Word and Wisdom. Om, the Egyptian's Holy Word, they frequently applied both to their incarnate Gods and to their sacred writings.

The practice of calling bibles "The Word of God" originated from the belief that, when the incarnate Word left the earth and returned to heaven, he infused a portion of his living spirits into the divine writings which contained his history and his doctrines, and which he himself had prompted his disciples to write as his "Last Revelation to man." They then must contain a portion of him, i. e., a portion of the Holy Word—hence, both were called "The Holy Word."

And this heathen custom Christians borrowed.

ORIGIN OF THE WORD AS CREATOR.

The motive which prompted a belief in the creative Word may be styled a theological necessity. It was believed that the principal God, like the rulers of earth, was too aristocratic to labor with his own hands. Hence, another God was originated to perform the work of creation, and called "The Word."

The origin of the creative Word is still further indicated by Blackwood's Magazine.

It says:—

"Creation became impossible to a being already infinite, and was a derogation to a being already perfect. Some lower God, some Avatar, must be interposed (as an emanation from the mouth of the God supreme) to perform the subordinate task of creation. Hence, originated and came forth the Word as Creator."

CHAPTER XXIV. THE TRINITY VERY ANCIENTLY A CURRENT HEATHEN DOCTRINE

"THERE are three that bear record in Heaven, the Father, the Word, and the Holy Ghost, and these three are one." (i John v. 7.) This text, which evidently discloses a belief in the existence of three separate and distinct beings in the Godhead, sets forth a doctrine which was anciently of almost universal prevalence. Nearly every nation, whether oriental or occidental, whose religious faith has been commemorated in history. discloses in its creed a belief in the trifold nature and triune division of the Deity. St. Jerome testifies unequivocally, "All the ancient nations believed in the Trinity."

And a volume of facts and figures might be cited here, if we had space for them, in proof of this statement A text from one of the Hindoo bibles, (the Puranas) will evince the antiquity and prevalence of this belief in a nation of one hundred and fifty millions of people more than two thousand years ago. "O you three Lords! ' ejaculated Attencion, "know that I recognize only one God. Inform me, therefore, which of you is the true divinity that I may address to him alone my vows and adorations." The three Gods, Brahma, Vishnu, and Siva, becoming manifest to him, replied, "Learn, O devotee, that there is no real distinction between us. What to you appears such is only by semblance. The single being appears under three forms by the acts of creation, preservation and destruction but he is one."

Now, reader, note the remark here, that the ancient Christian fathers almost universally and unanimously proclaimed the doctrine of the Trinity as one of the leading tenets of the Christian faith, and as a doctrine derived directly by revelation from heaven. But here we find it most explicitly set forth by a disciple of a pagan religion more than three thousand years ago, as the Christian missionary D. O. Allen states, that the Hindoo bible, in which it was found was compiled fourteen hundred years before Christ, and written at a still earlier period. And we find the same doctrine very explicitly taught in the ancient Brahmin, Persian, Chaldean, Chinese, Mexican and Grecian systems —all much older than Christianity.

No writer ever taught or avowed a belief in any tenet of religious faith more fully or plainly than Plato sets forth, the doctrine of the Trinity in his Phaedon, written four hundred years B. C. And his terms are found to be in most striking conformity to the Christian doctrine on this subject, as taught in the New Testament Plato's first term for the Trinity was in Greek—1. To Agathon, the supreme God or Father. 2. The Logos, which is the Greek term for the Word. And, 3. Psyche, which the Greek Lexicon defines to mean "soul, spirit or ghost"—of course, the Holy Ghost. Here we have the three terms of the Christian Trinity, Father, Word, and Holy Ghost, as plainly taught as language can express it, thus making Plato's exposition of the Trinity and definition of its terms, published four hundred years B. C., identical in meaning with those of St. John's, as found in his Gospel, and contained in the above quoted text. Where, then, is the foundation for the dogmatic claim on the part of the Christian professors for the divine origin of the Trinity doctrine?

We will here cite the testimony of some Christian writers to prove that the Trinity is a pagan-derived doctrine. A *Christian bishop*, Mr. Powell, declares, "I not only confess but I *maintain*, such a similitude of Plato's and John's Trinity doctrines as bespeaks a common origin." (Thirteenth letter to Dr. Priestley.) What is that you say, bishop? "A common origin." Then you concede both are heaven-derived, or both heathen-derived. If the former, then revelation and heathenism are synonymous terms. If the latter, then Christianity stands on a level with heathen mythology. Which horn of the dilemma will you choose? St. Augustine confessed he found the beginning of John's Gospel in Plato's Phædon, which is a concession of the whole ground.

Another writer, Chataubron, speaks of an ancient Greek inscription on the great obelisk at Rome, which reads—1. The Mighty God. 2. The Begotten of God as Christ is declared to be "the only begotten of the Father" (John i. 14). And, 3. "Apollo the Spirit"—the Holy Spirit or Holy Ghost—thus presenting in plain language the three terms of the Trinity. And Mr. Cudworth, in corroboration of this report, says, "The Greeks had a first God, and second God, and third God, and the second was begotten by the first. And yet for all that," continues Mr. Cudworth, "they considered all these one."

In the Platonic or Grecian Trinity, the first person was considered the planner of the work of creation, the second person the creator, and the third person the ghost or spirit which moved upon the face of the waters, and infused life into the mighty deep at creation—the same Holy Ghost which descended from heaven to infuse life into the waters at Christ's baptism; thus, the resemblance is complete. Mr. Basnage quotes a Christian writer of the fifth century as declaring, "The Athenian sage Plato marvelously anticipated one of the most important and mysterious doctrines of the Christian religion"—meaning the Trinity—an important concession truly.

The oldest and probably the original form of the Trinity is that found in the Brahmin and Hindoo systems—the terms of which are—i. Brahma, the Father or supreme God. 2. Vishnu, the incarnate Word and Creator. 3. Siva, the Spirit of God, i. e., the Holy Spirit or Ghost—each answering to corresponding terms of the Christian Trinity, and yet two thousand years older, according to Dr. Smith.

We have not allowable space for other facts and citations (as this work is designed as a mere epitome), although we have but entered upon the threshold of the evidence tending to prove that the Christian Trinity was born of heathen parents, that it is an offspring of heathen mythology, like other doctrines of the Christian faith, claimed by its disciples as the gift of divine revelation.

Here let it be noted as a curious chapter in sacred history that the numerous divine Trinities which have constituted a part of nearly every religious system ever propagated to the world were composed, in every case, of male Gods No female has ever yet been admitted into the triad of Gods composing the orthodox Trinity. Every member of the Trinity in every case is a male, and an old bachelor—a doctrine most flagrantly at war with the principles of modern philosophy.

For this science teaches us that the endowment of a being with either male or female organs, presupposes the existence of the other sex; and that either sex, without the other would be a ludicrous anomaly, and a ludicrous distortion of nature unparalleled in the history of science. As sexual organs create an imperious desire for the other sex, no male or female could long enjoy full happiness in the absence of the other party. What an unhappy, lonesome place, therefore, the orthodox heaven must have been, during the eternity of the past, with no society but old bachelors! The Trinity was constituted of males simply because woman has always been considered a mere cipher in society—a mere tool for man's convenience, an appendage to his wants. Hence, instead of having a place among the Gods she led the practical life of a servant and a menial, which accounts for her exclusion from the Trinity. But the time is coming when she will rule both heaven and earth with the omnipotent power of her love nature. Then we shall have no "war in heaven," and no fighting on earth.

CHAPTER XXV. ABSOLUTION, AND THE CONFESSION OF SINS, OF HEATHEN ORIGIN

SOME Christian writers have labored to make it appear that this is exclusively a Christian doctrine, while others have labored as hard to get it out of their bible, or make the people believe that it is not therein taught.

We shall show, upon scriptural and historical authority, that both are wrong.

There can be no question as to this rite having existed outside of Christianity, or of its being much older than Christianity. History proves both. Nor can it be successfully denied that it is taught in the Christian Scriptures, both the confessing of sins and that of forgiving sins. The apostle James, with respect to the former, is quite explicit. He enjoins, emphatically, "Confess your faults one to another." (James v. 16.) The practice of forgiving sins is also enjoined. "Forgiving one another" is recommended both in Ephesians (iv. 32) and Colossians. (iii. 13). "And whatsoever ye shall lose on earth shall be loosed in heaven" (Matthew xviii 18), is interpreted as conferring the power to forgive sins.

And then we remark that the practices both of confessing and forgiving sins are very ancient pagan rites and customs. Speaking of their prevalence in ancient India, the author of the Anacalypsis remarks, "The person offering sacrifices made a verbal confession of his sins, and received absolution." Auricular confession was also practiced among the ancient Mithriacs, or Persians, and the Parsees proper of the same country. Mr. Volney tells us, "They observed all the Christian sacraments, even to the laying on of hands in the confirmation." (211.) And the Christian Tertullian also tells us that "The priests of Mithra promised absolution from sin on confession and baptism," while another author adds, that "on such occasions Mithra marked his followers (the servants of God) in their foreheads," and that "he celebrated the sacrifice of bread, which is the resurrection."

In the collection of the Jewish laws called "The Mishna," we are told the Jews confessed their sins by placing their hands upon a calf belonging to the priest, and that this was called "the Confession of Calves." (See Mishna, tom. ii. p. 394.) Confessing sins was practiced in ancient Mexico; also under Numa of Rome, whose priests, we are informed, had to clear their consciences by confessing their sins before they could offer sacrifices. The practice of confessing and forgiving sins as recommended in the Christian bible, and practiced by some of the Christian sects, has been the source of much practical evil by furnishing a pretext and license, to some extent, for the commission of crime and sin. While sins can be so easily obliterated they will be committed—perpetrated without much remorse or restraint. "In China (says the Rev. Mr. Pitrat, 232), the invocation of Omito is sufficient to remit the punishment of the greatest crimes." The same author tells us, "The ancient initiation of the pagans had tribunals of penance, where the priests, under the name of *Roes*, heard from the mouth of the sinners themselves the avowal of their sins of which their souls were to be purified, and from the punishment of which they wished to be exempted." (Page 37.) The granting of absolution for sin or misconduct among the early primitive Christians was so common, St. Cyprian informs us, that "thousands of reprieves were granted daily," which served as an indirect license to crime. And thus the doctrine of divine forgiveness, as taught by pagans and Christians, has proved to be demoralizing in its effects upon society.

CHAPTER XXVI. ORIGIN OF BAPTISM BY WATER, FIRE, BLOOD AND THE HOLY GHOST

BAPTISM, in some of its various forms, is a very ancient rite, and was extensively practiced in several oriental countries. It was administered in a great varieties of forms, and with the use of different elements. Water was the most common, but fire and air, wind, spirit ghost were also used; and both the living and the dead were made the subjects of its solemn and imposing ceremonies.

We will notice each of these modes of baptism separate—appropriating a brief space to each.

1. Baptism by Water.

"Baptism by water," says Mr. Higgins, "is a very old rite, being practised by the followers of Zoroaster, by the Romans, the Egyptians, and other nations." It was also vogue among the ancient Hindoos at a still earlier day Their mode of administering it was to dip the candidate for immersion three times in the watery element, in the same manner as is now practiced by some of the Christian sects during the performance of which the hierophant would ejaculate the following prayer and ceremony: "O Lord this man is impure, like the mud of this stream! But as thou cleanse and deliver his soul from sin as the water cleanses his body." They believed that water possesses the virtue of purifying both soul and body—the latter from filth and the former from sin. The ancient Mexican, Persians, Hindoos and Jews were in the habit of baptizing their infants soon after they were born. And the water used for this purpose was called "the water of regeneration." Paul speaks of being "saved by the washing of regeneration." (See Titus iii. 5.) Those who touched these infants before they were baptized were deemed impure. And as this was unavoidable on the part of the mothers, they were required, as in the cases of the mothers of Chrishna and Christ, to present themselves on the eighth day after accouchement to the priest in the temple to be purified. The Romans chose the eighth day for girls and the ninth for boys. The child was usually named (christened) at the time it was baptized. And in India, the name, or God's name, or some other mark, was engraven or written on the forehead. This custom is several times recognized in the Christian bible, both in the old and in the New Testament. (See Ezek. ix 4; Rev. xiv. 9; xix. 20, etc.) John speaks of a mark being made on the forehead. (See Rev. xiii. 16.) Also of the name of God being written on the forehead. (Rev. iii. 12.)

THE DOVE DESCENDING AT BAPTISM.

At this stage of our inquiry it may be stated that several of the ancient religious orders had the legend of a dove or pigeon descending at baptism—a counterpart to the evangelical story of "the Spirit of God descending in bodily shape like a dove," and alighting on the head of Jesus Christ while being baptized by John in Jordan. (See Luke iii. 22.) It will be observed here that the spirit, or soul, of God descended not only in the manner, but in "bodily shape like a dove." This accords with the tradition anciently prevalent among the Hindoos, Mexicans, Greeks, Romans and Persians, or Babylonians, that all souls, or spirits, possessed, or were capable of assuming, the form of a dove. Hence, it is reported of Polycarp, Semiramis, Caesar and others, that at death their souls, or spirits, were seen to leave the body in "bodily shape like a dove" and ascend to heaven. "The Divine Love, or Eros," says Mr. Higgins, "was supposed by the oriental heathen to descend often in the form of a dove to bless the candidate for baptism." These traditions, doubtless, gave rise to the story of the dove descending at Christ's baptism—that is God in the shape of a dove, for that is clearly the meaning of the text. We are also informed by our author just quoted, that a dove stood for and represented, among the orientalists, the third person of the Trinity, as it does in the gospel story of Christ—he being the second member of the Christian Trinity of Father, Son and Holy Ghost. It was considered "the regenerator, or regenerating spirit," and persons being baptized were said to be "born again" into the spirit or the spirit into them; that is, the dove into or upon them.

What a master-key is furnished by these oriental religions for solving the mysteries of the Christian bible! How much more lucid than Divine Revelation—so-called!

We will quote again from Higgins: "Among all nations, from the very earliest period, water has been used as a species of religious sacrament. Because, as it dripped from the clouds, it was observed to have the power of reviving drooping nature and creating anew, or regenerating the whole vegetable kingdom in spring, it was hence chosen as an emblem of spiritual regeneration and a medium of baptism. Water was the element by means of which everything was born again through the agency of the Eros, Dove, or Divine Love." And, hence, the ceremony of dipping or plunging (or, as it is modernly termed, baptizing) came into vogue for the remission of sins and "the regeneration into a new and more holy life."

Some streams were supposed to have more efficacy in these respects than others. Hence, nearly all religious nations had their "Holy Rivers," "Holy Water," "Sacred Pools," etc. The Hindoos resorted to the "Holy Ganges," the Egyptians to the "Holy Nile," the Chaldeans and Persians to the "Holy Euphrates," the Greeks to their "Holy Lustral Water," the Italians to the river Po, and the Jews and Christians to their holy river Jordan. If Jordan was not called "holy," it was undoubtedly considered so, else why did Elisha order Naaman to wash seven times in that stream instead of Damascus, which was much nearer and more accessible? And why was Christ baptized in Jordan? "And all the land of Judea, and they of Jerusalem, were baptized in Jordan, confessing their sins." (Matt iii. vi.) Why, as several streams were handier to a large portion of the candidates, simply because Jordan was considered to be "more holy." And Christians had their sacred pool of Bethesda, as the Hindoos had their Sahar.

The rite of baptism was at first generally practiced in caves—as were also other religious rites; and as these caves were often difficult of access, and their mouths, doors or gates narrow and difficult to enter, they fully exemplify Christ's declaration, "Straight is the gate and narrow is the way that leadeth unto life." (Matt. vii. 14.) And when he declared, "Except a man be born of water and of the spirit he cannot enter the kingdom of heaven" (John iii. 5) he was only seconding the exhortation of the priests to enter these subterranean vaults and be baptized after the oriental and Jewish custom. Thus originated baptism by water in the form of dipping, or immersion.

BAPTISM BY SPRINKLING.

Owing to the scarcity of water in some countries, and its entire absence in others, and the fatal effects sometimes resulting from the practice of baptizing infants and invalids by immersion, a new mode of baptism eventually sprung up, now known as "sprinkling," in which sometimes water and sometimes blood was used. Virgil, Ovid and Cicero all speak of its prevalence amongst the ancient Romans or Latins. We are informed that the ancient Jews practiced it upon their women while in a state of nudity, the ceremony being administered by three rabbis, or priests. But the custom finally gave way to one more consonant with decorum. Blood, being considered "the life thereof" of man, was deemed more efficacious than water, and hence was often used in lieu of that element. The Greeks kept a "holy vessel" for this purpose, known as the Facina. The Romans used a brush, which may now be seen engraven upon some of their ancient coins and sculptured on their ancient temples. The Hindoos and Persians used a branch of laurel or some other shrub for sprinkling the repentant candidate, whether water or blood was used.

In some countries the rite was practiced as a talisman against evil spirits. The Mexicans never approached their altars without sprinkling them with blood drawn from their own bodies, as the Jews sprinkled the walls and door-posts of their temples with blood under the requisition of the Levitical code. This mode of fancied purification by sprinkling either with water or blood we find recognized, and apparently sanctioned, in the Christian bible, both in the Old and New Testaments. Ezekiel says, "I will sprinkle clean water on you." (Ezek. xxxvi. 25.) Peter uses the phrase, "The sprinkling of the blood of Jesus Christ." (1 Peter i. 2.) And Paul makes use of the expression, "The blood of sprinkling, that speaketh better things than that of Abel" (Heb. xii. 24), which we regard as an indirect sanction of the senseless heathen idea of effecting spiritual purification by drops of blood. (See Potter's Antiquities and Herbert's Travels.)

BAPTISM BY FIRE.

Baptism by fire was a form or mode of application which seems to have been introduced from the belief that it was productive of a higher degree of purification. There were several ways of using fire in the baptismal rite. In some cases the candidate for immortality ran through blazing streams of fire—a custom which was called "the baptism of fire." M. de Humboldt, in his "Views of the Cordilleras and Monuments of America," informs us it prevailed in India, Chaldea and Syria, and throughout eastern Asia. It appears to have been gotten up as a substitute for sun-worship, as this luminary was believed to be constituted of fire, though in reality there never was any such thing as sun or solar worship. Christian writers represent the ancient Persians as has having been addicted to solar worship. But Firdausi, Cudworth and other authors declare that neither they nor any other nation ever worshiped the sun, but merely an imaginary Deity supposed to reside in the sun. Heathen nations have been charged with many things of which they were not guilty; though it is true that in the spirit of Christ's exhortation, "Whosoever loseth his life for my sake shall find it," some of the candidates for the fiery ordeal voluntarily sacrificed their lives in the operation, under the persuasion that it was necessary to purify the soul, and would enable them to ascend to higher posts or planes of enjoyment in the celestial world. And some of them were taught that sins not expurgated by fire, or some other efficaciously renovating process in this life, would be punished by fire in the life to come. Here we will mention that there is a seeming recognition of this ancient heathen rite in both departments of the Christian's bible. Isaiah says, "When thou walkest through fire thou shalt not be burned." (lxiii. 2.) And the Baptist John recognizes three modes of baptism: "I indeed baptize

105

you with water, but he that cometh after me shall baptize you with fire and the Holy Ghost." (Matt. iii. 11). And Paul teaches the necessity of being purified by fire. (See i Cor. iii. 15.) So it is both a heathen and a Christian idea.

BAPTISM BY THE HOLY GHOST.

This fanciful ceremony is both a Christian and a heathen rite, and is undoubtedly of heathen origin. The mode of applying it was to breathe into or upon the seeker for divine favors. This was done by the priest, who, it was believed, imparted the Spirit of God by the process. The custom, Mr. Herbert informs us, was anciently quite common in oriental countries, and was at a later date borrowed by Christ and his apostles and incorporated into the Christian ceremonies. We find that Christ not only sanctioned it but practised it, as it is declared when he met his disciples after his resurrection "he breathed on them, and saith unto them, Receive ye the Holy Ghost." (John xx. 22.)

And the following language of Ezekiel is evidently a sanction of the same heathen custom: "Thus saith the Lord God, Come from the four winds, O breath, and breathe upon these slain, that they may live." (xxxvii. 9.) Let it be borne in mind here that breath, air, wind, spirit and ghost were used as synonymous terms, according to Mr. Parkhurst (see Chap. XXII.), and this breathing was supposed to impart spiritual life, being nothing less than the Spirit of God, the same as that breathed into Adam when "he became a living soul." (See Gen. ii. 7.) For a fuller exposition see Chapter XXII.

BAPTISM OF OR FOR THE DEAD.

It was customary among the Hindoos and other nations to postpone baptism till near the supposed terminus of life, in order that the ablution might extinguish all the sins and misdeeds of the subject's earthly probation. But it sometimes happened that men and women were killed, or died unexpectedly, before the rite was administered. And as it would not do for these unfortunate souls to be deprived of the benefit of this soul-saving ordinance, the custom was devised of baptizing the defunct body, or more commonly some living person in its stead. The method of executing the latter expedient, according to St. Chrysostom, was to place some living person under the bed or couch on which the corpse was reclining, when the defunct was asked if he would be baptized. The living man, responding for the dead, answered in the affirmative. The corpse was then taken and dipped in a vessel prepared for the purpose. This silly practice was in vogue among the early Christians, and Paul seems to regard it as an important custom. "Else what shall they do which are baptized for the dead, if the dead rise not at all." (i Cor. xv. 9.)

The inference derivable from this text is, that Paul held that the labor of baptizing the dead would be lost in the event of the falsification of the doctrine of the resurrection, but otherwise it would be valid—which evinces his faith in the senseless and superstitious practice. It will be observed from the historical exposition of this chapter that all the various ancient heathen modes and rites of baptism have been practiced by Christians, and are sanctioned by their bible.

CHAPTER XXVII. THE SACRAMENT OR EUCHARIST OF HEATHEN ORIGIN

AT the feast of the Passover, Christ is represented, while distributing bread to his disciples, to have said, "Take, eat; this is my body" (Matt. xxvi. 26); and while handing round the consecrated cup, he enjoined, "Drink ye all of it, for this is my blood of the new covenant, which is shed for many for the remission of sins" (xxvi. 27). Here is a very clear and explicit indorsement of what is generally termed "the Eucharist or Sacrament." And nothing can be more susceptible of proof than that this rite or ordinance is of pagan origin, and was practically recognized many centuries prior to the dawn of the Christian era.

So we observe, by the text above quoted, the Christian Savior and Lawgiver copied, or reproduced, an old pagan rite as a part of his professedly new and spiritual system, one of the most ancient and widely-extended formulas of pagandom. And stranger still, the catechisms of the Christian church represent this ordinance as having originated in the design and motive to keep the ancient Christian world in remembrance of the death and sufferings and sacrifice of Christ, while we find it existing long prior to his time, both among Jews and pagans, this being virtually admitted in the bible itself, so far as respects the pagans, thus proving that it did not originate with Christ, and therefore is not of Christian origin. For in Gen. viv. 18, we read, "And Melchisedek, king of Salem, brought forth bread and wine, and he was the priest of the Most High God." Because the Melchisedek here spoken of is represented as being "a priest of the Most High God," and showed so much respect to Abraham, it is presumed and assumed, by Christian writers, that he was a Jewish priest and king; and Mr. Faber (vol. i. p. 72) calls him "an incarnation of the son of God." But there is no intimation throughout the Jewish Scriptures of the Jews ever having had a king or priest by that name. And besides, Eupolemus (vol. i. p. 39), tells us that the temple of Melchisedek was the temple of Jupiter, in which Pythagoras studied philosophy. Then, again, according to some writers, the name is synonymous with Moloch, the God of war among the Greeks. Strange, then, that Melchisedek should be claimed as a priest and king among the Jews. Be this as it may, the case proves that the ceremony of offering bread and wine existed long before the era of Jesus Christ.

And then we have much more and much stronger proof of this fact than is here furnished. The Christian Mr. Faber virtually admits it, when he tells us, "The devil led the heathen to anticipate Christ with respect to several things, as the mysteries of the Eucharist, etc." "And this very solemnity (says St Justin) the evil spirit introduced into the mysteries of Mithra." (Reeves, Justin, p. 86.) Mr. Higgins observes, "It was instituted hundreds of years before the Lord's death took place." Amongst the ancient religious orders and nations who practiced this rite, we may name the Essenes, Persians, Pythagoreans, Gnostics, Brahmins and Mexicans. For proof of its existence and antiquity among the last-named nation, we refer the reader to the "Travels" (chap. ii.) of that Christian writer, Father Acosta. Mr. Marolles, in his Memoirs (p. 215) quotes Tibullus as saying, "The pagan appeased the divinity with holy bread." And Tibullus, in a panegyric on Marcella, wrote, "A little cake, a little morsel of bread, appeased the divinities."

And here we discover the idea which originated the ceremony. It was started, like animal sacrifices, for the purpose of appeasing the wrath or propitiating the favor of the angry Gods. Tracing the conception still further in the rear of its progress, and apparently to its primary inception, Mr. Higgins observes, "The whole paschal supper (the Lord's supper with the Christians) was in fact a festival of joy to celebrate the passage of the sun across the equinox of spring."

We find one pagan writer who had intelligence enough to ridicule this senseless ceremonial custom, called "the sacrament." Cicero, some forty years before Christ, shows up the doctrine of the sacrament, or substantiation, in its true light. He asks, "How can a man be so stupid as to imagine that which he eats to be a God?" A writer quoted above says, "Mass, or the sacrifice of bread and wine, was common to many ancient nations." (Anac. vol. ii. p. 62.) According to Alnetonae, the ancient Brahmins had a kind of Eucharist called "prajadam." And the same writer informs us that the ancient Peruvians, "after sacrificing a lamb, mingled his blood with flour, and distributed it among the people." Writers on Grecian mythology relate that Ceres, the goddess of corn, gave her flesh to eat, and that Bacchus, the God of wine, gave blood to drink. Nor is there any evidence that Christ and his followers made a better use, or different use, or a more spiritual application of the sacrament, or ceremonial offering of bread and wine, than the pagans did, though some have claimed this. It was a species of symbolism with both, notwithstanding Mr. Glover, a Christian writer, declares, that "in the sacrament of the altar are the natural body and blood of Christ, verily and indeed." (See Glover's Remarks on Bishop Marsh's Compendious Review.) It may be noted here that the Persians, Pythagoreans, Essenes and Gnostics used water instead of wine, and that this mode of practice was less objectionable than that of the Christians, who (as sad experience proves) have too often laid the foundation for the ruin of some poor unsuspecting devotee, by luring him to the fatal fascination of the intoxicating bowl, by holding the sacred and ceremonial wine to his lips, while administering the sacrament or the Lord's supper.

CHAPTER XXVIII. ANOINTING WITH OIL OF ORIENTAL ORIGIN

THE custom and ceremony of anointing with oil by way of imparting some fancied spiritual power and religious qualification seems to have been extensively practiced by the Jews and primitive Christians, and still more anciently by various oriental nations. Mark (xiv. 4), reports Jesus Christ as speaking commendingly of the practice, by which it was evident he was in favor of the superstitious custom. The apostle James not only sanctions it, but recommends it in the most specific language. "Is any sick among you, let him call for the elders of the church, and let them pray over him, anointing him with oil in the name of the Lord." (James v. 14.)

The practice of greasing or smearing with oil, it may be noted here, was in vogue from other motives besides the one here indicated. We find the statement in the New American Cyclopedia (vol. i. p. 620), that anointing with perfumed oil was in common use among the Greeks and Romans as a mark of hospitality to guests. And modern travelers in the East still find it a custom for visitors to be sprinkled with rose-water, or their head, face and beard "anointed with olive oil." "Anointing," we are also told, "is an ancient and still prevalent custom throughout the East, by pouring aromatic oils on persons as a token of honor.... It was also employed in consecrating priests, prophets and kings, and the places and instruments appointed for worship." (Ibid.) Joshua anointed the ten stones he set up in Jordan, and Jacob the stone on which he slept at the time of his great vision.

The early Christians were in the habit of anointing the altars, and even the walls, of the churches, in the same manner as the images, obelisks, statues, etc., had long been consecrated by the devotees of the oriental systems. Aaron, Saul, David, Solomon, and even Jesus Christ were anointed with oil in the same way. David Malcom, in his "Essay on the Antiquity of the Britons," p. 144, says, "The Mexican king was anointed with Holy Unction by the high priest while dancing before the Lord." Vide the case of David "dancing before the Lord with all his might." Dr. Lightfoot, in his "Harmony of the New Testament," speaks of the custom among the Jews of anointing the sick on the Sabbath day (see Works, vol. i, p. 333; also Toland, Sect. Naz. p. 54), as afterwards recommended by the apostle James, as shown above. This accords exactly with the method of treating the sick in ancient India and other heathen countries several thousand years ago. For proof consult Hyde, Bryant, Tertullian and other writers. The custom of anointing the sick, accompanied with prayer and other ceremonies, was quite fashionable in the East long before the birth of either Jesus or James. One writer testifies that "the practice of anointing with oil, so much in vogue among the Jews, and sanctioned by Christ and his followers, was held in high esteem in nearly all the Eastern religions."

The foregoing historical facts furnish still further proof that Christianity is the offspring of heathenism.

CHAPTER XXIX. HOW MEN, INCLUDING JESUS CHRIST, CAME TO BE WORSHIPED AS GODS

JESUS CHRIST A DEMIGOD, ACCORDING TO CHRISTIAN WRITERS.

IT is truly surprising to observe the damaging concessions of some of the early Christian writers, ruinous to the dogmas of their own faith with respect to the divinity of Jesus Christ, placing him, as they do, on an exact level with the heathen demigods, proving that the belief in his divinity originated in the same manner the belief in theirs did, by which it is clearly shown to be a pagan derived doctrine. Several Christian writers admit the belief in earth-born Gods (called Sons of

Gods), and their coming into the world by human birth was prevalent among the heathen long prior to the time of Christ. Hear the proof.

We will first quote St. Justin relative to the prevalence of the belief among the ancient Greeks and Romans. Addressing them, he says, "The title of Son of God (As applied to Jesus Christ) is very justifiable upon the account of his wisdom, considering you have your Mercury in your worship, under the title of Word or Messenger of God." (Reeves Apol. p. 76.) Here is the proof that the tradition of the Son of God coming into the world, and "the Word becoming flesh," was established amongst the ancient Greeks and Romans long prior to the era of Christianity, or the birth of Christ.

And yet more than a hundred millions of Christian professors can now be found, who, in their historic ignorance, suppose St. John was the first writer who taught the doctrine of "the Word becoming flesh," and that Jesus Christ was "the first and only begotten Son of God" who ever made his appearance on earth. How true it is that "ignorance is the mother of devotion" to creeds.

How "the man Christ Jesus" came to be worshiped as a God, is pretty clearly indicated by Bishop Horne, who shows that the doctrine of the incarnation was of universal prevalence long before Jesus Christ came into the flesh. He says, "That God should, in some extraordinary manner, visit and dwell with man, is an idea, which, as we read the writings of the ancient heathen, meets us in a thousand different forms." If, then, the tradition of God being born into the world was so universally established in heathen countries before the Christian era, as here shown, why should not, and why will not, our good Christian brethren dismiss their prejudices, and tear the scales from their eyes, so as to see that this universal belief would as naturally lead to the deification and worship of "the man Christ Jesus" as water flows down a descending plane?

And, certainly a thousand times more reasonable is the assumption that his deification originated in this way, than that, with all his frailties and foibles, he was entitled to the appellation of a God—a conclusion strongly corroborated by the testimony of that able Christian writer, Mr. Norton, who tells us that "many of the first Christians being converts from Gentileism, their imaginations were familiar with the reputed incarnation of heathen deities." How natural it would be for such converts to worship "the man Christ Jesus" as a God on account of his superior manhood!

Again, that ancient pillar of the Christian church, St. Justin, concedes that the ancient oriental heathen held all the cardinal doctrines of the Christian faith relating to the incarnation long prior to the introduction and establishment of Christianity. Hear him: Addressing the pagans, he says, "For by declaring the Logos the first begotten Son of God, our Master, Jesus Christ, to be born of a virgin without any human mixture, and to be crucified, and dead, and to have risen again into heaven, we say no more in this than what you say of those whom you style the sons of Jove." (Reeves, Apol. vol. i. p. 69.) Now, Christian reader, mark the several important admissions which are made here:—

1. Here is traced to ancient heathen tradition the belief in an incarnate Son of God.

2. The doctrine of a "first begotten Son of God."

3. Of his being born of a virgin.

4. Of his crucifixion.

5. Of his resurrection.

6. Of his final ascension into heaven.

All these cardinal doctrines of Christianity are here shown to have been in existence, and to have been preached by pagan priests long anterior to the Christian era, thus entirely oversetting the common belief of Christendom that these doctrines were never known or preached in the world until heralded by the first disciples of the Christian religion. A fatal mistake, truly! This suicidal admission of St Justin (a standard Christian writer) thus entirely uptrips all pretensions to originality in the fundamental doctrines of the Christian faith, and shows it to be a mere travesty of the more ancient heathen systems.

And we have still other testimony to corroborate this conclusion. The French writer Bazin says, "The most ancient histories are those of Gods becoming incarnate in order to govern mankind." Again he says, "The idea sprang up everywhere from confused ideas of God, which prevailed everywhere among mankind that Gods formerly descended upon earth. The fertile imagination of the people of various nations converted men into Gods."

And to the same effect is the declaration of Mr. Higgins, that "there was incarnate Gods in all religions." Sadly beclouded and warped indeed must be that mind which cannot see that here is set in as plain view as the cloudless sun at noonday, the origin of the deification of "the man Christ Jesus." No unbiased mind can possibly stave off the conclusion that such a universal prevalence of the practice of God-making throughout the religious world would cause such a man as Jesus Christ to be worshiped as a God—especially when we look at the various motives which promoted men to Gods, which we will now present.

MOTIVES TO INCARNATION, OR THE CAUSE OF MEN BEING WORSHIPED AS GODS.

The causes which led to the conception of Gods and Sons of God becoming clothed in human flesh—the manner in which the absurd idea originated of an infinite being descending from heaven, assuming the form of a man, being born of a pure and spotless virgin, and finally being killed by his own children, the subjects of his own government, are palpably plain and easily understood' in the light of oriental history.

And at the same time it is so shockingly absurd, that the rapid march of science and civilization will soon inaugurate the era when the man or woman who shall still be found clinging to these childish and superstitious conceptions—the offspring of ignorance, and the relics of barbarism, and a certain proof of undeveloped or unenlightened minds—will be looked upon as deplorably ignorant and superstitious. We will proceed to enumerate some of the causes which promoted men to the dignity of Gods.

1. God must come down to suffer and sympathize with the people.

111

The people of all ancient religious countries were so externally-minded, that they demanded a God whom they could know by virtue of his corporeity, really sympathized with their sorrows, their sufferings, their wrongs, and their oppressions, and, like Jesus Christ, "touched with a feeling of our infirmities" (Heb. iv. 15)—a God so far invested with human attributes, human frailties, and human sympathies, that he could shoulder their burdens and their infirmities, and take upon himself a portion of their sufferings. Hence it is said of Christ, "himself took our infirmities." (Matt. iii. 17.)

The same conception runs through the pagan systems. One writer sets forth the matter thus: "The Creator occasionally assumed a mortal form to assist mankind in great emergencies" (as Jesus Christ was afterward reported as being the Creator. See Col. i. 16.) "And as repeated sojourners on earth in various capacities, they (the Saviors) became practically acquainted with all the sorrows and temptations of humanity, and could justly judge of its sins while they sympathized with its weaknesses and its sufferings. When they again returned to the higher regions (heaven), they remembered the lower forms they had dwelt amongst, and felt a lively interest in the world they had once inhabited. They could penetrate even the secret thoughts of mortals."

The people then demanding a God of sympathy and suffering (as shown above), their credulous imaginations would not be long in finding one. Let a man rise up in society endowed with an extraordinary degree of spirituality and sympathy for human suffering; let him, like Chrishna, Pythagoras, Christ, and Mahomet, spend his time in visiting the hovels of the poor, or consoling their sorrows, laboring to mitigate their griefs, and in performing acts of charity, disinterested alms and deeds of benevolence, kindness and love, and so certain would he sooner or later command the homage of a God. For this was always the mode adopted, in an ignorant, undeveloped, and unenlightened age, for accounting not merely for moral greatness, but for every species of mental and physical superiority, as will be hereafter shown. We will proceed to notice the second cause of men being invested with divine attributes.

2. The people must and would have an external God they could see, hear, and talk to.

All the oriental nations, as well as Christian, taught that "God was a spirit," but no nation or class of people, not even the founders of Christianity, entertained a consistent view of the doctrine. Only a few learned philosophers saw the scientific impossibility of an infinite spirit being crowded into the human form. Hence they alone were contented to "worship God in spirit and in truth." Every religious nation went counter to the spirit of this injunction in worshiping for a God a being in the human form. Even the founders of Christianity, though making high claims to spirituality, were too gross, too sensuous in their conceptions, too externally-minded, and too idolatrous in their feelings and proclivities, to be content to "worship God in spirit." Hence their deification of the "man Christ Jesus" to answer the requisition of an external worship, by which they violated the command to "worship God as a spirit." That the practice of promoting men to the Godhead originated with minds on the external plane, and evinces a want of spiritual development, is clearly set forth by the author of "The Nineteenth Century" (a Christian writer) who tells us, "The idea of the primitive ages were wholly sensuous, and the masses did not believe in anything except that which they could touch, see, hear and taste." A true description, no doubt, of the ancient pagan worshipers of demigods. But we warn the Christian reader not to cast anchor here, for we have at our elbow abundance of Christian testimony from the pens of the very oracles of the church to prove that the same state of things, the same state of society, the same state of mind, the same proclivity for God-making, existed with the people among whom Christ was born, and that it was owing to this sensuous, idolatrous state of mind among his disciples that he received the homage and title of a God.

Hence the famous Archbishop Tillotson says, "Another very common notion, and rife in the heathen world, and a great source of their idolatry, was their deification of great men fit to be worshiped as Gods."... "There was a great inclination in mankind to the worship of a visible Deity. So God was pleased to appear in our nature, that they who were fond of a visible Deity might have one, even a true and natural incarnation of God the Father, the express image of his person." Now, we enjoin the reader to mark this testimony well, and impress it indelibly upon his memory. According to this orthodox Christian bishop, Jesus Christ appeared on earth as a God in condescension to the wishes of a people too devoid of spirituality, and too strongly inclined to idolatry, to worship God as a spirit. For he admits the worship of a God-man or a man-God is a species of idolatry. This tells the whole story of the apotheosis of "the man Christ Jesus." We have no doubt but that here is suggested one of the true causes of his elevation to the Deityship. Again he says, "The world was mightily bent on addressing their requests and supplications, not to the Deity immediately, but by some Mediator between the Gods and men." (See Wadsworth's Eccles. Biog. p. 172.) Here, then, we have the most conclusive proof that the belief in mediators is of pagan origin. We will now hear from another archbishop on this subject. In his "Caution to the Times" (p, 71), Archbishop Whately says, "As the Infinite Being is an object too remote and incomprehensible for our minds to dwell upon, he has manifested himself in his Son, the man Jesus Christ" Precisely so 1 just the kind of reasoning employed to account for the worship of man-Gods among the heathen. This logic fits one case as well as the other.

The Christian writer F. D. Maurice declares in like manner, "We accept the fact of the incarnation (of Jesus Christ), because we feel that it is impossible to know the absolute invisible God without an incarnation, as man needs to know him, and craves to know him." (Logical Essay, p. 79.) Here is more pagan logic—the same reasoning they employed to prove the divinity of their Saviors and demigods. And the Rev. Dr. Thomas Arnold declares, "It (the incarnation of Christ) was very necessary, especially at a time when men were so accustomed to worship their highest Gods under the form of men" (Sermon on Christian Life, p. 61.) Let the reader attentively observe the explicit avowal here made, and mark well its pregnant inferences. He makes Jesus Christ come into the world in condescension to the idolatrous rivalry of the Jews to be up with the heathen nations in worshiping God in the form of man; that is, the founders of Christianity, having been Jews, disclosed the true Jewish character in running after and adopting the customs of heathen countries then so rife—that of hunting up a great man, and making him a God—which was only one case out of many of the Jews adopting some of the numerous forms of idolatry and other religious customs of their heathen neighbors. Their whole history, as set forth in the Bible, proves, as we have shown in another chapter, that they were strongly prone to such acts. It is not strange, therefore, that they should and did convert "the man Christ Jesus" into a God. We will now listen to another Christian writer, the notable and noteworthy Dr. T. Chambers. "Whatever the falsely or superstitiously fearful imagination conjures up because of God being at a distance, can only be dispelled by God being brought nigh to us.... The veil which hides the unseen God from the eyes of mortals must be somehow withdrawn." (Select Works, vol. iii. p. 161.) Most significant indeed is this species of reasoning. It is the same kind of logic

113

which had led to the promotion of more than a score of great men to the Godhead among the ancient heathen. "The veil which hides the unseen God must be removed'" says Dr. Chambers; and so had reasoned in soliloquy a thousand pagans long before, when determined to worship men for Gods. It is simply saying, "We are too carnally-minded to worship God in spirit; we must and will have a God of flesh and blood—a God who can be recognized by the external senses;" he must "become flesh, and dwell amongst us." (See John i. 14.) Our author continues: "Now all this (removing the veil from the unseen God) has been done once, and done only once in the person of Jesus Christ." (Ibid.) Mistake, most fatal mistake, brother Chambers! It has been done more than a score of times in various heathen countries—a fact which proves you ignorant of oriental history.

Now let the reader mark the foregoing citations from standard Christian authors, setting forth some of the reasons which led the founders of Christianity to adopt a visible man-God in their worship in the person of Jesus Christ, Language could hardly be used to prove more conclusively that the whole thing grew out of an idolatrous proclivity to man-worship,—that is, the gross, sensuous, carnally-minded propensity to worship an extetnal, visible God,—proving, with the corroborative evidence of many other facts, that they were not a whit above the heathen in spiritual development. The reason employed by the Thibetan for the worship of the Hindoo Chrishna as a God, tells the whole story of the worship and the deification of Jesus Christ "We could not always have God behind the clouds; so we had him come down where we could see him." This is the same kind of reasoning made use of by the Christian writer above quoted, all of which discloses a state of mind among both heathen and Christians that would not long rest satisfied without deifying somebody, in order to have a visible God to worship. And hence Christians deified "the man Christ Jesus" for this purpose.

"The more externally minded (says Fleurbach), the greater was the determination to worship a personal God"—God in the form of man. And as the Jewish founders of Christianity (as every chapter of their history demonstrates) were dwelling on the external plane, it was not an act of direct innovation, therefore, for them to fall into the habit of worshiping the personal Jesus as a God. It involved no serious incursion on previous thoughts or habits. And warped and blinded, indeed, must be that mind which cannot here discover the true key to the apotheosis of Jesus— one of the real causes of his being stripped of his manhood, and advanced to the Godhead. It was as naturally to be expected from the then state of the religious world, and the state of the Jewish mind concerned in the founding of Christianity, as that an autumnal crop of fruit should succeed the bloom of spring.

Let it be specially noted, that all the Christian writers above cited tell us, in effect, that God sent his Son Jesus Christ into the world to be worshiped as a God in condescension to the ignorance and superstitious tendencies, and we will add, idolatrous proclivities of the people. From this stand-point we challenge the world to show why God may not have sent the oriental Saviors into the world for the same reason—that is, in condescension to the prejudices of the devout worshipers under the heathen systems. Why, then, is there not as much probability that he did do so? Why would he not be as likely to accommodate their ignorance and prejudices in this way as those of the founders of the Christian system. This question we shall keep standing before the Christian world till it is answered, and we challenge them to meet it, and overthrow it if they can.

3. Men deified on account of mental and moral superiority.

The ancient nations, in their entire ignorance of the philosophy of the human mind, and the laws controlling its actions, always accounted for the appearance of great men amongst them by supposing them to be Gods. Every country occasionally produced a man, who, by virtue of natural superiority, rose so high in the scale of moral and intellectual greatness as to fill the ideal of the people with respect to the characteristics of a God. So low, so limited, so narrow, so greatly circumscribed were the conceptions of deity, of the undeveloped and intellectually dwarfed minds of all religious countries in that age, that a man had to rise but a few degrees above the common level of the populace to become a God. He could "easily fill the bill," and exhibit all the qualities they assigned to the highest God in the heavens. And this is as true of the Jewish mind as that of any other nation, a portion of whom adored Jesus as a God. Or if they lacked anything in natural inclination, they made it up by imitation, a propensity which they possessed in no small degree, that is, a proneness to imitate the customs of other nations.

Mr. Higgins tells us that "men of brilliant intellects and high moral attainments, and great healers (of which Christ was one), were almost certain to be deified." In like manner Archbishop Tillotson says, "they deified famous and eminent persons by advancing them after their death to the dignity of an inferior kind of Gods fit to be worshiped by men on earth." Mark the expression, "after their death" We have shown in another chapter that Jesus Christ was not generally considered a God, even by his followers, till more than three hundred years after his death, when Constantine declared him to be "God of very God"—a circumstance of itself sufficient to establish the conclusion that he did not possess this character. A God would be adored as such by everybody while living, but a man's worshipers rise up after his death, as in the case of "the man Christ Jesus." Great mental endowments, or great moral attainments, would, in most countries, bring the most ignorant down on their knees to worship such a man as a God. But it re-quired years, and sometimes centuries, to get him fully established among the Gods. This is as true of Jesus Christ as the other human-descended deities. Whatever amount of homage Jesus might have received while living, any person who will institute a thorough, unbiased scrutiny in the case will discover that it was his great healing powers and superior mental qualities which finally deified him. His ignorant admirers knew no way of accounting for such extraordinary qualities but to suppose him to be the embodiment of infinite wisdom. Like the Chinaman who exclaimed, "See the God in that man," when an Englishman cured a young woman of partial blindness by anointing her eyes with kerosene. Such a deed would deify almost any man, in almost any country, before the dawn of letters and the recognition of the science of mind.

The missionary Rev. D. O. Allen's method of accounting for the deification of the Hindoo God Chrishna is so suggestive, that we here present it. He tells us that "as the exploits ascribed to Chrishna exceed mere human power, the difficulty was removed by placing him among the incarnations of Vishnu." (India, Ancient and Modern, p. 26.) Exactly so! We are glad of such historic information. We hope the Christian reader will note the lesson it suggests. For certainly, every reader, who has not had his reason shipwrecked on the shoals of a blind and dogmatic theology, can see here a key to unlock the great mystery of the Christian incarnation—the divinity of Jesus Christ As some of the exploits of Chrishna were supposed to "exceed mere human power," we are told the difficulty was explained by imagining him to be a God. How powerful the suggestion! how conclusive the explanation, not only for the Godhood of this sin-atoning Savior, but for that of "our Lord and Savior Jesus Christ," and all the other Lords, and Gods, and Saviors of antiquity! A single hint will sometimes explain whole volumes of obscure history, as does this of the Rev. Christian Hindoo missionary D. O. Allen. And surely, most deplorably blinded by superstition must be the two hundred millions of Christ worshipers, the three hundred millions who worship Chrishna, the one hundred and twenty million adorers of Confucius, the fifty millions of suppliants of Mithra the Mediator, and the one hundred and fifty millions of followers of Mahomet, who cannot see here a satisfactory solution of the deityship of all these Gods, and all the other man-Gods of antiquity.

The question is sometimes asked, How could two hundred millions of people come to believe that Jesus was a God merely because of his superiority as a man? We will answer by pointing to the history of the Hindoo Chrishna, and by asking the same question with respect to his Godhead. How could three hundred millions of people be brought to believe in his divinity, and worship him as a God, merely because he was a superior human being? One question is as easily answered as the other, and posterity will answer both questions alike. When we observe it taught as an important and easily learned lesson of history, and one based on a thousand facts, that no man could rise to intellectual greatness or moral distinction in the era in which Christ was born without being advanced to the dignity of a God, and worshiped as such, it is really a source of humility and sorrow to every unshackled lover of truth and humanity to reflect that there are so many millions of people whose mental vision is so beclouded by a dogmatic and inexorable theology that they cannot see the logical potency of these facts,—that they cannot be even moved by this great and overwhelming amount of evidence against the divinity dogma, and observe that it explodes it into a thousand fragments, but still cling to the delusion that "the man Christ Jesus," with all the human qualities and human frailties with which his own history (the Gospels) invest him, was nevertheless a God,—ay, the monstrous delusion that any being possessing a *finite form* could be an *infinite being*—a most self-evident and shocking absurdity. And we challenge all Christendom to show, or approximate one inch toward showing, that there was sufficient difference between Christ and Chrishna to require us to accept one as a man and the other as a God. It cannot be done.

We have shown, then, by the foregoing exposition, that one cause of the deification of men was simply an attempt to solve the problem of human greatness,—an attempt to account for the moral and intellectual superiority of men which enabled them to perform deeds and otherwise exhibit a character far above the capacity of the multitude to comprehend, and which they could find no other way to account for than to suppose them to be Gods, while the low and groveling conceptions which most religious nations, and especially the Jews, had formed of the character and essential attributes of the Infinite Deity (often investing him with the most ignoble human attributes, human passions, and human imperfections), made it perfectly easy to convert their great men by imagination into Gods. The Jews represented God not only as a coming down from heaven in propria persona, and walking, talking, wrestling, &c., as a man (on one occasion we are told he and Jacob scuffled all night), but he is often represented as acting the part of a wicked man, such as lying (see 2 Chron. v. 22), getting mad (see Deut. i. 37), swearing, sanctioning the highhanded and demoralizing crimes of stealing (see Ex. iii. 2), of robbery (see Ex. xii. 36), of murder (see Deut. xiii. 2) and even fornication (see Gen. xxxi. 1, and Num. xxxi) and thus they invested Diety with such mean, low, despicable attributes as to reduce his moral character to a level with the most immoral man in society. So that it was very easy, if not very natural, to elevate their great men (if it really required any elevation) to a level with their God.

Men and Gods were in character and conception so nearly alike, that it was easy to bring them on a level, or to mistake one for the other. And hence it is we find an incarnated God, Savior, Son of God, Redeemer, &c., figuring in the early history of nearly every oriental religious nation whose name and history has descended to us. Indeed, the practice of deifying men, or mistaking men for Gods, was once so common, so nearly universal, that it must require a mind very ignorant of oriental history to adore Jesus Christ as having been the only character of this kind who figured in the religious world. It was, as before suggested, deemed the most rational way of accounting for the marked superiority among men, to suppose that some men had a divine birth, and were begotten by the great Infinite Deity himself, and descended to the earth through the purest human (virgin) channel.

As Mr. Higgins remarks, "Every person who possessed a striking superiority of mind, either for talent or goodness, was supposed anciently to have a portion of the divine mind or essence incorporated or incarnated in him." The Jews had a number of men whose names imply a participation in the divine nature, among which we will cite Elijah and Elisha (El-i-jah and El-i-sha), El being the Hebrew name or term for God, while Jah is Jehovah (see Ps. lxviii. 4), and Sha means a Savior. Elijah, then, is an approximation to God—Jehovah, and Elisha is God—a Savior. The character of men and Gods were cast in molds so approximately similar, so nearly identical, as to make the transition, or change from one to the other, so slight and easy; either of men into Gods or Gods into men, that several nations went so far as to teach that a man might by his own natural exertions, his own voluntary powers, raise himself to a level with the Diety, and thereby become a God.

Mr. Ritter in his "History of Ancient Philosophy" (Chap. II.), tells us that some of the Budhist sect held that "a man by freeing himself by holiness of conduct from the obstacles of nature, may deliver his fellows from the corruption of the times, and become a benefactor and redeemer of his race, and also even become a God"—a "Budha"—i. e., a Savior and Son of God. Singular enough that the Christian should object to this doctrine as being rather blasphemous, when his own bible abundantly and explicitly teaches the same doctrine in effect!

We find the same thing substantially taught over and over again in the Christian Scriptures. "Be ye perfect even as your Father in heaven is perfect" (Matt. v. 18), requires a man to become morally perfect as God, which is all that the Budhist precept requires or contemplates, and no man can become perfect as God without becoming a God. But we are not left to mere inference in the matter, We have the doctrine several times expressed and unquestionably taught in the Christian bible of man's power and prerogative to become either a God or Son of God. "Said I not that ye are Gods?" (Ex. iv. 16). "Behold now, we are the sons of God." (i John i. 2.)

Here is the Budhist doctrine as explicitly stated as it can be taught. It is, then, a Christian bible doctrine as well as a pagan doctrine, that man can become a God, and that God can be born of woman, and thereby invested with all the frail and imperfect attributes of man. It cannot be considered a matter of marvel, therefore, that so many of the good, the great, and the wise men of almost every country, including "the man Christ Jesus," should be honored and adored with the

117

titles of Deity, and worshiped as God absolute, "Son of God," "Savior," "Redeemer," "Intercessor" "Mediator," &c.

4. God comes down and is incarnated to fight and conquer the devil. We will proceed to enumerate other causes and motives which conspired in various cases to invest some one or more of the great men of a nation with divine honors, and adore them as veritable Gods and Saviors "come down to us in the form of men." It was a tenant of faith with most of the ancient religions, that almost at the dawn of human existence a devil or evil principle found its way into the world, to the great discomfiture of man and the no small annoyance of the Supreme Creator himself, and that hence there must needs be a Savior, a Redeemer, an Intercessor to combat and if possible "destroy the devil and his works."

For this purpose appeared the Savior Chrishna, in India, the Savior Osiris, in Egypt, the God or Mediator Mithra, in Persia, the Redeemer Quexalcote, in Mexico, the Savior Jesus Christ, in Judea, &c. In the initiatory chapter on the transgression and fall of man, some of the oriental bibles graphically describe the scene of "the war in heaven"—a counterpart to the story of St. John, as found in the twelfth chapter of Revelation, wherein Michael and the dragon are represented as the captains and commander-in-chief of their respective embattled hosts, and in which the former was crowned as victor in the contest, as he succeeded in vanquishing and "casting out the evil one." In the pagan military drama the scene of the war in heaven is transferred to the earth. A God, a Savior (a Son of God), comes down to put a stop to the machinations of the "Evil One," i. e., to "destroy the devil and his works" as we are told Christ came for that purpose. (1 John iii. 8) See the Author's "Biography of Satan."

The Egyptian story runs thus: "Osiris appeared on earth to benefit mankind, and after he had performed the duties of his mission, and had fallen a sacrifice to Typhon (the devil, or evil principle), which, however, he eventually overcame ('overcame the wicked one,' 1 John ii. 11), by rising from the dead, after being crucified, he became the judge of mankind in a future state." (See Kerrick's "Ancient Egypt", also Wilkinson's "Egypt.")

The Budhist, or Hindoo, version of the story is on this wise: "The prince (of darkness), or evil spirit, Ravana, or Mahesa, got into a contest and a war with the divine hero Rama, in which the latter proved victorious, and put to flight the army of 'the wicked one,' but not till after considerable injury had been done to the human family, and the whole order of the universe subverted; to rectify which, and to achieve a final and complete triumph over Ravana (the devil) and his works, and thus save the human race from utter destruction, the gods besought Vishnu (the second person of the Trinity) to descend to the earth and take upon himself the form and flesh of man. And it was argued that as the mission appertained to man, the God Vishnu, when he descended to the earth in the capacity of a Savior, should become half man and half God, and that the most feasible way to accomplish this end was for him to be born of a woman."

And that the glory and honor of his triumph over Ravana, the devil, would be greater if achieved in this capacity than if he were to come down from heaven and conquer Ravana wholly with his attributes as a God, or wholly in his divine character—i.e., as absolute God, uninvested with human nature. The suggestion was approved by Vishnu, who descended and took upon himself "the form of man" ("the form of a servant"—Phil. ii. 7). And that his metamorphosis or earth-born life might be the purer, it was decided that he should be born of a woman wholly uncontaminated with man—that is, a virgin. And thus, far back in the midnight of mythology and fable, originated the story of divine Saviors and Gods being born of virgins—a conception now found incorporated in the religious histories of various ancient nations.

And now let us observe how substantially the Christian story of a Savior conforms to the above. Jesus, like the Saviors of India and Egypt, was believed to be a man-God—half man and half God, and reputedly he came into the world, like them, to "destroy the devil and his works," or the works of the devil—that is, to put an end to the evil or malignant principle introduced into the world by the serpent in the garden of Eden; as it is declared "the seed of the woman shall bruise the serpent's head" (Gen. iii. 15)—which is interpreted as referring to Christ. And like these and various other pagan Saviors Jesus is assigned the highest and most ennobling human origin—a birth from a virgin. And, as in the instances above named, Jesus had also several encounters with the devil; first in the wilderness, then on a mountain, and finally, like them, falls a sacrifice to his insidious, malignant power acting through the agency and mediumship of Judas Iscariot; for his betrayal is ascribed wholly to Satan, whom John called the serpent, entering into Judas and prompting the act. (See Rev. xii. 3). And thus Christ, like the other saviors, falls a victim to the serpentine or satanic power acting through the instrumentality of a Judas Iscariot; but finally, triumphed, like the Savior of Egypt (Osiris), by rising from the dead—"the first fruits of immortality." And thus the stories run parallel—the more modern Christian with the more ancient pagan.

```
(For a full exposition of the belief and traditions
respecting a devil and a hell in all ages and all countries,
see the Author's "Biography of Satan.")
```

CHAPTER XXX. SACRED CYCLES EXPLAINING THE ADVENT OF THE GODS

The Master-Key to the Divinity of Jesus Christ.

Extraordinary Revelations in History and Science.

RECENT explorations in the field of oriental sacred history have revealed to the antiquarian some curious and deeply interesting facts appertaining to traditions founded on, and growing out of, astronomical phenomena and changes in the visible heavens, which throw much light on, and go far toward elucidating and furnishing a satisfactory explanation of many of the "mysteries" of the Christian bible. The works which we have consulted, containing the reports and results of researches of this character, tend to elucidate and establish the following conclusions:—

1. That anciently, in religious countries, time was divided into Cycles, Aetas, or Neros.

2. That these measures of time grew out of, and represented periodical changes, or periodically occurring phenomena in the astronomical heavens.

3. That some religious nations had three Cycular periods of different lengths, representing three orders and degrees of miraculous births. In India the length of the first or shorter Cycle was thirty days, the length of one moon or month. Every change of the moon marked an important event in their religious history. Each change was supposed to denote the birth of some angel or celestial being known as an Eon. The second Cycular period was of six hundred years' duration, and was founded on a text of the sacred book of India, known as the Surya Sidhanta, which declares "the equinoctial point moves eastward one degree in thirty times twenty years" (thirty times twenty being 600). At every occurrence of this equinoctial change hightened by an eclipse of the sun or moon, or some other wonder-exciting phenomenon, a God was supposed to be born. Such a marvelous and terror-inspiring event, in the apprehensions of the credulous and superstitious populace of an unscientific age, could not be designed for anything less than the birth of a God or Divine Savior. Their theology teaches that such was the wickedness of man, that a God had to descend from heaven, and suffer and die for the people, in some way, every six hundred years.

And this period was announced by the God's causing a collision of the sun and moon, or some other terror-exciting phenomena in the heavens above or the earth beneath. When one of these six hundred Cycular periods was about to expire, and another commence, every remarkable phenomenon in the heavens was watched and interpreted as being connected with it. And some person born at that period, who exhibited any remarkable or extraordinary trait of character, was certain to be promoted to the Godhead, as being miraculously born and brought forth for the special occasion. He was the Avatar Savior or Messiah for that Cycle. There were two extraordinary events to be accounted for—one was the display of unusual and terror-exciting phenomena in the heavens, and the other the birth of extraordinary men on earth. And it was natural for an ignorant age to associate them together, and make one aid in accounting for the other. And as these celestial phenomena were only witnessed at intervals distant apart, the thought naturally arose, and the conclusion was easily established, that they came periodically, and for the special purpose of heralding the birth of a God.

And as tradition reported that similar events were witnessed six hundred years before the conviction was fixed in the popular mind, this was the established period intervening between these great epochs. And thus the six hundred year Cycular tradition became established in India, and finally spread through all the Eastern countries. We find traces of it in Egypt, Syria, Persia, Chaldea, China, Italy, and Judea. And the proof that the deification of great men in some countries grew out of this Cycular tradition is found in the fact that many of them were born at the commencement of Cycles. The Hindoos are able to recount the names of ten sin-atoning Saviors who made their appearance on earth at these regular intervals of six hundred years. The name of the first Avatar Mediator and Savior who forsook the throne of heaven to come down and die for the people was Matsa. Tradition and the sacred books fix his birth at about six thousand years B. C. The names and advent of the other sin-atoning Saviors occur in the following order: 2. Vurahay, 3. Kurma, 4. Nursu, 5. Waman, 6. Pursuram, 7. Kama, 8. Chrishna, 9. Sakia, 10. Salavahana. The last named Savior was cotemporary with Jesus Christ. The God and Savior Sakia was born six hundred years B. C. "Our Lord and Savior" and "Son of God," Chrisna, was immaculately conceived and miraculously born, according to Higgins, 1200 B. C.

120

A circumstance strongly confirming the conclusion that Cycular periods had much to do with the promotion of men to the dignity of Gods is, that most of the deified personages reported in history were, according to the best authorities, born near the commencement of Cycles. Recurring back to the eighth Cycle, we observe the advent of that period of Chrishna, Zoroaster 2d, Bali, Thammuz, Atys, Osiris, and several others. At the commencement of the ninth Cycle appeared Sakia, Quexalcote, Zoroaster 2d, Xion, Qairious, Prometheus, Mithra and many others.

The tenth Cycle brought in Jesus Christ, Salavhana, Apollonious, and others that might be named. Mahomet succeeded Jesus Christ just six hundred years (he was born in the year 600 A. D.), which inaugurated another Cycle. Many facts are recorded in history proving the prevalence and sacredness of the Cycle idea in different countries. The story in Egypt of the bird called the Phoenix, being hatched, according to tradition, just 600 years B. C., and living to be just six hundred years old, and having the power to renew itself every six hundred years, shows the prevalence of the Cycular tradition in that country.

We have the statement upon the records of history that when the first six hundred years after the foundation of Rome were about to expire, the people became greatly excited with the apprehension that some extraordinary event, must attend the occasion. And but for the influence of the philosophers, some extraordinary man would have been hunted up and promoted to divine honor as being the God born for that Cycle. The writings of Plato, Plutarch, Ovid, Cicero, Virgil, and Aristotle, all evince a belief in Cycles, and the belief that ten Cycles, or Aetas, were the measure, for the duration of the world. According to M. Faber, a new-born Savior was always expected to make his appearance at the commencement of one of these Cycles. Hence the deification of those personages above named, and many others that might be named. It is a remarkable circumstance that the Jewish bible should speak of Noah as being six hundred years old at the commencement of the flood, when it was a tradition amongst the ancient Egyptians that the ushering in of the six hundredth year Cycle was to be attended with a flood.

And the time antecedent to Noah after creation, was the measure of three Cycles, according to the chronology of the Samaritan bible, it being 6004-600+600= 1800 years from Adam to Noah. It is an interesting fact that those enigmatical figures made use of by Daniel, as also some of those found in the Apocalypse, are susceptible of a Cycular explanation. These occult prophecies, as they are supposed to be, which have puzzled and bewildered many thousands of Christian minds and bible expounders in their attempt to evolve their signification, are susceptible of a Cycular explanation. They are of easy solution on a Cycular basis, or with the Cycular key.

Take, for example, Daniel's famous prophecy (so called) of the seventy weeks, as found in the ninth chapter, announcing the advent of a Messiah at the end of that period. We find by a calculation based on Tyson's "Historical Atlas," and Haskell's "Chronology and Universal History," that Daniel lived in the hundred and tenth year of the ninth Cycle, at which time the prefigure seems to have been used. Assuming this as a basis, and multiplying seventy weeks by seven, to convert it into years, as Christian essayists are accustomed to doing, and we have as the result 70x7=490, which being added to one hundred and ten, the year that gave birth to the prophesy, makes six hundred, which exactly completes the Cycle, and furnishes a simple and beautiful explanation of a mystical figure, on which many thousands of conjectures, speculations, and guesses have been founded, but on which they have failed to throw any light.

The 70x70=490 years, were wanting to complete the Cycle; and when this rolled away, it brought a new Cycle, and with it a new sin-atoning Savior was always expected in some countries (the country in which Daniel lived being one of this number); a new Messiah (or sin-atoning Savior), and some great man born at that time, was fixed upon and deified as being that Messiah. Hence the Jews, in imitation of their neighbors, yielding to their strong proclivities to borrow from and copy after heathen nations, selected "the man Christ Jesus" as their Messiah and Savior. The mystical era of Daniel, signified by "a time, times, and the dividing of time" (Dan. vii. 25), or, as St. John has it, "a time, times, and a half time" (see Rev. xii. 14) is explainable by the same Cycular key.

Some writers have conjectured that Daniel was a Chaldean priest. If so, he must have had a knowledge of their astronomical Cycle of two thousand one hundred and sixty years, which completed the period of the precession of the equinoxes. Explained by this Cycle, his "time, times, and dividing of time, or half time," or "a time, another time, and a half time," as some writers have rendered it, would be 2160 f 2160-I-1080 5400; nine Cycles exactly, as 600X9= 5400. Add this to the Cycle in which he lived, and we have 5400+600=6000, the great Millennial Cycle, when not only a new Savior and Messiah was to be born, but a new world also. Both the long and short Cycle (and one was a measure of the other) were expected to expire at that time, according to a Chaldean tradition. And thus is beautifully explained another "deep, dark and unfathomable mystery," which thousands of devout minds have exhausted their ingenuity in trying to find a meaning for. Again, look at the frightful nightmare visions of Daniel and the author of the Apocalypse, in which they saw a monstrous beast with seven heads and ten horns, though Daniel mentions only the horns. The seven heads were, in all probability, the seven auspicious months of the year in which some of the nations revealed in the enjoyment of, and praised and celebrated their fruitful, bountiful blessings, the year being divided into two seasons, seven summer months and five winter months.

Now, let it be noted, St. John lived near the tenth Cycle, which answers to the ten horns of the beast. Hence is most forcibly suggested that interpretation of the figure. Daniel's ten horns should have been translated eleven horns, as he lived in the ninth Cycle, though so near the tenth, that he probably constructed his figure on the tenth. And Daniel's prophetic declaration (so considered), found in the eighth chapter, that it would be two thousand three hundred days until the sanctuary should be closed, is explainable in the same manner. According to Mr. Irving, Mr. Frere, and other writers, there was a large fraction over the three hundred days, making it nearer four hundred, and hence might have been so rendered, which would make 20004-400=2400; the exact length of four Cycles, 600x4=2400. And their are other mystical figures, frightful visions, and occult metaphors found in the Apocalypse susceptible of a Cycular solution. The Cycle is the true key for unlocking many of the ancient mysteries of various religions. The Chinese have always reckoned by Cycles of sixty years, instead of by centuries. (See New Am. Encyclop. vol. v. p. 105.)

We will now bestow a brief notice on the Millennial Cycle: the sacred period of 6000 years, composed of ten of the smaller Cycles, 600x10=6000. Dr. Hales says, "A tradition of Millennial ages prevailed throughout the east, and finally reached the west." (Chron. vol. i. p. 44.) We are told by astronomers that if the angle which the plane of the ecliptic forms with the plane of the Equator had decreased gradually, as it was once supposed to do, the two planes would coincide in about six thousand years—a period which comprises ten of the smaller Cycles, 600X10 =6000. And it was very easy and very natural for an ignorant and superstitious age to conclude that such a prodigious, astounding, and awful event as that of two stupendous orbits or planes coming in contact with each other, should be attended with some direful and calamitous event, and with a tremendous display of divine power. Nothing less than an entire revolution, if not the total destruction of the world, could comport with the majesty and magnitude of such an event.

And this great crisis was to bring down the Omnipotent Divine Judge from the throne of heaven; that is, the Almighty being who caused it was to come down, or send his Son to call the nations to judgment, and drown the world, or set it on fire. The first destruction according to the tradition of the Chaldeans, Persians, Assyrians, Mexicans, and some other nations, was to be by water, and the next by fire, when the oceans, seas, and lakes were to be converted into ashes. And Christ's apostles seemed to have cherished this tradition. Peter says, "whereby the world that was then, being overflowed by water, perished. But the heavens and the earth which are now, by the same word are kept in store, reserved unto fire against the day of judgment," (2 Peter iii. 6.) This was a pagan belief long prior to the era of Peter. Josephus says, "Adam predicted that the world would be twice destroyed, once by water, next by fire." A writer says, "A glorious, blissful future attends the destruction of the world by fire, and the reappearance of Vishnu (i. e., eleventh incarnation of Vishnu) has been for several thousand years the hopeful anticipation of India." "The last coming of Vishnu in power and glory," says another writer, "to consummate the final overthrow of evil, sin, and death, is so firmly fixed in the minds of the devotees, that they have an annual festival in commemoration of their prophesy referring to it, at which they exclaim, in a loud voice, 'When will the Divine Helper come? when will the Deliverer appear?'"

At the consummation of this event, "a comet will roll under the moon and set the world on fire;" so affirms their bible. And the Persian bible, the Zend-Avesta, in like manner predicts that "a star, with a tail in course of its revolution, will strike the earth and set it on fire." Seneca predicts that "the time will come when the world will be wrapped in flames, and the opposite powers in conflict will mutually destroy each other."

Ovid prophesies poetically,—

```
"For thus the stern, unyielding Fates decree.
That earth, air, heaven, with the capacious sea,
All shall fall victims to devouring fire,
And in fierce flames the blazing orbs expire."
Lucian, in a like spirit, exclaims,—

"One vast, appointed flame, by Fate's decree,
Shall waste yon azure heavens, the earth and sea."
```

The Egyptians marked their houses with red, to indicate that the world would be destroyed by fire. Orpheus, 1200 B. C., at the inauguration of the eighth Cycle, entertained fearful forebodings of the speedy destruction of the world by water or fire. Some nations held that the alternate destruction of the world by water and fire had already occurred, and would occur again.

Theopompus informs us that some of the orientalists believed that "the God of light and the God of darkness reigned by turn every six thousand years" (commencing with an astronomical Cycle of course), and that during this period the other was held in subjection, which finally resulted in "a war in heaven;" a counterpart to St. John's story. (See Rev. chap. xii.)

This accords with Volney's statement, that "it was recorded in the sacred books of the Persians and Chaldeans that the world, composed of a total revolution of twelve thousand periods, was divided into two partial revolutions of six thousand years each—one being the reign of good, and the other the reign of evil." (Ruins, p. 244.) This belief was disseminated through most of the nations. One of these revolutions was produced, some believed, by a concussion of worlds, which displaced the ocean and seas, and thus produced a general flood, which drowned every living thing on the earth. The next revolution will be caused by a collision of worlds, which will produce fire, and burn the earth to ashes.

Now, let it be noted that all of these grand epochs were founded on Cycles, and accompanied by the tradition of a God being born upon the earth (conceived by a virgin maid), or descending in person; that is, men were promoted to the Godhead. And in this way Jesus Christ was deified. Volney explains the matter thus: "Now, according to the Jewish computation, six thousand years had nearly elapsed since the supposed creation of the world (according to their chronology). This coincidence produced considerable fermentation in the minds of the people. Nothing was thought of but the approaching termination. The great Mediator and Final Judge was expected, and his advent desired, that an end might be put to their calamities." (Ruins, p. 168).

Mr. Higgins corroborates this statement, when he tells us that "about the time of the Cæsars, there seems to have been a general expectation that some Great One was to appear. And finally, when the Cycle had passed, the people, the Jew-Christians, began to look about to see who that Great One was. Some fixed on Herod, some on Julius Cæsar, and some on others. But finally public opinion settled on one Jesus of Nazareth, on account of his superiority in morals and intellect, while the Hindoos deified Salavahana, the Greeks Apollonious, &c." And thus science and history join hand in hand to explain most beautifully and conclusively the greatest mystery that ever brought two hundred millions of people daily upon their knees—the apotheosis, or deification of "the man Christ Jesus."

CHAPTER XXXI. CHRISTIANITY DERIVED FROM HEATHEN AND ORIENTAL SYSTEMS

MORE than twenty thousand sermons are preached in the Christian pulpits, on every recurring Sabbath, to convince the people that the religion and morality taught and practiced by Jesus Christ was of divine emanation, and was never before taught in the world,—that his system of morality was without a parallel, and his practical life without a precedent,—that the doctrine of self-denial, humility, unselfishness, benevolence, and charity,—also devout piety, kind treatment of enemies, and love for the human race, which he preached and practiced, had never before been exemplified in the life and teachings of any individual or nation. But a thorough acquaintance with the history and moral systems of some of the oriental nations, and the practical lives of piety and self-denial exemplified in their leading men long anterior to the birth of Christ, and long before the name of Christianity was anywhere known, must convince any unprejudiced mind that such a claim is without foundation. And to prove it, we will here institute a critical comparison between Christianity and some of the older systems with respect to the essential spirit of their teachings, and observe how utterly untenable and groundless is the dogmatic assumption which claims for the Christian religion either any originality or any superiority. Of course if their is nothing new or original, there is nothing superior.

We will first arrange Christianity side by side with the ancient system known as Essenism—a religion whose origin has never been discovered, though it is known that the Essenes existed in the days of Jonathan Maccabeus, B. C. 150, and that they were of Jewish origin, and constituted one of the three Jewish sects (the other two being Pharisees and Sadducees). We have but fragments of their history as furnished by Philo, Josephus, Pliny, and their copyists, Eusebius, Dr. Ginsburg, and others, on whose authority we will proceed to show that Alexandrian and Judean Essenism was identically the same system in spirit and essence as its successor Judean Christianity; in other words, Judean Christianity teaches the same doctrines and moral precepts which had been previously inculcated by the disciples of the Essenian religion.

A PARALLEL EXHIBITION OF THE PRECEPTS AND PRACTICAL LIVES OF CHRIST AND THE ESSENES.

We will condense from Philo, Josephus, and other authors.

1. Philo says, "It is our first duty to seek the kingdom of God and his righteousness so the Essenes believed and taught."

Scripture parallel. "Seek first the kingdom of God, and his righteousness, and all else shall be added." (Matt. vi. 33; Luke xii. 31.)

2. Philo says, "They abjured all amusements, all elegances, and all pleasures of the senses."

Scripture parallel. "Forsake the world and the things thereof."

3. The Essenes say, "Lay up nothing on earth, but fix your mind solely on heaven."

Scripture parallel. "Lay not up treasures on earth," &c.

4. "The Essenes, having laid aside all the anxieties of life," says Philo, "and leaving society, they make their residence in solitary wilds and in gardens."

Scripture parallel. "They wandered in deserts, and in mountains, and in dens, and in caves of the earth." (Heb. xi. 38.)

5. Josephus says, "They neither buy nor sell among themselves, but give of what they have to him that wanteth."

Scripture parallel. "And parted them (their goods) to all men as every man had need." (Acts ii. 45.)

6. Eusebius says, "Even as it is related in the Acts of the Apostles, all (the Esseues)... were wont to sell their possessions and their substance, and divide among all according as any one had need, so that there was not one among them in want."

Scripture parallel. "Neither was their any among them that lacked, for as many as were possessors of lands or houses sold them, and brought the price of the things that were sold, &c." (Acts iv. 34.)

7. Eusebius says, "For whoever, of Christ's disciples, were owners of estates or houses, sold them, and brought the price thereof, and laid them at the apostles' feet, and distribution was made as every one had need. So Philo relates things exactly similar of the Essenes."

Scripture parallel. (The text above quoted.)

8. "Philo tells us (says Eusebius) that the Essenes forsook father, mother, brothers and sisters, houses and lands, for their religion."

Scripture parallel. "Whosoever forsaketh not father and mother, houses and lands, &c. cannot be my disciples."

9. "Their being sometimes called *monks* was owing to their abstraction from the world," says Eusebius.

Scripture parallel. "They are not of the world, even as I am not of the world." (John xvii. 16.)

10. "And the name Ascetics was applied to them on account of their rigid discipline, their prayers, fasting, self-mortification, &c., as they made themselves eunuchs."

Scripture parallel. "There be eunuchs which have made themselves eunuchs for the kingdom of heaven's sake."

11. "They maintained a perfect community of goods, and an equality of external rank." (Mich. vol. iv. p. 83.)

Scripture parallel. "Whosoever will be chief among you, let him be your servant." (Matt. xx. 27.)

12. "The Essenes had all things in common, and appointed one of their number to manage the common bag." (Dr. Ginsburg.)

Scripture parallel "And had all things in common." (Acts ii. 44; see also Acts iv. 32.)

13. "All ornamental dress they (Essenes) detested." (Mich. vol. iv. p. 83.)

Scripture parallel. "Whose adorning let it not be that outward adorning of plaiting the hair, and of wearing of gold, and putting on of apparel." (1 Peter iii. 3.)

14. "They would call no man master." (Mich.)

Scripture parallel. "Be not called Rabbi, for one is your Master." (Matt, xxiii. 8.)

15. "They said the Creator made all mankind equal." (Mich.)

Scripture parallel. "God hath made of one blood all them that dwell upon the earth."

16. "They renounced oaths, saying, He who cannot be believed without swearing is condemned already." (Mich.)

Scripture parallel. "Swear not at all."

17. "They would not eat anything which had blood in it, or meat which had been offered to idols. Their food was hyssop, and bread, and salt; and water their only drink." (Mich.)

Scripture parallel. "That ye abstain from meat offered to idols, and from blood." (Acts xv. 29.)

18. "Take nothing with them, neither meat or drink, nor anything necessary for the wants of the body."

Scripture parallel. "Take nothing for your journey; neither staves nor script; neither bread, neither money, neither have two coats apiece."

19. "They expounded the literal sense of the Holy Scriptures by allegory."

Scripture parallel. "Which things are an allegory." (Gal. iv. 24.)

20. "They abjured the pleasures of the body, not desiring mortal offspring, and they renounced marriage, believing it to be detrimental to a holy life." (Mich.)

Scripture parallel. It will be recollected that neither Jesus nor Paul ever married, and that they discouraged the marriage relation. Christ says, "They that shall be counted worthy of that world and the resurrection neither marry nor are given in marriage." And Paul says, "The unmarried careth for the things of the Lord." (i Cor. vii. 32.)

21. "They strove to disengage their minds entirely from the world."

Scripture parallel. "If any man love the world, the love of the Father is not in him."

127

22. "Devoting themselves to the Lord, they provide not for future subsistence."

Scripture parallel. "Take no thought for the morrow, what ye shall eat and drink," &c.

23. "Regarding the body as a prison, they were ashamed to give it sustenance." (c. ii. 71.)

Scripture parallel. "Who shall change our *vile* bodies?" (Phil. iii. 21.)

24. "They spent nearly all their time in silent meditation and inward prayer." (c. ii. 71.)

Scripture parallel. "Men ought always to pray." (Luke xviii. 1.) "Pray without ceasing." (1 Thess. v. 17.)

25. "Believing the poor were the Lord's favorites, they vowed perpetual chastity and poverty." (c. ii. 71.)

Scripture parallel. "Blessed be ye poor." (Luke vi. 20.) "Hath not God chosen the poor?" (James ii. 5.)

26. "They devoted themselves entirely to contemplation in divine things." (c. ii. 71.)

Scripture parallel. "Mediate upon these (divine) things; give thyself wholly to them." (1 Tim. iv. 15.)

27. "They fasted often, sometimes tasting food but once in three or even six days."

Scripture parallel. Christ's disciples were "in fastings often." (2 Cor. xi. 27; see also v. 34.)

28. "They offered no sacrifices, believing that a serious and devout soul was most acceptable." (c. ii. 71.)

Scripture parallel. "There is no more offering for sin." (Heb. x. 18.)

29. "They believed in and practiced baptizing the dead." (c. ii. 71.)

Scripture parallel. "Else what shall they do which are baptized for the dead." (1 Cor. xv. 29.)

30. "They gave a mystical sense to the Scriptures, disregarding the letter."

Scripture parallel. "The letter killeth, but the spirit maketh alive." (1 Cor. iii. 6.)

31. "They taught by metaphors, symbols, and parables."

Scripture parallel. "Without a parable spake he not unto them." (Matt. xiii. 34.)

32. "They had many mysteries in their religion which they were sworn to keep secret."

Scripture parallel. "To you it is given to know the mysteries of the kingdom; to them it is not given." (Matt xiii. 11.) "Great is the mystery of godliness."

33. "They had in their churches, bishops, elders, deacons, and priests."

Scripture parallel. "Ordained elders in every church." (Acts xiv. 23.) For "deacons," see 1 Tim. iii. 1.

34. "When assembled together they would often sing psalms."

Scripture parallel. "Teaching and admonishing one another in psalms." (Col. iii. 16.)

35. "They healed and cured the minds and bodies of those who joined them."

Scripture parallel "Healing all manner of sickness," &c. (Matt iv. 23.)

36. "They practiced certain ceremonial purifications by water."

Scripture parallel. "The accomplishment of the days of purification." (Acts xxi. 26.)

37. "They assembled at the Sabbath festivals clothed in white garments."

Scripture parallel "Shall be clothed in white garments." (Rev. iii. 4.)

38. "They disbelieved in the resurrection of the external body."

Scripture parallel "It is sown a natural body, it is raised a spiritual body." (1 Cor. xv. 44.)

39. Pliny says, "They were the only sort of men who lived without money and without women."

Scripture parallel "The love of money is the root of all evil." (1 Tim. vi. 10.) Christ's disciples travelled without money and without scrip, and "eschew the lusts of the flesh."

40. "They practiced the extremest charity to the poor." (c. ii. 71.)

Scripture parallel "Bestow all thy goods to feed the poor." (1 Cor. xiii. 3.)

41. "They were skillful in interpreting dreams, and in foretelling future events."

Scripture parallel "Your sons and daughters shall prophesy, and your old men shall dream dreams." (Acts ii. 17.)

42. "They believed in a paradise,... and in a place of never-ending lamentations."

Scripture parallel "Life everlasting." (Gal. viii. 8.) "Weeping, wailing, and gnashing of teeth." (Matt. xiii. 42.)

43. "They affirmed," says Josephus, "that God foreordained all the events of human life."

Scripture parallel "Foreordained before the foundation of the world." (1 Peter.)

44. "They believed in Mediators between God and the souls of men."

Scripture parallel. "One Mediator between God and men." (1 Tim. ii. 5.)

45. "They practiced the pantomimic representation of the death, burial, and resurrection of God"—Christ the Spirit.

Scripture parallel. With respect to the death, burial, and resurrection of Christ, see 1 Cor. xv. 4.

46. "They inculcated the forgiveness of injuries."

Scripture parallel. "Father, forgive them; for they know not what they do." (Luke xxiii. 34.)

47. "They totally disapproved of all war."

Scripture parallel "If my kingdom were of this world, then would my servants fight." (John xviii. 36.)

48. "They inculcated obedience to magistrates, and to the civil authorities."

Scripture parallel. "Obey them which have the rule over you." (Heb. xiii. 17; xxvi. 65.)

49. "They retired within themselves to receive interior revelations of divine truth." (c. ii. 71.)

Scripture parallel. "Every one of you hath a revelation." (1 Cor. xiv. 26.)

50. "They were scrupulous in speaking the truth."

Scripture parallel "Speaking all things in truth." (2 Cor. vii. 14.)

51. "They perform many wonderful miracles."

Scripture parallel Many texts teach us that Christ and his apostles did the same.

52. "Essenism put all its members upon the same level, forbidding the exercise of authority of one over another." (Dr. Ginsburg.)

Scripture parallel. Christ did the same. For proof, see Matt. xx. 25; Mark ix. 35.

53. "Essenism laid the greatest stress on being meek and lowly in spirit." (Dr. Ginsburg.)

Scripture parallel. See Matt. v. 5; ix. 28.

54. "The Essenes commended the poor in spirit, those who hunger and thirst after righteousness, and the merciful, and the pure in heart." (Dr Ginsburg.)

Scripture parallel. For proof that Christ did the same, see Matt.

55. "The Essenes commended the peacemakers." (Dr. Ginsburg.)

Scripture parallel. "Blessed are the peacemakers."

56. "The Essenes declared their disciples must cast out evil spirits, and perform miraculous cures, as signs and proof of their faith." (Dr. Ginsburg.)

Scripture parallel. Christ's disciples were to cast out devils, heal the sick, and raise the dead, &c., as signs and proof of their faith. (Mark xvi. 17.)

57. "They sacrificed the lusts of the flesh to gain spiritual happiness."

Scripture parallel. "You abstain from fleshly lusts." (1 Peter ii. 11.)

58. "The breaking of bread was a veritable ordinance among the Essenes."

Scripture parallel. "He (Jesus) took bread, and gave thanks, and brake it." (Luke xxii. 19.)

59. "The Essenes enjoined the loving of enemies." (Philo.)

Scripture parallel. So did Christ say, "Love your enemies," &c.

60. The Essenes enjoined, "Doing unto others as you would have them do unto you."

Scripture parallel. The Confucian golden rule, as taught by Christ.

This parallel might be extended much further, but we will proceed to present the reader with a general description of Essenism, as furnished us by Philo, Josephus, and some Christian writers. Philo, who was born in Alexandria 20 B. C., and lived to 60 A. D., and who was himself an Essenian Jew, in his account of them, says, "They do not lay up treasures of gold or silver,... but provide themselves only with the necessities of life." Paul afterwards, having caught the same spirit, advises the same course of life. "Having food and raiment, therewith be content." Contentment of mind they regarded as the greatest of riches. They make no instruments of war. They repudiate every inducement to covetousness. None are held as slaves, but all are free, and serve each other. They are instructed in piety and holiness, righteousness, economy, &c. They are guided by a threefold rule: love of God, love of virtue, and love of mankind. Of their love of God they give innumerable demonstrations, which is found in their constant and unalterable holiness throughout the whole of their lives, their avoidance of oaths and falsehoods, and their firm belief that God is the source of all good, but of nothing evil. "Of their love of virtue they give proof in their contempt for money, fame, and pleasures, their continence, easy satisfying of their wants, their simplicity, modesty," &c. Their love of man is proved by their benevolence and equality, and their having all things in common, which is beyond all deception. They reverence and take care of the aged, as children do their parents. (Condensed from Philo's treatise, "Every Virtuous Man is Free.")

Josephus, 37 A. D., and who was also at one time a member of the Essenian Brotherhood, furnishes another fragmentary account of the Essenes in his "Jewish Wars," of which the following is the substance:—

"They love each other more than others (that is, are "partial to the household of faith"); they despise riches, and have all things in common, so that there is neither abjectness of poverty nor distinction of riches among them; they change neither garments nor shoes till they are worn out or become unfit for use; they neither buy nor sell among themselves; their piety is extraordinary; they never speak about wordly matters before sunrise; they are girt about with a linen apron, and have a baptism of cold water; they eat but one kind of a food at a time, and commence with a prayer, and the priest must say grace before any one eats (that is, breaks and blesses as Christ did); they also return thanks after eating, and then put off their white garments; strangers were made welcome at their tables without money and without price; they give food to the hungry and the needy and show mercy to all; they curb their passions, restrain their anger, and claim to be ministers of peace; an oath they regard as worse than perjury; they excommunicate offenders ('Go tell it to the churches, says Christ); they condemn finery in dress; though condemning in most solemn terms oaths, members were admitted to the secret brotherhood by an oath ('See thou tell no man,' said Christ); they endured pain with heroic fortitude, and regarded an honorable death as better than long life; they read and study their Holy Scriptures from youth, often prophesy, and it was very seldom they failed in their predictions."

Dr. Ginburg's testimony, abridged, is as follows:—

"The Essenes had a high appreciations of the inspired law of God. The highest aim of their lives was to become fit temples of the Holy Ghost (see i Cor. vi. 19); also to perform miraculous cures, and to be spiritually qualified for forerunners of the Messiah. They taught the duty of mortifying the flesh and the lusts thereof, and to become meek and lowly in spirit; they answered by yea, yea, and nay, nay (see Matt.), scrupulously avoiding oaths; they avoided impure contact with the heathen and the world's people, and lived retired from the world, being in numbers about four thousand; they strove to be like the angels of heaven; there were no rich and poor, or masters and servants, amongst them; they lived peaceably with all men; a mysterious silence was observed while eating; a solemn oath was required on becoming a member of the secret order, which required three things:

1. Love of God;

2. Merciful justice to all men, and to avoid the wicked, and help the righteous;

3. Purity of character, which implied love of truth, hatred of falsehood, and strict observance of 'the mysteries of godliness' to outsiders—that is, 'heathen and publicans;' they endured suffering for righteousness' sake, with rejoicings, and even *sought* it; regarding the body as a prison for the soul, they desired the time to come to escape from it; they recognized eight different stages of

132

spiritual growth and perfection: 1. Bodily purity; 2. Celibacy; 3. Spiritual purity; 4. The suppression of anger and malice, and the cultivation of a meek, lowly spirit; 5. The attainment of true holiness; 6. Becoming fit temples for the Holy Ghost; 7. The ability to perform miraculous cures, and raise the dead; 8. Becoming forerunners of the Messiah; and finally they took a solemn vow to exercise, piety toward God and justice toward all men, to hate the wicked, assist the good to keep clear of theft and unrighteous gains, to conceal none of their 'mysteries of godliness' from each other, or disclose them to others. 'Great is the mystery of godliness' ('See thou tell no man'); they were to walk humbly with God, shun bad society, forgive their enemies, sacrifice their passions, and crucify the lusts of the flesh; they disregarded bodily suffering, and even gloried in martyrdom, preaching and singing to God amid their sufferings; but in their domestic habits they were extremely filthy; they wore their clothes until they became ragged, filthy, and offensive, never changing them till they were wore out; their food consisted of bread and water, and wild roots and fruits of the palm tree; they enjoined their duty, not only of forgiving their enemies, but of seeking to benefit them, and of even blessing the destroyer who took life and property. Such was the religion, such the moral system, such the devout piety, and such the practical lives of the Essenian Jews, a religious sect which flourished in Alexandria and Judea several hundred years before the birth of Christ, and went out of history the hour Christianity came in.

Now, as the foregoing exposition shows that Essenism and Christianity are most strikingly alike in all their essential features, that the former system contains nearly every important doctrine and precept of the Christian religion, the question occurs here as one of momentous import, how is this striking resemblance, this identity of character of the two religions, to be accounted for? Does it not go far toward proving that Christianity is an outgrowth, a legitimate offspring, of Judean Essenism? Indeed, are we not absolutely driven to such a conclusion? Let us briefly recite some of the important facts brought to light by the investigation of the character and history of these two religions, and see if those facts do not bring them together and weld them as one system—as one and the same religion.

1. Both are alike, and Essenism is much the older system.

2. Both religions are an outgrowth of Judaism.

3. Both were known and taught in Judea and in Alexandria.

4. Josephus living in Judea, and Philo in Alexandria, neither of them speaks of Christianity, or refers to any such religion by that name, and yet both describe a religion inculcating the same doctrines and moral precepts, which they call Essenism.

Is not this very nearly conclusive proof that Essenism was only another name for Christianity— that it had not yet changed its name to Christianity? That famous standard author, Mr. Gibbon, was evidently of this opinion when he said, "Whether, indeed, the first of that sect (the Essenes) took the name of Christian when the appellation of Christian had as yet been nowhere announced, it is by no means necessary to discuss." (Book II. chap. xvi.) Here is evidence that Gibbon believed that the Essenes, after having borne that name for centuries, changed the appellation to Christian. And we find still stronger language than this in the writings of the same author expressive of this opinion. In a note to chapter xv. he says, "It is probable that the Therapeuts (Essenes) changed their name to Christians, as some writers affirm, and adopted some new articles of faith." Here the position is assumed that the Christian religion is an outgrowth of Essenism, that is, merely a continuation of that religion under a change of name, with a slight modification of its creed.

5. And then we have the declaration of Christian writers, expressed in the most positive terms, that Essenism and Christianity were the same religion, the former name being used at an earlier period. Hear Eusebius, a standard ecclesiastical writer of the fourth century. He asserts positively, "Those ancient Therapeuts (Essenes) were Christians, and their ancient writings were our gospels." (Eccl. Hist. p. 63.) Hark! Hark! my good Christian reader, here is one of your own sworn witnessess testifying that the Essenes originated and established the Christian religion; i. e., the religion now known by that name. Will you then give it up? If not, we have other testimony of a similar character, rendering the proposition still stronger. Robert Taylor declares, "The learned Basnage has shown that the Essenes were really Christians centuries before Christ, and that they were actually in possession of those very writings which are now our Gospels and Epistles." (p. 81.) And then we have the declaration of the author of "Christ the Spirit" (p. no), that "the Christians were the later Essenes—that is, the Essenes of the time of Eusebius under a changed name, that name having been made at Antioch, where the disciples were first called Christian." The same writer suggests that "their sacred books are our sacred books." We will now hear Eusebius again: "It is highly probable that their (the Essenes') ancient commentaries, which Philo says the Essenes have, are the very Gospels and writings of the Apostles."

Based upon this conclusion, he calls the Essenes "the first heralds of the gospel." "I find it, therefore, most probable," says Mr. Weilting, "that Jesus and John belonged literally to the society of the Essenes." And then the New American Encyclopedia furnishes us with the testimony of a very able English author of the last century (De Quincy), who concurs with all the writers cited above. "Mr. De Quincy (it says) identified the Essenes as being the early Christians; i. e., the early Christians were known as Essenes. Such testimony, coming from such a source, is entitled to much weight." (Vol. i. p. 157.) And to the same effect is the testimony of Bishop Marsh, who admits that our Gospels were drawn from those of the Essenes. (See his edition of Michaelis' translation of the New Testament.)

Thus far historical *writers*. We will now lay before the reader some historical *facts*, fraught with unanswerable logical potency, and pointing to the same conclusion. It is a fact, and one of deep logical import, and tending to corroborate the conclusion of some of the writers cited above, who tell us the Christian Gospels were first composed by the Essenes; that the language in which those Gospels were originally written was Greek, the language in which the Alexandrian Essenes always wrote, while the evangelical writers, Matthew, Mark, Luke, and John, being illiterate fishermen, could have had no knowledge of any but the Jewish, their own mother-tongue,—at least it is susceptible of satisfactory proof that they never wrote in any other language. Hence the conclusion is irresistible that they were not the original authors of the Gospels.

The works of several authors are now lying at our elbow, who express the conviction unequivocally that the Gospels were copied, if not translated, from older writings. Mr. Le Clerc, one of the ablest writers of his time, maintained this position, and did it ably. Another writer, a

Mr. Hatfield, was awarded a prize in 1793. by the theological faculty of Gottingen, for an essay, in which the position was ably argued that Matthew, Mark, Luke, and John were not the authors of the books which bear their names, but were mere copyists. Dr. Lessing and others concur with him in this conclusion. A circumstance confirming this verdict is found in the fact that the word *church* occurs in our Gospels, which were written before such an institution was established by those who were then called Christians.

"Go tell it to the church" (Matt, xviii. 17) was uttered before any steps had been taken by the then representatives of the Christian faith to organize such a body—an evidence this, that he alluded to the church of the Essenes, as there were no other churches in existence at the time; which leaves the inference patent and irresistible that he and his disciples were Essenes, perhaps then under the changed name of Christians. Centuries prior to that era the Essenes had not only churches, but their whole ecclesiastical nomenclature of bishops, deacons, elders, priests, disciples, scriptures, gospels, epistles, psalms, hymns, mystery, allegory, &c. If Christianity was re-established in the days of Christ and his apostles, they had nothing to originate, either with respect to doctrines, precepts, church polity, or ecclesiastical terms—all being established for them centuries before that era. With these facts in view, it seems impossible that the two religious orders—Essenes and Christians—could have been in existence at the same time as separate institutions. The former must have ended when the latter commenced.

Josephus says, "the Essenes were scattered far and wide, and were in every city," being quite numerous in Judea in his time. But he makes no reference to any sect or religious order by the title of Christian—a strong inferential evidence, upon sound priori reasoning, that Christianity as yet was sailing under another name. Josephus must have known and named the fact, had there been a Christian sect or disciple there bearing that name. Impossible otherwise. We are then (upon the logical force of these and many other facts) driven to the conclusion that Christianity began when Essenism ended, and the change was only in name. I challenge the whole Christian world to find the historical proof that Christianity commenced one hour before the termination of Essenism, or of Essenism overlapping the Christian religion so far as to survive one day beyond or after its birth. I will confront them with the logic of dates, and defy them to find any proof except their own unauthorized, unauthenticated, and fictitious chronology, that a Christian was ever known in any country by that name prior to the time of Tacitus, 104 A.D., who is the first of the three hundred writers of that era that makes any mention of Christianity, Christ, or a Christian. This was long after Josephus' time, which accounts most satisfactory for his omitting any allusion to Christ or Christianity. That religion had not yet dropped the name of Essenism and adopted that of Christianity.

Now, hard indeed must distorted reason fight the ramparts of logic and history to resist the conviction, in view of the foregoing facts, that Christianity is simply an outcropping of Essenism, either direct or through Buchism. And even if it were possible to prove that the two religions never became welded together, yet it is not possible to disprove the striking identity of their doctrines, and the spirit of their precepts, and the practical lives of their disciples. And this identity, coupled with the fact that Essenism is the older system, is of itself most superlatively fatal to all pretension or claim to originality for the doctrines of the Christian faith.

It is a matter of no importance whether Christianity was originally known by another name, so long as it can be shown that its doctrines had all been preached and proclaimed to the world centuries prior to the date assigned for its origin. And this is proved by the long list of paralellisms presented in the incipient pages of this chapter. And this proof explodes the pretensions of Christianity to an "original divine revelation," and brings it down to a level with pagan orientalism. And the fact that it sprang up in a country where its doctrine had long been taught by pagans and orientalists, must produce the conviction, deep and indelible, in all unbiased minds, that orientalism was the mother and heathenism the father of the Christian religion, even in the absence of any other proof. In fact, no other proof can be needed.

And what are the arguments, it may be well here to inquire, with which orthodox Christians attempt to meet, combat, and vanquish the overwhelming mass of historical facts and historical testimonies we have presented in preceding pages, tending to prove and demonstrate the oriental origin of their religion and its identity with Essenism? Their whole argument is comprised in the naked postulate of the Rev. Mr. Paideaux, D. D., that "the Essenes did not believe in the resurrection of the physical body (but believed in a spiritual resurrection), and omit from their creed the Trinity and Incarnation doctrine, and therefore they could not have been the originators of the Christian religion;" but this argument is as easily demolished as a cobweb, as the following facts will prove:—

1. We have but a fragment of the Essenian religion,—but one end of their creed,—mere scraps furnished us by Philo, Josephus, and Pliny. We have none of their sacred books apart from the Christian New Testament.

2. They had secret books, as we have shown, in which doctrines were taught which they regarded as *too sacred to be thrown before the public*, as "pearls before swine." And no doctrines were regarded as more sacred or secret in that age than the doctrines of the Trinity and Incarnation. Christ's injunction, "See thou tell no man," was probably their motto, which prevented the publicity of a portion of their doctrines. And as their sacred books, containing their doctrines, perished with the extinction of the sect (except those now found in the Christian New Testament), a full knowledge of their doctrines, therefore, never reached the public mind. All religious sects had secret doctrines, designated as "Mysteries of Godliness," including the principal Jewish sects and the earliest Christian churches. It is, therefore, highly probable that if we were in possession of all their sacred books, we would be in possession of the proof that they believed and taught in their monasteries the doctrines above named. But we are not left to mere inference that the Essenes' creed did include the doctrines of the Trinity and the Divine Incarnation. We find skeletons of these doctrines scattered along the line of their history. Philo himself, an Essene teacher, most distinctly teaches the doctrine of "the Incarnation of the Divine Word or Logos." And "Son of God," "Mediator," "Intercessor," and "Messiah," were familiar words with him. The idea often reappears in his writings, that the "Word could become flesh;" that the Son of God could appear as a personality, and return to the bosom of the Father. Moreover, one writer informs us that the Essenes celebrated the birth and death of a Divine Savior as a "Mystery of Godliness." And they claimed in their earlier history to be "forerunners of the Messiah"—a claim which would soon bring a Messiah before the world, that is, lead them to deify and worship some great man as "*The Messia*."

136

As for the doctrine of the Trinity, we have the authority of Eusebius that they taught this doctrine too. So that it is not true that they did not recognize these two prime articles of the Christian faith, the Incarnation and Trinity doctrines. Some modern Christians assert that the Essenes not only omitted to teach these doctrines, but that, on the other hand, they taught other doctrines not taught in the Christian New Testament. This is not improbable. For the Christian religion has been characterized by frequent changes in its doctrines in every stage of its practical history, as was also the Jewish religion which preceded it, and from which it emanated. Judaism is a perpetual series of changes. It changed even the name of its God from Elohim to Jehovah. Its leader and founder Abram was changed to Abraham, and his grandson and successor from Jacob to Israel. And we have the works of many Christian writers in our possession who prove by their own bible that the Jews made many changes in their religious polity and religious doctrines. This is more especially observable when they came in contact with nations teaching a different religion. Their whole history shows they were prone to imitate, and borrow, and always did borrow on such occasions, and engraft the new doctrines thus obtained into their own creed, and thus effected important changes in their religion. We have the authority of Dr. Campbell for saying the Jews never believed and taught the doctrine of future punishment (and other doctrines that might be named) till after they were brought in contact with Persians in Babylon who had long taught these doctrines. (See Dissertation VI.) And Dr. Enfield declares their theological opinions underwent thorough changes during this period of seventy years' captivity. Even their national title was changed at one period from Israelites to Jews. With all these changes of names, titles, and doctrines in view, it is not incredible that one of the Jewish sects should change its name from Essenes to Christians, and with this change modify some of the doctrines. And more especially as their title, according to Dr. Ginsburg, had been changed before from Chassidim to Essenes. And Philo at one period calls them Therapeuts, while Eusebius says the Therapeuts were Christians. Put this and that together, and the question is forever settled.

Now, with all this overwhelming mass of historical evidence before us, "piled mountain high," tending to prove the truth of the proposition that Christianity is the offspring and outgrowth of ancient Judean Essenism, we feel certain that no sophistry, from interested charlatans or stereotyped creed worshipers, can stave off or obliterate the conviction in unprejudiced minds, that the proposition is most amply proven.

We will now collate Christianity with another ancient religious system, which we are certain it will not be disputed, after the comparison is critically examined, contains the sum total of the doctrines and teachings of Christianity in all their details.

CHAPTER XXXII. THREE HUNDRED AND FORTY-SIX STRIKING ANALOGIES BETWEEN CHRIST AND CHRISHNA

I. THEIR MIRACULOUS HISTORY AND LEADING PRINCIPLES.

1. The advent of each Savior was miraculously foretold by prophets.

2. The fallen and degenerate condition of the human race is taught in the religion of each.

3. A plan of restoration or salvation is provided for in each case.

4. A divine Savior is considered necessary in both cases.

5. The necessity of atoning for sin is taught in the religion of each.

6. A God, or Son of God, is selected as the victim for the atoning sacrifice in each case.

7. This God is sent down from heaven in each case in the form of a man.

8. The God or Savior in each case is the second person of the Trinity.

9. Chrishna, as well as Christ, was held to be really God incarnate.

10. The mission of each Savior is the same.

11. There is a resemblance in name-Chrishna and Christ.

12. Chrishna, as well as Christ, was incarnated and born of a woman.

13. The mother in each case was a holy virgin.

14. The same peculiarities of a miraculous conception and birth are related of each.

15. Each had an adopted earthly father.

16. The father of Chrishna, as well as that of Christ, was a carpenter.

17. God is claimed as the real father in both cases.

18. A Spirit or Ghost was the author of the conception of each.

19. There was rejoicing on earth when each Savior was born.

20. There was also joy in heaven at the birth and advent of each.

21. Chrishna, as well as Christ, was of royal descent.

22. Their mothers were both reputedly pious women.

23. The names of two mothers are somewhat similar—Mary and Maia.

24. Each had a special female friend—Elizabeth in the one case, and the wife of Nanda in the other.

25. Neither Savior was born in a house, but both in obscure situations.

26. Both were born on the 25th of December.

27. Both, at birth, were visited by wise men and shepards.

28. The visitors conducted by a star in each case.

29. The rite of purification observed by the mothers of each.

30. An angel warning of impending danger in each case.

31. The incumbent ruler was hostile in each case.

32. A bloody decree in each case for the destruction of the infant Savior.

33. A flight of the parents takes place in both cases.

34. The parents of one sojourned at Muturea, the other at Mathura.

35. Each Savior had a forerunner—John the Baptist in one case, Bali Rama in the other.

36. Both were preternaturally smart in childhood.

37. Each disputed with and vanquished learned opponents.

38. Both became objects of search by their parents.

39. And both occasioned anxiety, if not sorrow, to their parents.

40. The mother of each had other children—that is children begotten by man as well as God.

41. Both Saviors retired to, and spent considerable time in the wilderness.

42. The religious rite of "fasting" was practiced by each Savior.

43. Each delivered a noteworthy sermon, or series of moral lessons.

44. Chrishna, as well as Christ, was called and considered God.

45. Each was both God and the Son of God (so regarded).

46. "Savior" was one of the divine titles of each.

47. Each was designated "the Savior of man," "the Savior of the world," &c.

48. Both expressed a desire to "save all."

49. Each sustained the character of a Messiah.

50. Chrishna, as well as Christ, was a Redeemer.

51. Each Savior was called "Shepard."

52. Both were believed to be the Creator of the world.

53. Each is sometimes spoken of, also, as only an agent in the creation.

54. Both were the "Light and Life" of men.

55. Each "brought life and immortality to light."

56. Both are represented as "the seed of the woman bruising the serpent's head."

57. Was Christ a "Dispenser of grace," so was the Hindoo Savior.

58. One was "the lion of the tribe of Judah," the other "the lion of the tribe of Saki."

59. Christ was "the Beginning of the End," Chrishna "the Beginning, the Middle, and the End."

60. Both proclaimed, "I am the Resurrection."

61. Each was "the way to the Father."

62. Both represented emblematically "the Sun of Righteousness."

63. Each is figuratively represented as being "all in all."

64. Both speak of having existed prior to human birth.

65. A dual existence—an existence in both heaven and earth at once—is claimed by or for both.

66. Chrishna, as well as Christ, was "without sin."

67. Both assumed the divine prerogative of forgiving sins.

68. The mission of each was to deliver from sin.

69. Both came to destroy the devil and his works.

70. The doctrine of the "atonement" is practically realized in each case.

71. Each made a voluntary offering for the sins of the world.

72. Both were human as well as divine.

73. Chrishna, as well as Christ, was worshiped as God absolute.

74. Each was regarded as "the Lord from Heaven."

75. Chrishna, as well as Christ, had applied to him all the attributes of God.

76. Was Christ omniscient, so was Chrishna.

77. Was one omnipotent, so was the other (so believed).

78. And both are represented as being omnipresent.

79. Each was believed to be divinely perfect.

80. Was one "Lord of lords," so was the other.

81. Each embodied the "power and wisdom of God."

82. All power was committed unto each (so claimed).

83. Chrishna performed many miracles as well as Christ.

84. One of the first miracles of each was the cure of a leper.

85. Each healed "all manner of diseases."

86. The work of casting out devils constitutes a part of the mission of each.

87. Each practically proved his power to raise the dead.

88. A miracle appertaining to a tree is related of both.

89. Both could read the thoughts of the people.

90. The power to detect and eject evil spirits was claimed by both.

91. Both had the keys or control of death.

92. Each led an extraordinary life.

93. Each had a character for supernatural greatness.

94. Both possesed or claimed a oneness with the Father.

95. A "oneness with his Lord and Master" is claimed, also, for the disciples of each.

96. A strong reciprocal affection between Master and disciple in each case.

97. Each offers to shoulder the burdens of his disciples.

98. A portion of the life of each was spent in preaching.

99. Both made converts by their miracles and preaching.

100. A numerous retinue of believers springs up in each case.

101. Both had commissioned apostles to proclaim their religion.

102. Each was an innovator upon the antecedent religion.

103. A beautiful reform in religion was inaugurated by each Savior.

104. Each opposed the existing popular priesthood.

105. Both abolished the law of lineal descent in the ancient priesthood.

106. Each was an object of conspiracy by his enemies.

107. Humility and external poverty distinguished the life of each.

108. Each denounced riches and rich men, and loathed and detested wealth.

109. Both had a character for meekness.

110. Chastity or unmarried life was a distinguishing characteristic of each.

111. Mercy was a noteworthy characteristic of each.

112. Both were censured for associating with sinners.

113. Each was a special friend to the poor.

114. A poor widow woman receives marked attention by each.

115. Each encounters a gentile woman at a well.

116. Both submitted unresistingly to injuries and insults.

117. General practical philanthropy and impartiality marks the life of each Savior.

118. Each took more pleasure in repentant sinners than in virtuous saints.

119. Both practically disclosed God's attempt to reconcile the world to himself.

120. The closing incidents in the earth-life of each were strikingly similar.

121. A memorable last supper marked the closing career of both.

122. Both were put to death by "wicked hands."

123. Chrishna, as well as Christ, was crucified.

124. Darkness attended the crucifixion of each.

125. Both were crucified between two thieves.

126. Each is reported to have forgiven his enemies.

127. The age of each at death corresponds (being between thirty and thirty-six years).

128. Each, after giving up the ghost, descends into hell.

129. The resurrection from the dead is a marked period in the history of each.

130. Each ascends to heaven after his resurrection.

131. Many people are reported to have witnessed the ascension in each case.

132. Each is reported as having both descended and ascended.

133. The head of each, while living on earth, was anointed with oil.

II. DOCTRINES.

134. There is a similarity in the doctrines of their respective religions.

135. The same doctrines are propagated by the disciples of each.

136. The doctrine of future rewards and punishments is a part of each system.

137. Analogous views of heaven are found in each system.

138. A third heaven is spoken of in each system.

139. All sin must be punished according to the bible teachings of each.

140. Each has a hell provided for the wicked.

141. Both teach a hell of darkness and a hell of light.

142. An immortal worm finds employment in the hell of each system ("the worm that dieth not.")

143. The arch-demon of the under world uses brimstone for fuel in one case, and oil in the other.

144. The motive for future punishment is in both cases the same.

145. Each has a purgatory or sort of half-way house.

146. Special divine judgments on nations are taught by each.

147. A great and final day of judgment is taught by each.

148. A general resurrection also is taught in each religion.

149. That there is a "Judge of the dead" is a doctrine of each.

150. Two witnesses are to report on human actions in the final assizes.

151. We are furnished in each case with the dimension of heaven or "the holy city."

152. Man is enjoined to strive against temptation to sin by each.

153. And repentance for sin is a doctrine taught by the bible of each.

154. Each has a prepared city for a paradise.

155. The bibles of both teach that we have no continuing city here.

156. Souls are carried to heaven by angels, as in the instance of Lazarus, in each case.

157. A belief in angels or spirits is a tenant of each religion.

158. The doctrine of fallen or evil angels is found in both system.

159. Obsession by wicked or evil spirits is taught by each.

160. Both teach that sickness or disease is caused by evil spirits.

161. Each has a king-devil or arch-demon with a posse of subalterns or evil spirits.

162. Both bibles record the story of a "hellaballoo" or war in heaven.

163. Both teach that an evil man can neither do nor speak a good thing.

164. Both teach that sin is a disadvantage in the present life as well as in the future.

165. The doctrine of free will or free agency is taught by each.

166. Predestination seems to be inferentially taught by each.

167. In each case man is a prize in a lottery, with God and the devil for ticket-holders.

168. Both make the devil (or devils) a scape-goat for sin.

169. Both teach the devil or evil spirits as the primary cause of all evil.

170. The destiny of both body and soul is pointed out by each.

171. The true believers are known as "saints" under both systems.

172. Saints with "white robes" are spoken of by each.

173. Both specify "the Word of Logos" as God.

174. Wisdom, too, is personified as God by the holy Scriptures of each.

175. Both teach that God may be known by his works.

176. The doctrine of one supreme God is taught in each bible.

177. Light and truth are important words in the religious nomenclature of each.

178. Both profess a high veneration for truth.

179. "Where the treasure is, there is the heart also," is taught by each.

180. "Seek and ye shall find" is a condition prescribed by each.

181. Religious toleration is a virtue professed by both.

182. All nations are professedly based on an equality by each.

183. Both, however, enjoin partiality to "the household of faith."

184. The doors of salvation are thrown open to high and low, rich and poor, by each.

185. Each professes to have "the only true and saving faith."

186. There is a mystery in the mission of each Savior.

187. "Rama" is a well known word in the bible of each.

188. "The understanding of the wise" is a phrase in each.

189. Both speak figuratively of "the blind leading the blind."

190. "A new heaven and a new earth" is spoken of by each.

191. The doctrine of a Trinity in the Godhead is taught by each.

192. Baptism by water is a tenant and ordinance of each.

193. "Living water" is a metaphor found in each.

194. Baptism by fire seems also to be recognized by each.

195. Fasting is emphatically enjoined by each.

196. Sacrifices are of secondary importance in each system, and are partially or wholly abandoned by each.

197. The higher law is paramount to ceremonies in each religion.

198. The bible of each religion literally condemns idolatry.

199. Both also make concessions to idolatry.

200. Polygamy is not literally encouraged nor openly condemned by either.

201. The power to forgive sins is conferred on the disciples of each.

202. The doctrine of blasphemy is recognized by each.

203. Pantheism, or the reciprocal in-being of God in nature and nature in God, is taught by both.

III. BIBLES AND HOLY SCRIPTURES.

204. Each has a bible which is the idolized fountain of all religious teaching.

205. Both have an Old Testament and a New Testament, virtually.

206. The New Testament inaugurates a new and reform system of religion in each case.

207. "All Scripture is given by inspiration of God" is the faith of the disciples of each.

208. Each system claimed to have its inspired men to write its scriptures.

209. Both hold a spiritual qualification necessary to understand their bibles.

210. It is a sin to become "wise beyond what is written" in their respective bibles.

211. Both recommend knowing the Scriptures in youth.

212. Alteration of their respective bibles is divinely interdicted.

213. The bible is an infallible rule of faith and practice in both cases.

214. "All scripture is profitable for doctrine" is the faith of each.

215. Both explain away the errors of their bibles.

IV. SPIRITUALITY OF THE TWO RELIGIONS.

216. The religion of Chrishna is pre-eminently spiritual no less than Christ's.

217. Both teach that "to be carnally minded is death."

218. External rites are practically dispersed with in each religion.

219. The spiritual law written on the heart is recognized by each.

220. "God is within you," Budhists teach as well as Christians.

221. Both recognize an invisible spiritual Savior.

222. "God dwells in the heart," say Hindoo as well as Christians.

223 An inward recognition of the divine law is amply seen in both.

224. Both confess allegiance to an inward monitor.

225. The doctrine of inspiration and internal illumination is found in both.

226. The indwelling Comforter is believed in by both.

227. Both also teach that religion is an inward work.

228. Both speak of being born again—i. e., the second birth.

229. A spiritual body is also believed in by both.

230. "Spiritual things are incomprehensible to the natural man" say each.

231. God's spiritually sustaining power Budhists also acknowledge.

232. Both give a spiritual interpretation to their bibles.

233. Each has a new and more interior law superseding the old law.

234. The spiritual cross—self-denial or asceticism—is a prominent feature of each religion.

235. The duty of renouncing and abandoning the external world is solemnly enjoined by each.

236. Budhists renounce the world more practically than Christians.

237. Withdrawal or seclusion from society is recommended by each.

238. Bodily suffering as a benefit to the soul is encouraged by each.

239. Voluntary suffering for righteousness' sake is a virtue with each.

240. The cross is a religious emblem in each system.

241. Both glory in "the religion of the cross" as better than a religion without suffering.

242. Hence both teach "the greater the cross the greater the crown."

243. Earthly pleasures are regarded as evil by both.

244. Contempt for the body as an enemy to the soul is visible in both.

245. Retirement for religious contemplation is a duty with each.

246. The forsaking of relations is also enjoined by each.

247. Spiritual relationship is superior to external relationship with both.

248. "To die is great gain" we are taught by each.

249. A subjugation of the passions is a religious duty with each.

250. The road to heaven is a narrow one with each.

251. The same state of religious perfection is aspired to by the disciples of each.

V. THE DOCTRINE OF FAITH OR BELIEF.

252. Faith is an all-important element and doctrine with each.

253. Heresy, or want of faith, is a sin of great magnitude with both.

254. Faith in the Savior is a condition to salvation by both.

255. Confessing the Savior is also required in both cases.

256. "Believe or be damned" is the condition or profess to believe the terrible sine qua non to salvation by each.

257. Skeptics or unbelievers are with both the chief of sinners.

258. "Faith can remove mountains," either with a Bud-hist or a Christian.

259. Both contrast faith with works.

260. Faith without works is dead—so teach both Bud-hists and Christians.

VI. THE DOCTRINE AND PRACTICE OF PRAYER.

261. Prayer is an important rite in each religion.

262. Private or secret prayer is recommended by both.

263. Each has also a formula of prayer.

264. "Pray without ceasing" is a Budhist as well as a Christian injunction.

265. Praying to their respective Saviors in sickness and in health is a custom with both.

266. The custom of praying for the dead is recognized in each system.

VII. TREATMENT OF ENEMIES.

267. It is a Hindoo as well as a Christian injunction to treat enemies kindly.

268. Passive submission to injuries and abuse is enjoined by both.

269. The holy Scriptures of both require us to pray for enemies, and feed them.

270. And even love to enemies is a part of the spirit of each religion.

149

VIII. THE MILLENNIUM.

271. Hindoos, like Christians, prophesy of a great millennial era.

272. There is a remarkable similarity in their notions with respect to it.

273. Both anticipate a second advent or new Savior on the occasion.

274. The destruction of the world also is to take place in both cases.

275. And an entire renovation and a new order of things are to be established in each case.

IX. MIRACLES.

276. There is almost a constant display of miraculous power in each system.

277. The disciples of both are professedly endowed with this power.

278. Miraculous cures of the lame, the blind, and the sick are reported in both cases.

279. Miracles of handling poisonous reptiles with impunity are reported by both.

280. Swallowing deadly poison is enjoined by Christians and practiced by Hindoos.

281. Many cases of the miraculous ejection of devils are reported by both.

282. The miracle of thought-reading is displayed by both.

283. The saints in both cases are reported as raising the dead.

X. PRECEPTS.

284. "The kingdom of heaven" was to be sought first of all things in each case.

285. Love to God is a paramount obligation under each system.

286. And the worship of God is an essential requisition in each religious polity.

287. "Cease to do evil and learn to do well" is virtually enjoined by each.

288. An inward knowledge of God is taught as essential by both systems.

289. A reliance on works is discouraged by both.

290. Purity of heart is inculcated by Hindoos as well as Christians.

291. Speak and think evil of no man is a gospel injunction of each.

292. A love of all beings is more prominently the spirit of Budhism than that of Christianity.

293. The practice of strict godly virtue is enjoined by both.

294. Moderation and temperance are recommended by both.

295. Patience is a virtue in each religion.

296. The duty of controlling our thoughts is taught by each.

297. Charity has a high appreciation by each.

298. Both make the poor objects of attention.

299. The practice of hospitality is recommended by each.

300. Humility is a duty and a virtue under both systems.

301. Mirthfulness or light conversation is forbidden by each.

302. Purity of life is a duty with Hindoos as well as Christians.

303. Chasteness in conversation is inculcated by both.

304. "Respect to persons" is a sin in the moral polity of both.

305. Alms-giving is religiously enjoined by the holy Scriptures of both.

306. Both teach that "it is better to give than to receive."

307. Loyalty to rulers is a moral requisition of each system.

308. Honor to father and mother is esteemed a great virtue by both.

309. The correct training of children is with each a scriptural duty.

310. "Look not upon a woman" is more than hinted by each.

311. The reading of the holy Scriptures is enjoined by both.

312. Lying or falsehood is with each a sin of great magnitude.

313. Swearing is discountenanced by both religions.

314. Theft or stealing is specially condemned by both.

315. Both deprecate and condemn the practice of war.

316. Both discountenance fighting.

317. Neither of them professes to believe in slavery.

318. Drunkenness and the use of wine are more specifically condemned by the Hindoo religion.

319. Adultery and fornication are heinous sins in the eyes of both.

320. Both condemn covetousness as a great sin.

321. Budhists more practically condemn anger than Christians do.

XI. MISCELLANEOUS ANALOGIES.

322. Both have their apocryphal as well as their canonical Scriptures.

323. Stories are found in the bible of each which would be rejected if found elsewhere.

324. Both make their bible a finality in matters of faith.

325. Both have had their councils and commentaries to reveal theis bibles over again.

326. Numerous schisms, divisions, sects, and creeds have sprung up in each.

327. Various religious reforms have sprung up under each.

328. Conversion from one religious sect to another is common to both.

329. Both religions have been troubled with numerous skeptics or infidels.

330. Both have often resorted to new interpretations for their bibles to suit the times.

331. The unconverted are stigmatized by each.

332. "Knock and it shall be opened" is the invitation of each.

333. Public confession of sins in class-meetings is known to each.

334. Death-bed repentance often witnessed under both religious systems.

335. A belief in haunted houses incident to the religious countries of both.

336. A superior respect for woman claimed by each.

337. An idolatrous veneration for religious ancestors by each.

338. Each sustain a numerous horde of expensive priests.

339. A divine call or illumination to preach claimed by each.

340. Religious martyrdom the glory of each.

341. Both have encountered "perils by sea and land" for their religion.

342. He who loseth his life (for his religion) shall find it, say both.

343. Both in ancient times suffered much persecution.

344. The disciples of both have suffered death without flinching from the faith.

345. Each sent numerous missionaries abroad to preach and convert.

346. And, finally, each cherished the hope of converting the world to their religion.

The author has in his possession historical quotations to prove the truth of each one of the above parallels. He has all the historical facts on which they were constructed found in and drawn from the sacred books of the Hindoo religion and the works of Christian writers descriptive of their religion. But they would swell the present volume to unwieldy dimensions, and far beyond its proper and prescribed limits, to present them here; they are therefore reserved for the second volume, and may be published in pamphlet form also.

In proof of the correctness of the foregoing comparative analogies, we will now summon the testimony of various authors setting forth the historical character of the Hindoo God Chrishna, and the essential nature of his religion, so far as it approximates in its doctrines and moral teachings to the Christian religion. We will first hear from Colonel Wiseman, for ten years a Christian missionary in India.

"There is one Indian (Hindoo) legend of considerable importance" says this writer... "This is the story of Chrishna, the Indian Apollo. In native legends he is represented as an Avatar, or incarnation of the Divinity. At his birth, choirs of Devitas (angels) sung hymns of praise, while shepherds surrounded his cradle. It was necessary to conceal his birth from the tyrant ruler, Cansa, to whom it had been foretold that the infant Savior should destroy him. The child escaped with his parents beyond the coast of Lamouna. For a time he lived in obscurity, and then commenced a public life distinguished for prowess and beneficence. He washed the feet of the Brahmins, and preached the most excellent doctrines; but at length the power of his enemies prevailed.... Before dying, he foretold the miseries which would take place in the Cali-yuga, or wicked age (Dark Age) of the world."

153

"Chrishna (says another writer) taught his followers that they alone were the true believers of the saving faith; throwing down the barriers of caste, and elevating the dogmas of their faith above the sacerdotal class, he admitted every one who felt an inward desire to the ministry to the preaching of their religion. A system thus associating itself with the habits, feelings, and personal advantages of its disciples could not fail to make rapid progress." (Upham's History. Doctrines of Budhism.)

"Budhism inculcates benevolence, tenderness, forgiveness of injuries, and love of enemies; and forbids sensuality, love of pleasure, and attachment to worldly objects." (Judson).

"At the moment of his (Chrishna's) conception a God left heaven to enter the womb of his mother (a virgin). Immediately after his birth he was recognized as a divine personage, and it was predicted that he would surpass all previous divine incarnations in holiness. Every one adored him, saluting him as 'the God of Gods.' When twenty years of age he went into a desert, and lived there in the austerest retirement, poverty, simplicity, and virtue, spending his whole time in religious contemplation. He was tempted in various ways, but his self-denial resisted all the seductive approaches of sin. He declared, 'Religion is my essence.' He experienced a lively opposition from the priests attached to the ancient creeds (as Christ subsequently did). But he triumphed over all his enemies after holding a discussion with them (as Christ did with the doctors in the Temple). He revised the existing code of morals and the social law. He reduced the main principles of morality to four, viz: *mercy, aversion to cruelty, unbounded sympathy for all animated beings and the strictest adherence to the moral law.* He also gave a decalogue of commandments, viz.: 1. Not to kill. 2. Not to steal. 3. To be chaste. 4. Not to testify falsely. 5. Not to lie. 6. Not to swear. 7. To avoid all impure words. 8. To be disinterested. 9. Not to take revenge. 10. And not to be superstitious. This code of morals was firmly established in the hearts of his followers." (Abridged from Hardy's Manual of Budhism.)

"It was prophesied in olden times that a person would arise and redeem Hindostan from 'the yoke of bondage.' At midnight, when the birth of Chrishna was taking place, the clouds emitted low music, and poured down a rain of flowers. The celestial child was greeted with hymns by attending spirits.

"The room was illuminated by his light, and the countenances of his father and mother emitted rays of glory, and they bowed in worship.' 'The people believed he was a God.' They eagerly caught the words which fell from his lips, which taught his divine mission, and they called him the 'Holy One,' and finally the 'Living God.' He performed miraculous cures. At his birth a marvelous light illumined the earth. His followers baptised, and performed miraculous cures. And he, when a child, attracted attention by his miracles. While attending the herds with his foster-father a great serpent poisoned the river, which caused the death of cows and shepherd-boys when they drank of it, whom Chrishna restored to life by a look of divine power. His life was devoted to mercy and charity. He left paradise from pure compassion, to die for suffering sinners. He sought to lead men to better paths and lives of virtue and rectitude. He suffered to atone for the sins of the world; and the sinner, through faith in him, can be saved. Christ and Chrishna both taught the equality of man. Prayers addressed to Chrishna were after this fashion: 'O thou Supreme One! thy essence is inscrutable. Thou art all in all. The understanding of man cannot reach thy Almighty Power. I, who know nothing, fly to thee for protection. Show mercy unto me, and enable me to see and know thee.' Chrishna replies, 'Have faith in me. No one who worships me can perish. Address thyself to me as the only asylum. I will deliver thee from sin. I am animated with equal benevolence toward all beings. I know neither hatred nor partiality. Those who adore me devoutly are in me and I in them'"—"Christ within you the hope of glory." (Abridged from Mr. Tuttle.)

"If we consider that Budhism proclaimed the equality of all men and women in the sight of God, that it denounced the impious pretensions of the most mischievous priesthood the world ever saw, and that it inculcated a pure system of practical morality, we must admit that the innovation was as advantageous as it was extensively spread and adopted." (Hue's Journey through China, chap. v.)

"To Chrishna the Hindoos were indebted for a code of pure and practical morality, which inculcated charity and chastity, performance of good works, abstinence from evil, and general kindness to all living things." (Cunningham.)

"Budhism never confounds right or wrong, and never excuses any sin" (Catharine Beecher.)

"He (Chrishna) honored humanity by his virtues." (St Hilaire.)

"It is probable that every incident in his (Chrisna's) life is founded in fact, which, if separated from surrounding fable, would afford a history that would scarce have any equal in the importance of the lessons it would teach." (Hardy's Manual of Budhism.)

"He (Chrishna) undertakes and counsels a constant struggle against the body. In his eyes the body is the enemy of man's soul (as Paul thought when he spoke of 'our vile bodies.') He aims to subdue the body and the burning passions which consume it.... He requires humility, disregard of wordly wealth, patience and resignation in adversity, love to enemies, religious tolerance, horror at falsehood, avoidance of frivolous conversation, consideration and esteem for women, sanctity of the marriage relation, non-resistance to evil, confession of sins, and conversion." (St. Hilaire.)

"Budhism has been called the Christianity of the East." (Abel Remuset.)

"The doctrine and practical piety of their bible (the Baghavat Gita) bear a strong resemblance to those of the Holy Scriptures. It has scarcely a precept or principle that is not found in the (Christian) bible. And were the people to live up to its principles of peace and love, oppression and injury would be known no more within their borders... It has no mythology of obscene and ferocious deities, no sanguinary or impure observances, no self-inflicting tortures, no tyrannizing priesthood, no confounding of right and wrong by making certain iniquities laudable in worship. In its moral code, its description of the purity and peace of the first ages, and the shortening of man's life by sin, it seems to follow genuine traditions. In almost every respect it seems to be the best religion ever invented by man." (Rev. H. Malcom's Travels in Asia.)

"If the morality of Budhism be examined, its exhortations to guard the will, to curb the thoughts, to exercise kindness towards others, to abstain from wrong to all, it propounds a very high standard of practice." (Upham's Doctrines and History of Budhism.)

155

"It seeks the highest triumphants of humanity in the exercise of devotion, self-contemplation, and self-denial." (Theogony of the Hindoos, by Bjornsjerma.)

"And the doctrines of Budhism are not alone in the beauty of their sentiments and the excellence of much of their morality. 'It is not permitted to you to return evil for evil' is one of the sentiments of Socrates." (Rev. H. S. Hardy's Eastern Monachism.)

"Budhism insists on the necessity of taking the intellectual faculties for guides in philosophical researches." (Tiberghien.)

"It sought to wean mankind from the pleasures and vanities of life by pointing to the transitoriness of all human enjoyment." (Smith's Mongolia.)

"The principal characteristics of Budhism are the doctrines of mildness and the universal brotherhood of man." (Ibid.)

"Life is a state of probation and misery, according to Budhism." (Upham, chap. vi.)

"The Brahmins found fault with him (Chrishna) for receiving as disciples the outcasts of Hindoo society (as the Jews did Christ for fellowshipping publicans and sinners). But he (Chrishna) replied, 'My law is a law of mercy to all.'" (Hue's Voyages through China.)

"Budhism attracted and furnished consolation for the poor and unfortunate." (Ibid.)

"Budhism is a rationalistic and reform system as compared with Brahminism. Landresse expresses his high admiration of the heroism with which the Budhist missionaries before Christ crossed streams and seas which had arrested armies, and traversed deserts and mountains upon which no caravans dared to venture, and braved dangers and surmounted obstacles which had defied the omnipotence of the emperors." (A note on Landresse's *Foe Koui Ki.*)

"If we addressed a Mogul or Thibetan this question, Who is Chrishna? the reply was, instantly, 'The Savior of men.'" (Hue's Journey through China.)

"Chrishna, the incarnate Deity of the Sanscrit romance continues to this hour the darling God of the women of India.... Chrishna was the person of Vishnu (God) himself in the human form." (Asiat. Researches, 260).

"Respectable natives told me that some of the missionaries had told them that they were even now almost Christians" (owing to the two religions being so nearly alike). (Ibid)

"All that converting the Hindoos to Christianity does for them is to change the object of their worship from Chrishna to Christ." (Robert Cheyne.)

"Brahminism or Budhism in some of its forms is said to constitute the religion of considerably more than half the human race. It teaches the existence of one supreme eternal, and uncreated God, called Brahma, who created the world through Chrishna, the second member of the

156

Trinity." Paul says, God created the world through Jesus Christ, the second member of the Christian Trinity. (Eph. iii. 9.) How striking the resemblance! "The doctrine of the incarnation, the descent of the Deity upon earth, and his manifestation in a human form for the redemption of mankind, seems to have existed in the shape of prophecy or fact in all ages of the world. Hindooism teaches nine of these incarnations. Furthermore, it teaches the doctrine of the Trinity, the fall and redemption of man, and a state of future rewards and punishments in a future life.... This religion in chief of Asia is traceable to remote ages. The doctrine of the Trinity is represented in the Elephantine cavern, and taught in the Mahabarat, which goes back for its origin nearly two thousand years before Christ." (New York Sunday Despatch, 1855.)

"In the year 3600, Chrishna descended to the earth for the purpose of defeating the evil machinations of Chivan (the devil), as Christ 'came to destroy the devil and his works.' (See John iii. 8.) After a fierce combat with the devil, or serpent, he defeated him by bruising his head—he receiving, during the contest, a wound in the heel. ('It [the serpent] shall bruise thy head, and thou shalt bruise his heel.'—Gen. iii. 15.) He died at last between two thieves.... He lead a pure and holy life, and was a meek, tender, and benevolent being, and enjoined charity, hospitality, and mercy, and forbade lying, prevarication, hypocrisy, and overreaching in dealing, and pilfering, and theft, and violence toward any being." (Lecture before the Free Press Association in 1827.)

"The birthplace of the Hindoo hero (Chrishna) is called Mathura, which is easily changed, and by correct translation becomes Maturea, the place where Christ is said to have stopped, between Nazareth and Egypt... To show his humility he washed the feet of the Brahmins (as Christ is said to have washed the feet of the Jews—see John xiii. 14). One day a woman came to him and anointed his hair with oil, in return for which he healed her maladies. One of his first miracles was that of healing a leper, like Christ (See Mark i. 4). Finally, he was crucified, then descended to Hades. (It is said of Christ, 'his soul was not left in hell.'—Acts ii. 31.) He (Chrishna) rose from the dead and ascended to Voicontra (heaven.)" (Higgin's Anacalypsis, vol. ii. p. 239).

Now, we ask, is it any wonder, in view of the foregoing historical exposition, that Eusebius should exclaim, "The religion of Jesus Christ is neither new nor strange?" (Eccl. Hist. ch. iv.) Truly did St. Augustine say, "This, in our day, is the Christian religion, not as having been unknown in former times, but as having recently received that name."

Here, then, we pause to ask our good Christian reader, *Where is your original Christianity now?* or what constitutes the revealed religion of Jesus Christ? or where is the evidence that any new religion was revealed by him or preached by him, seeing we have all his religion, as shown by the foregoing historical citations, included in an old heathen system more than a thousand years old when Jesus Christ was born? We find it all here in this old oriental system of Budhism—*every essential part, particle and principle* of it. We find Christianity all here—its Alpha and Omega, its beginning and end. We find it here in all its details,—its root, essence, and entity,—all its "revealed doctrines," religious ideas, beautiful truths, senseless dogmas and oriental phantoms. Not, a doctrine, principle, or precept of the Christian system, but that is here proclaimed to the world ages before "the angels announced the birth of a divine babe in Bethlehem." Will you, then, persist in claiming that "truth, life, and immortality came by Jesus Christ," and that "Christ came to preach a new gospel to the world, and to set forth a new religion never before heard amongst men" (to use the language of Archbishop Tillotson), when the historical facts cited in this work demonstrate a hundred times over that such a position is palpably erroneous? Will you still persist, with all those undeniable facts staring you in the face (proving and reproving, with overwhelming demonstration, that the statement is untrue), in declaring that "the religion of Jesus Christ is the only true and soul-saving religion, and all other systems are mere straw, stubble, tradition, and superstition" (as asserted by a popular Christian writer), when no mathematician ever demonstrated a scientific problem more clearly than we have proved in these pages that all the principle systems of the past, by no means excepting Christianity, are essentially alike in every important particular—all of their cardinal doctrines being the same, differing only in unimportant details?

Seeing, then, that all systems of religion have been found to be essentially alike in spirit and in practice, the all-important question arises here, What is the true cause assignable for this striking resemblance? How is it to be accounted for? Perhaps some of our good Christian readers, unacquainted with history, may cherish the thought that all the oriental systems brought to notice are but imitations of Christianity; that they were reconstructed out of materials obtained from that source; that Christianity is the parent, and they the off-spring. But, alas for their long-cherished idol, those who entertain such forlorn hopes are "sowing to the wind, and are doomed to disappointment." With the exception of Mahomedanism alone, Christianity is the youngest system in the whole catalogue. The historical facts to prove this statement are voluminous. But as it needs no proof to those who have read religious history, but little space will be occupied with citations for this purpose. With respect to the antiquity of the principal oriental system, we need only to quote the testimony of Sir William Jones, a devout Christian writer, who spent years in India, and whose testimony will be accepted by any person acquainted with his history. He makes the emphatic declaration, "That the name of Chrishna, and the general outline of his history, were long anterior to the birth of our Savior, and probably to the time of Homer (900 b. C.) we know very certainly." (Asiat. Res. vol. i. p. 254.) No guess-work about it. "*We know very certainly.*"

And being a scholar, a traveler, and a sojourner among the Hindoos, and well versed in their history, no person ever had a better opportunity to know than he. We will hear this renowned author further. "In the Sanscrit dictionary, compiled more than two thousand years ago, we have the whole history of the incarnate deity (Chrishna), born of a virgin, and miraculously escaping in his infancy from the reigning tyrant of his country (Cansa). He passed a life of the most extraordinary and incomprehensible devotion. His birth was concealed from the tyrant Cansa, to whom it had been predicted that one born at that time, and in that family, would destroy him;" i. e., destroy his power. (Asiat. Res. vol. i. p. 273.) This writer also states that the first Christian missionaries who entered India were astonished to find there a religion so near like their own, and could only account for it by supposing that the devil, foreseeing the advent of Christ, originated a system of religion in advance of his, and "just like it." Stated in other words, he got out the second edition of the gospel plan of salvation before the first edition was published or had an existence. Rather a smart trick this, thus to outwit God Almighty.

With respect to the vast antiquity of the Hindoo oriental religion, which indicates it as being not only the source from which the materials of the Christian religion were drawn, but as being the parent of all the leading systems, with their three thousand subordinate branches which existed at

158

a much earlier period than Christianity, we need only point to the deep chiseled sculptures and imperishable monuments enstamped on their time-honored temples, tombs, altars, vases, columns, pagodas, ruined towers, &c., which, with contemporary inscriptions, warrant us in antedating the religion of the Himmalehas far beyond the authentic records of any other religion that has floated down to us on the stream of time. The numerous images of their crucified Gods, Chrishna and Saki, emblazoned on their old rock temples in various parts of the country, some of which are constructed of clay porphyry, now the very hardest species of rock, with their attendant inscriptions in a language so very ancient as to be lost to the memory of man, vie with the Sanscrit in age, the oldest deciphered language in the world.

All these and a hundred corroboratory historical facts fix on India as being the birthplace of the mother of all religions now existing, or that ever had an existence, while the great workshop in which they were subsequently remodeled was in Alexandria in Egypt, whose theological schools furnished the model for nearly every system now found noticed on the page of history— Christianity of course included. So much for the unrivaled antiquity of the Hindoo religion. Now, the more important query arises, What relationship does ancient heathen or Hindoo Budhism bear to Christianity? What is the evidence that the latter is an outgrowth of the former? As an answer to this question, the reader will please note the following facts of history:—

1. Alexandria, the home of the world's great conqueror, was at one period of time the great focal center for religious speculation and propagandism, the great emporium for religious dogmas throughout the East, and a place of resort for the disciples of nearly every system of religious faith then existing.

2. In this capital city, comprising about five hundred thousand inhabitants, were established a voluminous library, and vast theological schools, in which men of every religious order, and of every phase of faith, met and exchanged religious ideas, and borrowed new doctrines, with which they remodeled their former systems of faith, amounting in some cases to an entire change of their long-established creeds.

3. In these theological schools the Jewish sect, which afterward became the founders of Christianity, were extensively represented; for, let it be noted, its first disciples and founders had all been Jews, probably of the Essene sect. "For a long time the Christians were but a Jewish sect," says M. Reuss' "History of Christian Theology." Alexander had, previous to this time (that is, about 330 b. c.), subjected the whole of Western Asia to his dominions, including, of course, "The Holy Land"—Judea.

4. By this act a large portion of the Jewish nation were transferred from their own country to Alexandria. And this number was afterward vastly increased by Alexander's successor, Ptolemy Sotor, who carried off and settled in that credal city one hundred thousand more Jews.

5. As the result, in part, of these repeated calamities, "the Lord's chosen people" were literally broken up. They lost their law, lost their leader and lawgiver, lost their language, lost the control of their country, the *"Promised Land"* which (they verily believed) the Lord had deeded to them *in fee simple*, and ratified in the high court of heaven, and had declared they should hold and

possess forever. And finally they partially lost their nationality, being literally dissolved and broken up; and were finally almost lost to history—the ten tribes disappearing entirely.

6. The Jews had ever manifested a proneness for copying after the religious customs of their heathen neighbors, and engrafting their doctrines into their own creeds, as their bible history furnishes ample proof.

7. In Alexandria a very superior opportunity was afforded for doing this, excelling in this respect any previous period of their history.

8. The shattered condition of their own religion, with all its conventional creeds, customs, and ceremonies, now suspended and literally prostrated, as above shown, vastly augmented the temptation ever rife with them to make another change in their religion, and subject their creed to another installment of new doctrines, by which it became Christianity.

9. The liberal character and tolerant spirit of the political and religious institutions of the kingdom of Alexandria, with its vast and attractive library of two hundred thousand volumes, established principally by Ptolemy Phila-delphus, with other attractive features already pointed out, furnished great facilities, as well as increased temptations to religious propagandists to absorb new theories, and make new creeds out of the vast medley of religious doctrines and speculative dogmas preached and propagated in that royal city by the disciples and representatives of nearly every religious system then in existence, brought together by the attractions above specified.

10. Hence every consideration would lead us to conclude, taken in connection with the facts above stated, and the well-known borrowing proclivity and imitative propensity of the Jews, that they would not, and could not, withstand the overweening and overpowering temptation to make another radical change in their religion by a new draught on the boundless reservoir of speculative ideas, religious tenets, and specious theories then glowing in the popular schools of Alexandria.

11. All the facts above enumerated would impel us to the conclusion that the Jews would—and every page of history touching the matter proves they did—make important changes in their religion by this contact with the oriental systems, as they had repeatedly done before. Some of this proof we will here present, to show how they originated Christianity.

12. "The schools of Alexandria" says Mr. Enfield, a Christian writer, "by pretending to teach sublime doctrines concerning God and divine things, enticed men of different countries and religions, and among the rest the Jews, to study its mysteries, and incorporate them with their own.... The Jewish faith mixed with the Pythagorean, and afterward with the Egyptian oriental theology" (that is, they became Essenes in the Grecian school of Pythagoras, who taught the doctrines of that religious order, then Bud-hists in the Egyptian schools of Alexandria). And finally, with Christ as their leader, who taught the doctrines of both schools (they being essentially alike), they assumed the name of Christian in honor of him, and thus is Christianity from Essene Budhism.

13. Beers in his "History of the Jews," sustains the above statement by the declaration that the Essenian Jews "fled to Egypt at the time of the Babylonian captivity, and there became acquainted with the Pythagorean philosophy, and ingrafted it upon the religion of Moses," which would make them Essenian Budhists—for Cunningham assures us that "the doctrine of Pythagoras were intensely Budhistic." (Philsa. Topus, chap. x.)

14. We will condense a few more historical testimonies relative to the entire change of the Jewish faith, while in Alexandria, as well as on other occasions, to show how easy and natural it was for that portion of the Jews who afterward became the founders of Christianity to slide into and adopt Essenian Budhism, whose doctrines they took to constitute the Christian religion.

15. Mr. Gibbon (chap. xxi.) declares that the theological opinions of the Jews underwent great changes by their contact with the various foreigners they found in Alexandria. Mr. Tytler likewise, in his "Universal History," assures us that the Jewish religion "became *totally changed by the intermixture of heathen doctrines*." Dr. Campbell also testifies that "their views came pretty much to coincide with those of the pagans." (See his Dissertation, vi.) And the author of "*The Expositor* for 1854" complains that the pagan "theology stole upon them from every quarter, and mingled in all the views of the then known tribes, so that by the year 150 b. c., it had wrought visible changes in their notions and habits of thought." (P. 423.) Here we have the proof that the whole Jewish religion underwent a change in Alexandria.

16. Now, most, certainly a nation or sect professing a religion so easily changed, and possessing a character so fickle, or so irrepressible as to yield on every slight occasion, and embrace every opportunity to imbibe new religious ideas and doctrines, would easily, if not naturally, slide into the adoption of the religious system then promulgated in Alexandria under the name of Budhism, and afterward remodeled or transformed, and called Christianity.

17. The Jews of the Essenian order, as we have in part shown in a previous chapter, set forth in their creed all the leading doctrines now comprised in the Christian religion hundreds of years before the advent of Christ, not excepting the doctrine of the divine incarnation and its adjuncts, as these concomitants of the present popular faith, we will now prove, were not unknown to the Jewish theology, but constituted a part of the religion of some of the principal Jewish sects. That standard Christian author, Mr. Milman, in his "History of Christianity," tells us that "the doctrine of the incarnation ('God manifest in the flesh') was the doctrine from the Ganges, and even the shores of the Yellow Sea to the Ilissus. It was the fundamental principle of the Indian Budhist religion and philosophy. It was the basis of Zoroasterism. It was pure Platonism. It was Platonic Judaism in the Alexandrian school." Here it is positively declared, by a popular Christian writer, whose work is a part of nearly every popular library in Christiandom as a standard authority, that the appearance of God amongst men in the human form, by human birth, was a doctrine of the Jewish religion in some of its branches, especially the Essenian branch—further proof that Christianity originated nothing, and gave utterance to no new doctrine or precepts, and performed no new miracles. Where, then, is the claim for its originality? On what ground is it predicated? Please answer us, good Christian brother.

18. It is a question of no importance, if it could be settled, whether Christianity is a direct outgrowth from one of the new-fangled sects of Judaism, or whether it derived a portion of its

doctrines from this source and the balance from ascetic Budhism. Yet we regard it as an incontrovertible proposition that it all grew out of Budhism originally, either directly or indirectly.

19. Christ may have received his doctrines secondhanded, all or a portion from the Essenian Jews; for that sect held all the leading doctrines of Budhism (as we have shown in a previous chapter), which now goes under the name of the religion of Jesus Christ.

20. Or we may indulge the not unreasonable hypothesis that the founders of Christianity, who republished the doctrines of Budhism and adopted them as their own, received them all direct from the disciples of that religious order; for "they were everywhere," as one writer (Mr. Taylor) declares, speaking of their extensive travels to propagate their doctrines through the world. And it was about that period, as Mr. Goodrich informs us, they sent out nine hundred missionaries, who made six millions of converts,—a small fraction of their present number (three hundred and eighty millions, as given by some of our geographies),—one third more than the entire census of Christendom, and six times the number of believers in the Christian religion, if we omit Greeks and Catholics. "It is." as a writer remarks, "the oldest and most widely spread religion in the world." And, whatever hypothesis may be adduced to account for the fact, Christianity is now all Budhism.

21. It is impossible, with the historic darkness which at present environs and beclouds our pathway, to determine at what period or in what manner Christ became an Essene,—whether he was born of Essenian parents, or became a convert to the faith,—because the whole period of his life, with the exception of about three years, is a total blank in history. There is but one incident related of his movements by his bible biographers prior to his twenty-seventh year, leaving more than a quarter of a century of his probably active life unreported—a period that may have witnessed several important changes in his religion. We have not even his ancestry reported in his scriptural biography, in either parental line, unless we assume Joseph to have been his father. The parental lineage of his mother is entirely omitted Had we his line of ancestry, or could we trace him back to his national or family origin, we doubt not but we should there find a clue to the origin of his religion. We should find his ancestors were Essenian Jews.

22. Nor can we fix the date when Essenian Budhism among the Jews received the name of Christianity for a similar reason. There is a link—a chain of events of four hundred years left out of the bible between Judaism and Christianity—thus lacking four hundred years of connecting the two religions together, or of showing how the latter grew out of the former. Malachi, the last book of the Old Testament, antedates the first events of Christian history four centuries, or twelve generations, thus leaving a wide and dark gap between them. And besides, we cannot find the name of Christ or Christianity mentioned in any of the contemporary histories of that era till one hundred and four years after the time fixed for Christ's birth by Christendom; Tacitus being the first writer who names either, and this was at that date.

23. These facts disclose the whole secret with respect to the mystery and darkness thrown around the origin of the Christian religion—the how, the when, and the where of its origin. That chapter of Christian history is left out of the record. The bible account itself is but fragmentary, as it leaves nine tenths of Christ's history a blank,—twenty-seven years out of the thirty,—and omits

all mention of his ancestors beyond his grandmother, and leaves even the time of his birth a blank. "The researches of the learned," says Mr. Mosheim (a standard Christian author), "though long and ably conducted, have been unable to fix the time of Christ's birth with certainty." (Eccl. Hist. p. 23.) Wonderful admission, truly, as it is an evidence that nothing else can be fixed "with certainty," with respect to the history of "the man Christ Jesus," only that his doctrines and precepts were all borrowed perhaps during the twenty-seven dark and mysteries years of his life, if not an Essene by birth.

24. There is no escaping the conclusion that Christianity is a *borrowed system*—an outgrowth and remodeling of Budhism, with a change of name only. A thousand facts of history prove and proclaim it, and the verdict of posterity will be unanimous in affirming it.

25. From the almost endless chain of analogies, exhibiting a striking resemblance even in their minute details of Christianity and Budhism, we are compelled to conclude that one furnished the materials for the other; that one is the offspring—the legitimate child—of the other. And as it is a settled historical fact that Budhism is much the older system, there is hence no difficulty in determining which is the parent and which is the child.

26. In the Hindoo story of the creation of the human race, we find Adimo and Heva given as the names of the first man and woman answering to our Adam and Eve. And our Shem, Ham, and Japheth are traceable to their Sherma, Hema, and Jiapheta; the difference in the mode of spelling is probably owing to the difference in the languages. And under the new era we have Christ Jesus answering to their Chrishna Zeus, as some writers give the name of the eighth Avatar. And for Maia, a godmother, we have Mary. And other similar analogies might be pointed out besides the long string of strikingly similar events previously presented in the history of the two Saviors (Christ and Chrishna), amounting to hundreds.

27. Such an almost countless list of similar and nearly identical incidents bids defiance, and absolutely sets at naught all attempts to account for it as a mere fortuitous accident. There is no other explanation possible but that Christianity is a re-vamp or re-establishment of Budhism.

28. Here let it be noted that Christianity was not the only religion which was rehabilitated in the Alexandrian schools. On the contrary, all the popular oriental systems then in active being had long previously passed through the same representative theological schools and creed-making institutions of that royal and commercial city. All were remodeled in its theological workshops— a fact which accounts most conclusively for the same train of religions ideas and historical incidents being found in the later sacred books of each. And besides, Sir William Jones says, "The disciples of these various systems of religion had intercourse with each other long before the time of Christ, which would necessarily bring about a uniformity in the doctrines and general character of each system."

29. The disciples of all the religious systems cited their initiatory miracles as a proof of being on familiar terms with God Almighty. They all (as is claimed) healed the sick; all restored the deaf, the dumb, and the blind; all cast out devils, and all raised the dead. (See chapter on Parallels.) In fact, all their miracles and legendary marvels run in parallel lines, because all were recast in the

same creed-mold in Alexandria. A coincidence is thus beautifully explained, which would otherwise be hard to account for.

30. Mr. Gibbon says, "It was in the school of Alexandria that the Christian theology appears to have assumed a regular and scientific form" (Decline, &c., chap. xv.); that is, the regular and scientific form of Budhism or Essenism.

31. Pregnant with meaning is the text, "It was in the city of Antioch the disciples were first called Christians." (Acts xi. 36.) Here is conclusive proof that the disciples of the Christian faith were not always known by the same name, and were not at first called Christians. Then what were they called during the earlier years of their history?

Here is a great and important query, and one involving a momentous problem. Couple the two facts together, that the disciples were first known as Christians at Antioch, and that the Essenian order of believers expired and went out of history about that period, and the question is at once and forever satisfactorily settled. It was not an infrequent act on making important changes in a religion, and adopting some new items of faith to change the title of the system, and give it a new name.

After Alexander Campbell had made some modifications in his previous religious faith, and started a new church, his followers were popularly called Campbellites. Elias Hicks ingrafted some reform ideas into the Quaker faith, and instituted a new society of that order. Hence, and henceforth, his disciples were known as Hicksites. In like manner Jesus Christ having made some innovations in his inherited Jewish faith (which was of the Essene stamp) by ingrafting more of the Budhist doctrine into it, his followers were henceforth called Christians. How complete the analogy! Here let it be borne in mind, as powerfully confirmatory of this conclusion, that the first Christians were (as history affirms) "merely reformatory Jews." The twelve chosen were all Jews, probably of the Essene order. According to the Rev. Mr. Prideaux (Jewish History), the Jews of this order were first called Israelites, in common with the other tribes; then Chassidim; and thirdly Essenes. And finally, after the Essenian Jesus Christ, with some new radical ideas, proclaimed, "Ye have heard it hath been said by them of old time" thus and so, "but I say unto you" differently. The title was again changed, and they adopted or received the name of Christians—the Essenes going out of history at the very date Christians first appear in history. Put this and that together, and the chain is welded. Thus we can as easily trace the origin of Christianity as we can trace the origin of a root running beneath the soil in the direction of a certain tree. History, then, proclaims that to the honest, pious, deeply-devout, self-denying, yet ignorant, slothful, and filthy Budhistic Essenes must be awarded the honor or dishonor of giving birth to that system of religion now known as Christianity.

CHRISHNA AS A GOD—ADDITIONAL FACTS.

The following additional facts relative to the history, character, life, and teachings of Zeus Chrishna, or Jeseus Christna (as styled by one writer) are drawn mostly from the Vedas, Baghavat, Gita (Bible in India).

164

1. *His Virgin Mother, her Character.*—The holy book declares, that "through her the designs of God were accomplished. She was pure and chaste; no animal food ever touched her lips; honey and milk were her sustenance; her time was spent in solitude, lost in the contemplation of God who showered upon her innumerable blessings; she looked upon death as the birth to a new and better life; when she traveled, a column of fire in the heavens went before her to guide her. One evening, as she was praying, she heard celestial music, and fell into a profound ecstasy, and being overshadowed by the spirit of God, she conceived the God Chrishna." (Baghavat, Gita).

2. *Chrishna, his Life and Mission.*—This sin-atoning God was about sixteen when he commenced active life. Like Christ, he chose twelve disciples to aid him in propagating his doctrines. "He spent his time working miracles, resuscitating the dead, healing lepers, restoring the deaf and the blind, defending the weak against the strong, and the oppressed against the oppressor, and in proclaiming his divine mission to redeem man from original sin, and banish evil, and restore the reign of good." (Baghavat, Gita.) It is declared that he came to teach peace, charity, love to man, self-respect, the practice of good for its own sake, and faith in the inexhaustible goodness of the Creator; also to preach the immortality of the soul, and the doctrine of future rewards and punishments, and to vanquish the prince of darkness, Rakshas. It is further declared that "Brahma sent his son (Chrishna) upon the earth to die for the salvation of man." "His lofty precepts and the purity of his life spread his fame throughout all India, and finally won for him more than three millions of followers." "He inculcated the sublimest doctrines, and the purest morals, and the grand principles of charity and self-denial." "He forbade revenge, and commanded to return good for evil, and consoled the feeble and the unhappy." "He lived poor, and loved the poor." "He lived chaste, and enjoined chastity." "Problems the most lofty, and morals the most pure and sublime, and the future destiny of man, were themes which engaged his most profound attention."

"Chrishna, we will venture to say (says the Bible in India) was the greatest of philosophers, not only of India, but of the entire world." "He was the grandest moral figure of ancient times." (Bible in India.) "Chrishna was a moralist and a philosopher." "We should admire his moral lessons, so sublime and so pure." "He was recognized as the 'Divine Word.'" "He received the title of Jeseus, which means pure Essense." Chrishna signifies the "Promised of God," the "Messiah." "When he preached, he often spoke from a mount. He also spoke in parables. 'Parable plays a great part in the familiar instructions of this Hindoo Redeemer.'" He relates a very interesting parable of a fisherman who was much persecuted by his neighbors, but who in the time of a severe famine, when the people were suffering and dying for the want of food, being so noble as to return good for evil, he carried food to these same persecuting enemies, and thus saved them from starvation. "Therefore," said he "do good to all, both the evil and the good, even your enemies."

His addresses to the people were simple, but to his disciples they were elevated and philosophical. Such was the wisdom of his sermons and his parables, that the people crowded around him, eager to behold and hear him, "saying, This is indeed the Redeemer promised to our Fathers." Great multitudes followed him, exclaiming, "This is he who resuscitates the dead, and heals the lame, and the deaf, and the blind." On one occasion, as he entered Madura (as Christ once entered Jerusalem), "the people came out in flocks to meet him, and strewed branches in his way." On another occasion two women approached him, anointed him with oil, and worshiped him. When the people murmured at this waste, he replied, "Better is a little given with an humble heart than much given with ostentation." Such was his sense of decorum, that he admonished some girls he once observed playing in a state of nudity on the bank of a river after bathing. They repented, asked his forgiveness, and reformed. "The followers of Chrishna practiced all the virtues, and observed a complete abnegation of self (self-denial), and lived poor, hoping for a reward in the future life. They occupied all their time in the service of their Divine Master. Pure and majestic was their worship." Chrishna had a favorite disciple *Adjaurna*, who sustained to him the relation of John to Christ, while Angada acted the part of Judas by following him to the Ganges and betraying him.

3. *His last Hours.*—"When Chrishna knew his hour had come, forbidding his disciples to follow him, he repaired to the bank of the River Ganges; and having performed three ablutions, he knelt down, and looking up to heaven, he prayed to Brahma." While nailed to the cross, the tree on which he was suspended became suddenly covered with great red flowers, which diffused their fragrance all around. And it is said he often appeared to his disciples after his death "in all his divine majesty."

4. *The second Advent of Chrishna.*—"There is not a Hindoo or a Brahmin who does not look upon the second coming of Chrishna as an established article of faith." Their holy bibles (the Vedas and Gita) prophesy of him thus: "He shall come crowned with lights; he shall come, and the heavens and the earth shall be joyous; the stars shall pale before his splendor; the earth will be too small to contain him, for he is infinite, he is Almighty, he is Wisdom, he is Beauty, he is all and in all; and all men, all animated beings, beasts, birds, trees, and plants, will chant his praises; he will regenerate all bodies, and purify all souls." "He will be as sweet as honey and ambrosia, and as pure as the lamb without spot, or as the lips of a virgin. All hearts will be transported with joy. From the rising to the setting of the sun it will be a day of joy and exultation, when this God shall manifest his power and his glory, and reconcile the world unto himself." Such are a few of the prophetic utterances of his devout and prayerful disciples.

"We find," says a writer, "in all the theogonies of different countries the hope of the advent of a God (either his first or his second coming)—a hope which sprang from a sense of their own imperfections and sufferings, which naturally induced them to look for a divine Redeemer."

5. *Precepts of Chrishna.*—Numerous are the prescriptive admonitions found in the holy books which set forth the religion of "this heathen demigod" (so called by Christian professors). They appertain to all the duties of life, but are too numerous to be quoted here. Those appertaining to woman enjoin the most sacred regard for her rights, such as "woman should be protected with tenderness, and shielded with fostering solicitude." "There is no crime more odious than to persecute woman, or take advantage of her weakness." "Degrade woman and you degrade man." For other similar precepts, see Chapter XXXII. The injunctions to read their holy bible (the Vedas, &c.) are quite numerous, such as, "Let him study the holy Scriptures unceasingly" "Pray night and morning, and read the holy Scriptures in the attitude of devotion." And many of them read it through upon their knees. (See Chap. XLIV.) We have not space for a further exposition of this subject here; but it will be found more fully set forth in the pamphlet, "Christ and Chrishna Compared," which will, perhaps, become an Appendix to this work.

166

It may be objected that there are precepts and stories to be found in the religion of this Hindoo God (Chrishna), which reflect but little credit or honor upon that religion. This is true. And similar reflections would materially damage the religion of Christianity also. The story of Christ beating and maltreating the money-changers in the temple, his cursing an innocent, unoffending, and unconscious fig tree, and his indulgence in profane swearing at his enemies,—"O ye fools and blind, ye generation of vipers, how can you escape the damnation of hell!"—does not reflect any credit upon his religion, viewed as a system. Defects, then, may be found in both systems. In viewing the analogies of the two religions, it should be noted that the Hindoos claim, with a forcible show of facts and logic, that the religion of Christianity grew out of theirs. It has not been long since a learned Hindoo maintained this position in a public debate with a missionary. If all these facts effect nothing in the way of inducing the Christian clergy to confess the falsity of their position in claiming their religion to be a direct emanation from God, it will be a sad commentary upon either their intelligence or their honesty.

These historical facts, with those set forth in the preceding chapters, prove that the religion called Christianity, instead of being, as Christians claim, "the product of the Divine Mind," is the product of "heathen" minds; i. e., a spontaneous outgrowth of the moral and religious elements of the human mind. And therefore, for God to have revealed it over again to the founders of Christianity would have been superfluous, and a proof of his ignorance of history.

Note.—The author deems it proper to state here, with respect to the comparison between Christ and Chrishna, that some of the doctrines which he has selected as constituting a part of the religion of the Hindoo Savior, are not found in the reported teachings of that deified moralist. But as they appear to breathe forth the same spirit, it is presumed he would have indorsed them, had they come under his notice. As Christians assume the liberty to arrange the doctrines of Paul and Peter under the head of Christianity because claimed to be in consonance with the religion of Christ, though not all taught by him, the author, in like manner, has assumed, that some doctrines taught by other systems and religious teachers of India accord with those taught by Chrishna, and hence has arranged them with his. The author's purpose is not to set forth the doctrines of any sect, any system, or any religious teacher, but to show that all the doctrines of Christianity are traceable to ancient India. But whether taught by this sect or that sect, it is foreign to our purpose to inquire; and hence, for convenience, he has arranged them all into one system, and designated them Chrishnianity (borrowing a new term). There can be no more impropriety, he presumes, in arranging the doctrines of the various conflicting sects of India into one system (including even Brahminism and Budhism), than to arrange, as Christians do, the doctrines taught by the antagnostic system of Catholicism and Protestantism, and their six hundred conflicting sects, under the head of Christianity. Hence, Christians, of course, will not fault the arrangement. The classification above alluded to comprises, in part, the religion of many of the Hindoo sects, but does not set forth all their doctrines, only those analogous to Christianity. Chrishna was a Vishnuite, and not a Brahmin, as some writers assume. He and Christ were both reformers, and departed from the ancient faith. Vishnuism appears to have finally centered in Budhism.

CHAPTER XXXIII. APOLLONIUS, OSIRIS, MAGUS, ETC.—GODS

MIRACULOUS ACHIEVEMENTS OF OTHER GODS AND DEMI-GODS OF ANTIQUITY.

THE age in which Christ flourished, as before remarked, was pre-eminently an age of miracle. The practice of thaumaturgy, and the legends invested with the display of the miracle-working power, both preceding and subsequent to that era, rose to a great height. "All nations of that time," says a writer, "were mightily bent on working miracles." And the disciples who acted the part of biographers for the various crucified Gods and sin-atoning Saviors, throughout the East, seemed to vie with each other in setting off the lives and histories of their favorite objects of worship respectively, with marvelous exploits and the pageantry of the most astounding prodigies. And the miracles in each case were pretty much of the same character, thus indicating a common course for their origin,—all probably having been cast in the same mold—in the theological schools of the once famous, world-renowned city of Alexandria, the capital of Egypt. Having, in the preceding chapters, presented the miraculous achievements of the Hindoo Gods, Chrishna and Saki, we will here bring to notice those of other Gods.

THE MIRACLES RECORDED OF ALCIDES, OSIRIS, AND OTHER GODS OF EGYPT.

1. We have the miraculous birth by a virgin in the case of Alcides.

2. Osiris, while a sucking infant in his cradle, killed two serpents which came to destroy him.

3. Alcides performed many miraculous cures.

4. According to Ovid he cured by a miracle the daughter of Archiades.

5. Also the wife of Theogenes, after the doctors had given her up.

6. And both these Gods converted water into wine.

7. Both of them frequently cast out devils.

8. Julius declares Alcides raised Tyndarus and Hippo-litus from the dead.

9. When Zulis was crucified, the sun became dark and the moon refused to shine.

10. Both he and Osiris were resurrected by a miracle.

12. Both ascend to heaven in sight of many witnesses.

12. And finally we are told that from Alexandria the whole empire became filled with the fame of these miracle-workers, who restored the blind to sight, cured the paralytic, caused the dumb to

speak, the lame to walk, &c. All these miracles were as credibly related of these Gods as similar miracles of Jesus Christ.

MIRACLES PERFORMED BY PYTHAGORAS AND OTHER GODS OF GREECE.

1. Pythagoras was a spirit in heaven before he was born on earth.

2. His birth was miraculously foretold.

3. His mother conceived him by a specter (the Holy Ghost).

4. His mother (Pytheas) was a holy virgin of great moral purity.

5. Plato's mother, Paretonia (says Olympicdorus), conceived him by the God Apollo.

6. Pythagoras in his youth astonishes the doctors by his wisdom.

7. Was worshiped as the "Son of God," "Paraclete," "Child of Divinity," &c.

8. Coaid see events many ages in the future (says Richardson, his biographer).

9. Could bring down the eagle from his lofty height by command.

10. Could approach and subdue the wild, ferocious Daunian bear.

11. Could, like Christ, appear at two places at once.

12. Could walk on the water and travel on the air.

13. Could discern and read the thoughts of his disciples.

14. Could handle poisonous reptiles with impunity.

15. Cured all manner of diseases.

16. Restored sight to the blind.

17. He "cast out devils."

18. Jamblicus says he could allay storms on the sea.

19. Raised several persons from the dead.

20. And, finally, "a thousand other wonderful things are told of him," says Jamblicus.

With respect to his character, it is said that "for humility, and practical goodness, and the wisdom of his moral precepts, he stood without a rival." He discarded bloody sacrifices, discouraged wars, forbade the use of wine and other intoxicating drinks, enjoined the forgiveness of enemies and their kind treatment, and also respect to parents. He was a special friend to the poor, and taught that they were the favorites of God. "Blessed are ye poor." He practiced and recommended the silent worship of God. He retired from the world, and often fasted, and was a great enemy to riches (like Jesus Christ). He considered poverty a virtue, and despised the pomp of the world. He recommended (like Christ) the abandonment of parents, relations, and friends, houses and lands, &c., for religion's sake. His disciples, like those of Christ, had a common treasury and a general community of goods, to which all had free access, so that there was no poverty or suffering amongst them while the supply lasted. All shared alike. In fact, with respect to the spirit of his precepts, his moral lessons, and nearly his whole practical life, he bore a striking resemblance to Jesus Christ, and presented the same kind of evidence, and equally convincing evidence, of being a God. And as he was born into the world five hundred and fifty-four years before Christ, the latter probably obtained the materials of his moral system from that Grecian teacher, or in the same school of the Essenian Budhists, in which both Pythagoras and Christ appear to have taken lessons.

MIRACLES OF THE ROMAN GODS QUIRINUS AND PROMETHEUS.

1. Prometheus was honored with a miraculous birth.

2. Quirinus was miraculously preserved in infancy, when threatened with destruction by the tyrant ruler Amulius.

3. He performed the miracles, according to Seneca and Hesiod, of curing the sick, restoring the blind, raising the dead, and casting out devils.

4. Both these Gods were crucified amid signs, and wonders, and miracles.

5. All nature was convulsed, and the saints arose when they were crucified.

6. The sun was also darkened, and refused to shine.

7. Both descended to hell, and rose from it by divine power.

8. And Prometheus was seen to ascend to heaven.

We cite these lists of miraculous events as if real facts, not because we believe they were such, but as possessing the same degree of credibility as those related of Jesus Christ.

MIRACLES AND RELIGION OF APOLLONIUS OF TYANA.

1. Everything was subject to his miraculous power.

2. He performed many miraculous cures.

170

3. He restored sight to the blind.

4. He cast out devils, which sometimes "cut up" like those of Christ

5. He enabled the lame to walk.

6. He re-animated the dead.

7. He could read the thoughts of bystanders.

8. Sometimes disappeared in a miraculous manner.

9. Caused a tree to bloom, while Christ made another tree to wither away.

10. The laws of nature obeyed him.

11. Could speak in many languages he had never learned.

12. Was at one time transfigured, like Christ

13. His birth was miraculously foretold by an angel.

14. Was born of a spotless virgin.

15. There were demonstrations of joy and singing at his birth.

16. Exhibited proofs in infancy of being a God.

17. Manifested extraordinary wisdom in childhood.

18. He was called "the Son of God."

19. Also "the image of the Eternal Father manifested in the flesh."

20. He was also styled "a prophet."

21. Like Christ, he retired into mystic silence.

22. His religion was one of exalted spirituality.

23. He taught the doctrine of "the Inner Life."

24. He possessed exalted views of purity and holiness.

25. Like Christ, he was a religious ascetic.

26. His religion, as in the case of Christ, forbade him to marry.

27. He ate no animal food, and would wear no woolen garments.

28. Gave his substance to the poor.

29. Eschewed love for wine and women.

30. Refrained from artificial ornaments and sumptuous living.

31. He was a high-toned moral reformer.

32. He condemned external sacrifices.

33. Also condemned gladiatorial shows.

34. He religiously opposed dancing and sexual pleasures.

35. He recommended the pursuit of wisdom.

36. Was of a serene temper, and never got angry.

37. Was a true prophet, foresaw and foretold many future events.

38. Foresaw a plague, and stopped it after it had commenced.

39. Crowds were attracted by his great miracles and his wisdom.

40. He disputed with and vanquished the wise men of Greece and Asia, as Christ did the learned doctors in the temple.

41. When imprisoned by Domitian and loaded with chains, he disinthralled himself by divine power.

42. He was followed by crowds when entering Alexandria, like Christ when entering Jerusalem.

43. Was crucified amidst a display of divine power.

44. He rose from the dead.

45. Appeared to his disciples after his resurrection.

46. Like Christ, he convinced a Tommy Didymus by getting him to feel the print of the nails in his hands and feet.

47. Was seen by many witnesses after his resurrection, and was hailed by them as the "God Incarnate," "the Lord from Heaven."

48. He finally ascended back to heaven, and now "sits at the right hand of the Father," pleading for a sinful world.

49. When he entered the temple of Diana, "a voice from above was heard saying, 'Come to heaven.'"

50. Accordingly he was seen no more on earth only as a spirit

The reader will observe that the foregoing list of analogies, drawn from the history of Apollonius, as furnished us by his disciple Damos and his biographer Philostratus, are found also, in almost every particular, in the history of Jesus Christ. And the list might have been extended. It is declared, "A beauty shone in his countenance, and the words he uttered were divine," which reminds us of Christ's transfiguration. And his "staying a plague at Ephesus" revives the case of Christ stilling the tempest on the waters. Now, the question very naturally arises here, How came the histories of Apollonius and Christ to be so strikingly alike? Was one plagiarized from the other? As for the miraculous history of Apollonius being reconstructed from that of Jesus Christ, as some Christians have assumed, there is not the slightest foundation for such a conclusion, as the following facts will show, viz.:—

1. The Cappadocian Savior (Apollonius) was born several years anterior to the advent of the Christian Savior, and appeared at an earlier date upon the stage of active life, and thus got the start of Christ in the promulgations of his doctrines and the exhibition of his miracles. Christ's active life, Christians concede and the bible proves, did not commence till about his twenty-eighth or thirtieth year, which was long after Apollonius had inaugurated his religion, and long after he had commenced the promulgation of his doctrines, and attested them by wonderful miracles, according to his biographer Philostratus.

2. The New American Cyclopedia tells us, "Apollonius labored for the purity of Paganism, and to sustain its tottering edifice against the assaults of the Christians." So that, being placed in a hostile attitude toward the representatives of the Christian faith, it is not likely he would condescend to borrow their doctrines and the miraculous history of their incarnate God, to invest his own life with. He was probably one of the "anti-Christs" spoken of in the New Testament; but this circumstance reflects nothing dishonorable upon his character; for some of those distinguished personages denounced as "anti-Christ," by Christ's gospel biographers, were, according to impartial history, noble, honest, and righteous men. Their only offense consisted in robbing Christ of his divine laurels, by claiming similar titles, and claiming to perform the same kind of miracles; and there is as much proof that they did achieve these prodigies as that Christ did.

3. The early Christian writers conceded that Apollonius and the other oriental Gods did perform the miracles which are ascribed to them by their respective disciples, but accounted for it by the childish expedient of obsession. Christ was assumed to perform miracles by divine power, they

by the power of the devil—a childish and senseless distinction truly, and one which can have no logical force in this enlightened age.

MIRACLES AND CLAIMS FOR SIMON MAGUS. B. C.

1. It is declared, "he was in the beginning with God."

2. That "he existed with God from all eternity."

3. That "he took upon himself the form of a man."

4. That "he was the Son of God," "the Word," &c.

5. That "he was the second person in the godhead."

6. That "he came down to destroy the devil and his works."

7. That "he was the image of the Eternal Father."

8. That "he was the first-born Son of God."

9. That he could control the elements.

10. That he could walk on the air as Christ did on the water.

11. Could move anything by the command, "Be thou removed."

12. That he could raise the dead.

13. That he could transform himself into the image of any man.

14. That he was "the Paraclete, or Comforter."

15. That he came to "redeem the world from sin."

16. Finally, he was the world's "Savior," "Redeemer," "the Only Begotten of the Father," and "through his name men are to be saved."

The reader will call to mind that this Simon Magus is mentioned and condemned in the Acts of the Apostles, for offering to pay Peter for a bestowment of the gift of the Holy Ghost. And yet every philosopher in this age must concede that Magus' assumption in the case is more sensible and philosophical than that of Peter's. For the latter calls it "a gift from God," whereas every person now acquainted with the nature, principles, and science of animal magnetism, knows that such manifestation as that which Peter ascribes to God and the Holy Ghost, is a simple natural phenomenon; and that, consequently, it can be no more a violation of the rules of propriety to pay for the labor of making such developments than it is to pay a teacher for developing the mind of a child. It was certainly a greater act of courtesy to offer to pay for it than to demand it as a gratuitous favor. Hence we infer he excelled Peter in his demeanor as a gentleman, especially as he bore Peter's severe reprimand with patience, and apparently with a better spirit than that which dictated it. And we may remark here, also, that notwithstanding this Samaritan Jew is so unsparingly denounced by the godly Peter, and by the early Christian fathers also, yet we have the historical proof that he was an honest, pious, and ardently devout man. His whole life was absorbed in the cause of religion, and his whole soul devoted to his religious duties and the worship of his God. Hence we think Peter's rebuke was uncalled for.

Let the reader note the fact here that there are three circumstances amply sufficient to account for bibles and religious books being profusely supplied with the reports of groundless miracles.

1. As everybody then believed in miracles (at least everybody who dared speak) there was nobody to investigate the reports of such occurrences, to learn whether they were true or false.

2. The few who attempted to disprove the truth of those miraculous occurrences now found reported in sacred history, had their books burned, as in the case of Porphyry and Celsus, in the early history of Christianity, who called in question the truth of bible miracles.

3. These marvelous facts were not usually recorded till long after the period in which they are said to have occurred, when the witnesses had left the stage of time, and every event exciting ay attention had grown to a monstrous prodigy. These circumstances, in an age of boundless credulity and scientific ignorance, which magnified every phenomenon, and looked upon every natural event as a direct display of divine power, accounts most fully and satisfactorily for the burdensome repetition of groundless miraculous stories found upon nearly every page of the sacred history of every religious nation. without driving us to the necessity of challenging the veracity of the writers who recorded them. They may all have been honest men.

CONFUCIUS OF CHINA, BORN 551 B. C.

This moral teacher, religious chieftain, and philosopher, though not subjected to the ignominious death of the cross, deserves a passing notice for the excellency of his morals and the acquisition of a world-wide fame. In the following particulars his history bears a strong analogy to that of Jesus Christ.

1. He commenced as a religious teacher when about thirty years of age.

2. The Golden Rule (see Chap. XXXIV.) was his favorite maxim.

3. Most of his moral maxims were sound and of a high order. The New American Cyclopedia says (vol. v. p. 604), "His writings approach the Christian standard of morality;" and in some respects they excel.

4. He traveled in different countries, preaching and teaching his doctrines.

5. He made a host of converts, amounting now to one hundred and fifty millions.

6. His religion and morals have been propagated by apostles and missionaries, some of whom are now traveling in this country, laboring to convert Christians to their superior religion and morals. "There was a time," says the work above quoted, "when European philosophers vied with each other in extolling Confucius as one of the sublimest teachers of truth among mankind."

In the following respects his teachings were superior to those of Christ:—

1. He taught that "the knowledge of one's self is the basis of all real advances in morals and manners." A lesson Christ neglected to teach.

2. "The duties man owes to society and himself are minutely defined by Confucius," says the Cyclopedia. Another important work Christ partially omitted.

He constructed several hundred beautiful and instructive moral maxims, which we have not space for here, and which amply prove that "the holiest truths were inculcated by pagan philosophers."

CHAPTER XXXIV. THE THREE PILLARS OF THE CHRISTIAN FAITH—MIRACLES, PROPHECIES, AND PRECEPTS

WHEN Christians are asked for the proof of the divinity of Jesus Christ, they point to his miracles and precepts, and the Messianic prophecies, said to have been fulfilled by his coming. And the same kind of evidence is adduced to prove the divine claims of their bible and its religion, including the Old Testament, which contains the prophecies. Their divine origin and supernatural character are claimed to be proved by the miracles, prophecies, and precepts found recorded in the Holy Book. All, then, stand or fall together—the divinity of Christ, and the divinity of the bible and its religion, all, rest on this threefold argument. All, it is claimed, are attested and proved by a threefold display of divine power, manifested,—

1. By the performance of various acts, transcending human power and the laws of nature, called Miracles.

2. By the discernment of events lying in the future which no human sagacity or prescience could have foreseen, unless aided by Omniscience; the display of such power being called Prophecy.

3. By the enunciation of Moral Precepts beyond the mental capacity of human beings to originate.

These three propositions cover the whole ground. They constitute the three grand pillars of the Christian faith, which, if shown to be untenable, must prostrate the whole superstructure to the ground. We will examine each separately, commencing with miracles.

I. Miracles the first Pillar of the Christian Faith.

We will not occupy space in discussing the various meanings assigned to the word miracle by different writers, but take the popular definition as given above, and proceed to inquire how much evidence can be deduced from the miracles represented as having been performed by Jesus Christ, toward proving his divinity and the truth of his religion. In the first place, it should be borne in mind that Christianity is not the only religion which appeals to miracles as a proof of its divine authorship. More than three hundred systems and sects are reported in history, most of which have, from time immemorial, gloried in being able to wield this knock-down argument as they claim it to be, in support of the truth and divine authenticity of their various systems of faith. We have briefly noticed some of the miraculous achievements reported in their sacred books, and ascribed to their Gods and sin-atoning Saviors, and compare them with similar ones related of Jesus Christ, commencing with Pagan Miracles.

As the whole pathway of religious history is thickly be-studded with miracles wrought in all ages and countries, and every page of the oriental bibles and religious books is literally loaded down with the relation of these marvelous prodigies said to have been wrought by their Gods, Demigods, and crucified Saviors, it places a writer in a quandary to know where to begin to make a selection. We will express no opinion here as to whether these astounding feats were ever witnessed or not; but will merely state that they come to us as well authenticated as those reported in the Christian bible. There is as much evidence that Zoroaster, at the request of King Gustaph, caused a tree to spring up in a man's yard forthwith, of such magnificent proportions that no rope could be found large enough to reach around it, as that Jesus Christ caused a fig tree to wither away by merely cursing it. And we have the same kind of evidence that the Hindoo Messiah, Chrishna, of India, restored two boys to life who had been killed by the bites of serpents, as that Jesus Christ resurrected Lazarus and the widow's son of Nain; and as much proof that Bacchus turned water into wine, as that Jesus performed this act six hundred years after. And a hundred other similar comparisons might be drawn. The evidence of the truth of these performances in both cases, pagan and Christian, is simply the report of the writer. If there are any exceptions to be made in either case of better evidence, it will be found in favor of pagan religion; for its adherents are able in many cases to point to imperishable monuments of stone erected in commemoration of their miracles. And Mr. Goodrich tells us this is the highest species of evidence that can be offered to prove the truth of any ancient event. But as Christians, on the other hand, can find no such evidence to prove the performance of any miracles reported in their bible, it will be seen at once that the pagan miracles are the best authenticated. The famous historian Pausanias states upon current authority that Esculapius raised several persons from the dead, and names Hippolytus among the number, and then points to a stone monument erected as a proof of the occurrence—thus furnishing, according to Christian logic, the most conclusive proof of one of the most astounding miracles ever wrought. And yet no philosopher or man of science in this age can credit the literal truth of the story. But a spiritualist can easily conceive that he and others might have mistaken the risen spirits of those resurrected persons for their physical bodies, because they know that many mistakes of this kind have occurred in modern times.

We might refer to many other cases of pagan miracles attested by monumental evidence if our space would permit—such as the names of many persons engraven upon the walls of the Temple of Serapis, miraculously carved by the God Esculapius. Strabo tells us the ancient temples are full of tablets describing miraculous cures performed by virgin-born Gods of those times, and names a case of two blind men being restored to sight by the son of God Alcides in the presence of a large multitude of people, "who acknowledged the miraculous power of the God with loud acclaim." Many spiritualists at the present day know by practical experience how these "miraculous cures" were performed. Without continuing the citation of cases, suffice it to say, the sin-atoning Gods of the orientals are reported as performing the same train of miracles assigned to Jesus Christ, such as performing astonishing cures, casting out devils, raising the dead, &c. Now, sadly warped indeed by education must be that mind which cannot see that if the account of such prodigies, reported in the history of Jesus Christ, can do anything towards proving him to have been a God, then the world must have been full of Gods long before his time. It is impossible to dodge or evade such a conclusion.

Christians are in the habit of assuming that all the miraculous reports in the bible are unquestionably true, while those reported in pagan bibles are mere fables and fiction. But if they will reverse this proposition, it can be easier supported, because we have shown their miracles are better attested and authenticated. Their own bible admits that the heathen not only could and did perform miracles, but miraculous prodigies of the most astonishing character, equal to anything reported in their own religious history—such as transmuting water into blood, sticks into serpents, and stones into frogs. In a word, it is admitted they performed all the miraculous feats of Moses with the single exception of turning dust into lice. But certainly making lice was not a more difficult achievement than that of making frogs, and this is admitted they did do successfully.

Hence it will be seen that the Egyptian pagans made as great a display of divine or miraculous power as "God's Holy People," according to the admission of the bible itself. And there is no intimation that the mode of performing the miracles was not the same in both cases, but a strong probability exists that it was, a conclusion confirmed by the bible report of the case which leads us to infer that they performed the miracles in the same way Moses did. For it is said, "The Egyptians did so with their enchantments"—that is, with the "enchanting rod" used on such occasions by the Egyptians, Assyrians, Babylonians, and other nations, including also the Jews. Now, as Moses always used the "enchanting rod" in performing miracles, called by him "the rod of God, the rod of divination," &c. (see Ex. iv.), there is thus furnished the most satisfactory proof that he performed his miracles on this occasion, as well as all other occasions, by the same stratagem as the Egyptians and other nations did. And even if the mode adopted by the Egyptians had been different, it is still admitted they performed the miracles. In the name of reason and common sense, then, we ask if such facts as here presented with the case just referred to do not forever prostrate and annihilate all arguments based on miracles toward proving the divine character or divine origin of the religion of the bible, or towards proving

Jesus Christ, or any other being reported to have performed miracles, as possessing divine attributes?

CATHOLIC MIRACLES.

Some of the most astonishing and best authenticated miracles ever performed by any religious sect we find reported in the history of the Roman Catholic church, looked upon and styled by the Protestants "the mother of Harlots and Abomination." And yet there is much stronger proof that the Catholic religion has the divine sanction, if miracles can furnish such proof. The editor of "The Official Memoirs" declares that during the Italian war in 1797, several pictures of the virgin Mary, situated in different parts of the country, were seen to open and shut their eyes for the space of six or seven months, and that no less than sixty thousand people actually saw this miracle performed, including many bishops, deacons, cardinals, and other officers of the church, whose names are given. And Forsyth's Italy (p. 344), written by a highly accredited author, tells us that a withered elm tree was suddenly restored to full life and vigor by coming in contact with the body of St. Zenobis, and that this miracle took place in the most public part of the town, in the presence of many thousands of people; that "it is recorded by contemporary historians, and inscribed upon a marble column now standing where the tree stood."

Now, the question may be asked here, Would the people have allowed such an impudent trick to insult them as the erection of a monument for an event that never took place? If not, how is the matter to be explained? These are only specimens of a hundred more Catholic miracles of an astonishing character at our command. Several queries may be entertained in the solution of these stories. 1st, Were some phenomena really witnessed on which these stories were constructed, but which got magnified from a molehill to a mountain before they found their way into history? or, 2d, Were they manufactured as a pious fraud, which was rather a fashionable business with the early disciples of the Christian faith, according to Mr. Mosheim? Whatever answer may be given to these questions will explain the miracles of the Christian bible, excepting those which can be accounted for on natural principles.

SATANIC MIRACLES.

Among all the workers of miracles reported in the bible the devil seems to have been pre-eminent, and hence must come in for the better end of the argument toward proving him to have been a God. No miracle could excel the act of his "transforming himself into an angel of light," as stated in 2 Cor. xi. 14. It is not transcended by any other case, not even by Christ's transfiguration. And according to Paul he was endowed "with all power, and signs, and lying wonders." (Thess. ii. 9.) If, then, he possessed "all power," Christ, and no other God, could have possessed a miraculous power superior to his, for "all" comprehends the whole, beyond which nothing can reach. Where, then, is the evidence to come from to prove that Christ was a God, because he was a miracle-worker, or his religion divine, because attested by miracles—seeing the devil performed some of the most difficult miracles ever wrought? Should we not then change his title from that of a demon to a God, and place his religion amongst the divinely endowed systems? St. John represents the "Evil One" as having power to make "fire come down from heaven in the sight of men," and 'to deceive those that dwell on the earth by means of those miracles which he hath power to do." (Rev. xiii.)

Here the question arises, What can a miracle prove, what end can it serve, or what good can possibly arise from the display of the miracle-working power, when it is liable "to deceive those that dwell upon the earth?" Certainly, therefore, it proves nothing, and accomplishes nothing. And may not the apostles themselves have been deceived in ascribing some of the miracles they record to Jesus instead of the devil? Certainly we are drifted upon the quicksands of uncertainty by such a display of the miracle-working power, and are obnoxious to most fatal deception, which proves the total inutility and futility of such prodigies.

CHRIST'S MIRACLES NOT HIS OWN, BUT WROUGHT THROUGH HIM AND NOT BY HIM.

How could Christ's miracles, assuming they were wrought, do anything toward proving his divinity, when he did not claim to be their author, but merely the agent or instrument in the hands of the Father, like the apostles, who are reported to have performed the same miracles? "The Father he doeth the work," is his own declaration. And the Apostles seem to have accepted his word, and his view of the matter. For proof listen to Peter: "Ye men of Israel, hear these words: Jesus of Nazareth, a man approved of God among you by miracles, and wonders, and signs, which God did by him in the midst of you, as ye yourselves do know." (Acts ii. 22.) Let it be noted, then, the Christ's miracles were not performed by him as a God, but as "a man approved of God;" he was the mere medium or instrument in the case—a fact which banishes at once all grounds for controversy relative to his miracles serving the purpose of attesting his divinity, especially when it is conceded that men, magicians, and devils could achieve the same feats.

CHRIST'S MIRACLES DID NOT CONVINCE THE PEOPLE.

As the miracles of Christ seem to have had little effect toward convincing the people of his claims to the godhead, it is evident they could have been but little superior to those performed by others, and therefore not designed, at least not calculated, to convince them that he was a God. The frequent instances in which he upbraids the people for their unbelief, and calls them fools, "slow of heart," &c., is a proof of this statement.

CHRIST'S MIRACLES NOT DESIGNED TO CONVINCE THE PEOPLE.

A circumstance involving pretty strong proof that Christ's miraculous achievements were not considered as evidence of his divinity, is the fact that they were frequently performed in private, sometimes in the night, and often under the injunction of secrecy. "See thou tell no man," was the injunction, after the feat was performed, perhaps, in a private room. How can such facts be reconciled with the assumption that his miracles were designed to convince the people of his claims to the Divine Entity, as Christians frequently assert, when the people were not allowed to witness them, nor his disciples even to report them? Who can believe that he was a Divine Being, or Messiah, when he charged his disciples to "tell no man" that he was such a Being? Such incongruities verge to a contradiction. It is a logical contradiction to say that private miracles were designed to dissolve public skepticism. And yet many, if not most, of his reputed miraculous achievements were of this character. When he cured a blind man, he not only "led him out of the town" (Mark viii. 23), but forbid him, when his sight was restored, returning to the city, for fear he would publish it. When he resurrected Lazarus, he did not call the whole country around to witness it, but performed the act before a private party. The reanimation of Jairus's daughter was in the same concealed manner, in a private room, where nobody was admitted but his three confidential disciples (Peter, James, and John) and the parents, none of whom make any report of the case. How, therefore, the reporter (Mark) found it out, when he was not present, and none of the party were allowed to tell it to anybody, or why he should betray his trust by publishing it, if he was informed of it, is a "mystery of Godliness" not easily divined.

When Christ cleansed the leper, he sent him to the priest, enjoining him to "say nothing to any man." The dumb, when restored to speech, was not allowed to exhibit any practical proof of the fact by using his tongue. His miraculous perambulation on the surface of the sea (walking on the water) was not only alone, but in the dark. His transfiguration, likewise, according to Dr. Barnes, took place in the night, his three favorite companions being the only witnesses, and they "heavy with sleep." And finally, the crowning miracle of all, the resurrection, is not only represented as taking place in the night, but without one substantial or terrestrial witness to report it. Verily such facts as these are not calculated to augment the faith or work the conviction of a skeptic that these miracles were ever performed, seeing so few are reported as witnessing them, and even their testimony is not given. We have not the testimony of one person who claims to have been present and seen these wonders performed. Such facts are calculated to cast distrust upon the whole matter, especially when taken in connection with the fact that nine tenths of his life form a perfect blank in history. Is it possible, we ask, to reconcile such a fact with the belief of his divinity? Is it possible a God could lead a private life, or live twenty-seven years on earth, and do nothing worthy of note—a God known to nobody and noticed by nobody? Most transcendingly absurd is such a thought. Had Christ possessed the character that is claimed for him, not an hour of his life could have passed unaccompanied by some remarkable incident that would have been heralded abroad, and its record indelibly engraven upon the page of history; but instead of this, his acts were too commonplace to be noticed.

ALL HISTORY IGNORES HIM.

The fact that no history, sacred or profane,—that not one of the three hundred histories of that age,—makes the slightest allusion to Christ, or any of the miraculous incidents ingrafted into his life, certainly proves, with a cogency that no logic can overthrow, no sophistry can contradict, and no honest skepticism can resist, that there never was such a miraculously endowed being as his many orthodox disciples claim him to have been. The fact that Christ finds no place in the history of the era in which he lived,—that not one event of his life is recorded by anybody but his own interested and prejudiced biographers,—settles the conclusion, beyond cavil or criticism, that the godlike achievements ascribed to him are naught but fable or fiction. It not only proves he was not miraculously endowed, but proves he was not even naturally endowed to such an extraordinary degree as to make him an object of general attention. It would be a historical anomaly without a precedent, that Christ should have performed any of the extraordinary acts attributed to him in the Gospels, and no Roman or Grecian historian, and neither Philo nor Josephus, both writing in that age, and both living almost on the spot where they are said to have been witnessed, and both recording minutely all the religious events of that age and country, make the slightest mention of one of them, nor their reputed authors. Such a historical fact banishes the last shadow of faith in their reality.

It is true a few lines are found in one of Josephus's large works alluding to Christ. But it is so manifestly a forgery, that we believe all modern critics of any note, even of the orthodox school, reject it as a base interpolation. Even Dr. Lardner, one of the ablest defenders of the Christian faith that ever wielded a pen in its support, and who has written ten large volumes to bolster it up, assigns nine cogent reasons (which we would insert here if we had space) for the conclusion that Josephus could not have penned those few lines found in his "Jewish Antiquities" referring to Christ. No Jew could possibly use such language. It would be a glaring absurdity to suppose a leading Jew could call Jesus "The Christ," when the whole Jewish nation have ever contested the claim with the sternest logic, and fought it to the bitter end. "It ought, therefore" (says Dr. Lardner, for the nine reasons which he assigns), "to be forever discarded from any place among the evidences of Christianity." (Life of Lardner by Dr. Kippis, p. 23.)

As the passage is not found in any edition of Josephus prior to the era of Eusebius, the suspicion has fastened upon that Christian writer as being its author, who argued that falsehood might be used as a medicine for the benefit of the churches. (See his Eccles. Hist.) Origen, who lived before Eusebius, admitted Josephus makes no allusion to Christ. Of course the passage was not, then, in Josephus. One or two other similar passages have been found, in other authors of that era, which it is not necessary to notice here, as they are rejected by Christian writers. It must be conceded, therefore, that the numerous histories covering the epoch of the birth of Christ chronicle none of the astounding feats incorporated in his Gospel biographies as signalizing his earthly career, and make no mention of the reputed hero of these achievements, either by name or character. The conclusion is thus irresistibly forced upon us, not only that he was not a miracle-worker, but that he must have led rather an obscure life, entirely incompatible with his being a God or a Messiah, who came "to draw all men unto him." And it should also be noted here that none of Christ's famous biographers, Matthew, Mark, Luke, or John, are honored with a notice in history till one hundred and ninety years after the birth of Christ. And then the notice was by a Christian writer (Ireneus).

"We look in vain," says a writer, "for any cotemporary notice of the Gospels, or Christ the subject of the Gospels, outside of the New Testament. So little was this 'king of the Jews' known, that the Romans were compelled to pay one of his apostles to turn traitor and act as guide before they could find him. It is impossible to observe this negative testimony of all history against Christ and his miracles, and not be struck with amazement, and seized with the conviction that he was not a God, and not a very extraordinary man." Who can believe that a God, from off the throne of heaven, could make his appearance on earth, and while performing the most astounding miracles ever recorded in any history, or that ever excited the credulity of any people, and be finally publicly crucified in the vicinity of a great city, and yet all the histories written in those times, both sacred and profane, pass over with entire silence the slightest notice of any of these extraordinary events. Impossible—most self-evidently impossible!! And when we find that this omission was so absolute that no record was made of the day or year of his birth by any person in the era in which he lived, and that they were finally forgotten, and hence that there are, as a writer informs us, no less then one hundred and thirty-three different opinions about the matter, the question assumes a still more serious aspect. From the logical potency of these facts we are driven to the conclusion that Christ received but little attention outside of the circle of his own credulous and interested followers, and consequently stands on a level with Chrishna of India,

Mithra of Persia, Osiris of Egypt, and other demigods of antiquity, all whose miraculous legends were ingrafted in their histories long after their death. This leads us to consider

HOW CHRIST'S INCREDIBLE LEGENDS GOT INTO HIS HISTORY.

There is a remarkably easy and satisfactory way of accounting for all the marvelous feats and incredible stories found in the Gospel narratives of Jesus Christ, without assuming their reality or any intentional fraud or falsehood by the writers. When we learn that none of his evangelical biographies were penned (as Dr. Lardner affirms) till long after his death, we are no longer puzzled for a moment to understand exactly how many statements wholly incredible and morally impossible crept into his history, without challenging or calling in question the veracity or honesty of the writer. Perhaps the most powerful cord of moral conviction which holds the Christian professor to a belief in the divinity of Jesus Christ, is the difficulty of bringing himself to believe that the numerous miracles ascribed to him in the Gospels are merely the work of fiction, fabricated without a basis of truth, when they were evidently penned by men of the deepest piety and the strictest moral integrity. We ourselves were once environed with this difficulty. But it stands in our way no longer. We are disenthralled. We have solved the problem. We have found the true explanation. The key and clew to the whole secret is found in the simple fact, admitted by Christian writers and evidenced by the bible itself, that *no history of Christ's practical life was written out by a person claim-ing to have been an eyewitness* of the events reported, nor until every incident and act of the noble-minded Nazarene had had ample time to become enormously magnified and distorted by rumor, fable, and fiction; so that it was impossible to discriminate or separate the real from the unreal, the true from the false, in his partly-forgotten life. It could not be done. A true history could not then be, nor have been written under such circumstances. It is manifestly impossible. The time for writing each Gospel is fixed by Dr. Lardner as follows, viz.: Matthew 62 A. D., Mark 64 A. D., Luke 63 or 64 A. D., and John 68 A. D.; thus allowing ample time for every noteworthy incident of his life to grow from molehills to mountains, and to swell into fiction, fable, and prodigy, a tendency to which was then very rife and very prevalent in all religious countries. Having made a note of this fact, let the reader treasure in memory, as another equally important fact, that the biography of no man of note who figured in that era, or who lived prior to the dawn of letters (if penned many years after his death, as was frequently the case), is free from a large percentage of extravagant detail, and simple incidents magnified into miracles. This was the uncurbed tendency of the age which ultimated into universal custom.

The simplest incident in every man's life, who exhibited mind enough to attract attention, by rolling from year to year, and passing from mouth to mouth, invariably got to be finally swelled into such undue and enormous proportions, that it could only be accounted for by assuming the actor to have been a God. In this way many men of different countries, who had made a mark in the world, received divine honors and divine attributes, including such characters as Chrishna of India, Mithra of Persia, Quirinus of Rome, Eras of the Druids, Quexalcote of Mexico, Jesus Christ of Judea, and many others who might be mentioned. This circumstance deified them. The evidence of history to prove this declaration is abundant and irresistible.

POSTHUMOUS HISTORIES ALONE DEIFIED MEN.

To the two important facts above cited, viz., that Jesus Christ's evangelical histories were all written long after his death, and that unwritten histories of great men always become swollen and distorted with the lapse of time, let the reader add the equally significant fact that there is in all cases a vast difference in the biographies of famous men, penned during their actual lives, or immediately subsequent to their death, while every act and incident of their career was fresh and vigorous in the minds and memories of the cotemporaneous people, and before the ball of exaggerated rumor was set rolling, compared with those written at a later date, after molehills of fact had become mountains of fiction. The former are natural and reasonable, the latter unnatural and extravagant, and often fabulous. We will cite a few cases in proof. Let the reader compare the biographical sketches of Alexander the Great written near the epoch of his practical life, and those composed since the dawn of the Christian era, and he will find that the posthumous notices of him alone contain the story of the sun becoming obscured, and the earth developed in darkness, at the time of his mortal exit. It will be found, also, that Virgil's account of "the sheeted dead," rising from their graves at the time of Caesar's death, and which was written long after that famous hero left the stage of action, is omitted in all the cotemporary notices of that monarch, having crept in subsequently.

In like manner, the various miracles recorded of Pythagoras by his biographer Jamblicus,—such as his walking on the air, stilling the tempest, raising the dead, &c.,—are not related of him by any cotemporaneous writers who lived in the era of his practical life. And let the reader compare, also, Damos' life of Apollonius with that of his later biography by Philostratus, as an illustration of the same historical fact. Mahomet and his biograhers might be included in the same category. It is a remarkable circumstance that neither Mahomet himself nor any of his immediate followers claim for him more than the humble title of prophet, or "God's holy prophet," while his later admirers and devout disciples have elevated him to the throne of heaven, and given him a seat among the Gods.

And this historical analysis might be extended much farther if necessary. But cases enough have been cited to prove the principle and establish the proposition. And what is the lesson taught by these facts? A deeply-instructive and all-important one. From the foregoing historical illustrations we are impelled to the important conclusion, that the tissue of extravagant and incredible stories of demigod performances which run as a vein of fiction through the Gospel narrations of Jesus Christ, all grow out of long-continued rumor, in an age when the imagination was untamed and unbounded, and credulity uncurbed by a practical knowledge of the principles of science, and consequently the pen of the historian had lawless scope. All difficulty then vanishes, and the question is put forever at rest by assuming that if the Gospel histories of Jesus had been written by men who claimed to record only what they saw and heard themselves, we should have a more credible and instructive history of the great Judean reformer, freed from those Munchausen prodigies and that wild romance which mar the beauty and credibility of those now in popular use. This conclusion is not only natural, but irresistible, to a mind untrammeled by education and unbefogged by priestcraft. All that is wanting to convince us that miracles constitute no part of the real history of Christ, is a cotemporary instead of a posthumous biography—a history written in the age which knew him, and by an unprejudiced writer who witnessed all his movements. And we are perfectly willing to risk our reputation in this life, and our salvation in the next, by stating our conviction that this will be the unanimous verdict of posterity before fifty generations pass away.

184

CHRIST'S MIRACLES RECONSTRUCTED FROM FORMER MIRACLES.

There are other circumstances than those noticed in the preceding chapter, which can aid us very materially in solving the problem of Christ's divinity; or, in other words, can aid us in tracing his miracles to their origin, and thus confirm the truth of the preceding proposition. Moses and the prophets were considered by the evangelists antetypes or archetypes of the coming Savior. Hence some of the more important incidents of their lives were hunted up and worked over again, to make them fit the life of Christ as the Messiah, reconstructed and applied to him as the second Moses, and a new prophet; for Moses is represented as saying, "A prophet shall the Lord your God raise up like unto me." Hence Moses comes in with the prophets as an antetype of Christ. The transfiguration of Christ is therefore constituted after the model of the transfiguration of Moses on Mount Sinai. And Christ is represented as raising the dead, not only because Elijah and Elisha had performed such miracles, but did it under circumstances which prove, as they suppose, he possessed superior power. For while they could only reanimate the body immediately after the breath had left it, Christ could raise a man after he had been dead four days (the case of Lazarus). Hence the New Prophet was superior to the old, and more like a God—the thing they desired to prove. Both Elijah and Christ are represented as raising a widows son,— Elijah being considered the special prototype of Christ, who, many believed, had re-appeared under the changed name of Elias. (See John v. 17.) And then we observe that while Elisha exhausted his skill in making three gallons of oil, Christ could make thirty gallons of wine— another proof of the superiority of the New Prophet. Then, again, the miracle of feeding one hundred men with twenty loaves is far excelled by the latter, who feeds five thousand men with five loaves. And both prophets, Elisha and Christ, encountered unfordable streams in their travels; the expedient of the former is to make a passage, but Christ performed the greater miracle of walking on the surface. And while Moses had to send the leper without the camp before he could heal him, Christ could heal him instantly with a single touch. The same slaughter of the infants is commanded by Herod, in order to destroy Christ, that Pharaoh had ordered to effect the destruction of Moses. And thus many of the miracles of Jesus can be accounted for as reconstructions of former miracles. It was simply a competition or rivalry between the New Messianic prophet and the old prophets. The New Prophet excels and comes off victorious in every case, and is thus considered to be a God. The object of the competition is to show that while the prophets, assisted by God, could perform marvelous deeds, Christ, being God himself, could perform greater. This was to be the proof of his being a God, that he could outvie the servants of God in every miraculous thing ascribed to them. This was one way adopted to prove his divinity.

CHRIST'S MIRACLES MANUFACTURED FROM PROPHECIES.

Several of Christs miracles seem to have grown out of the Messianic prophecies; that is, were manufactured in order to fulfill the prophecies. There was, as we learn by the Gospels, an impression deep and wide-spread among the disciples of Christ, that the Old Testament was full of texts foretelling the advent of their Messiah, and foreshadowing his practical life. Under this conviction, a number of passages are quoted in the Gospels from the prophets as referring to Christ, but which, however, the context shows could not possibly have been written with any such thought or intention. Matthew has five miracles appertaining to Christ, built on prophecies, in his first two chapters. And they are represented as taking place "in order that the prophecy might be fulfilled," that is, Matthew, writing sixty-four years after Christ's advent, assumes those miracles had taken place because the prophecy required their performance, and hence recorded it as a fact without knowing it to be such. A great deal of that kind of license was assumed in that and subsequent ages, as the facts of history are ample to prove. It was done under the religious conviction that the cause of God and the church required it to be done, and that therefore it was justifiable.

STRICT VERACITY NOT REQUIRED OR OBSERVED.

It is by no means necessary to assume that the recorders of the New Testament miracles knew they had been performed, or that they would hesitate to record them as facts because they did not know them to be such. We are under no moral obligation to suppose they knew anything about it. People in that age were not so nice or so morally exact, as to require proof of a thing before they stated it, or never to state it unless they had the proof for its being true. We would be Very far from accusing the apostolic writers of malicious falsehood, or criminal misrepresentation. But we find that the disciples of all religions, in that age of the world, considered it not only allowable, but a religious duty, in the absence of knowledge, to supply omissions by guess-work or conjecture; that is, to use assumption in the place of proof, and to state that a thing was so when there was no proof of it whatever, and even when the proof was against it. All religious history is full of the exhibition of this kind of elasticity of conscience. Even a species of pious lying was considered justifiable in many cases. Paul furnishes evidence of this, when he says, "If the truth of God hath more abounded through my lie unto his glory, why am I judged a sinner?" (Rom. iii. 16.) "No sin to lie for the glory of God," seems to be the teaching of this text. Although Paul does not clearly disclose for what purpose this policy was employed, yet it can easily be inferred. A part of the important business of the New Testament writers was to build a reputation for Christ and his inspired band of disciples for working miracles. A fame for achieving "signs and wonders" was the great set off of the age. There seems to have been an almost boundless competition amongst the disciples of the various religious orders, including Jews, Pagans, and Christians, as to who could, or whose God could outstrip all competitors in achieving astonishing prodigies that should set the laws of nature at defiance. And no devout disciple, who had good inventive powers, would allow any rival to outdo him. Nothing could authenticate the claim of the adopted Messiah to the throne or heaven, or a participation in the Divine Essence, like a miraculous display of divine power. Hence the history of all the Gods and demi-gods of the illiterate ages, including that of Christ, is loaded down with miraculous feats. There is the clearest proof that Christ's disciples were in this general rivalry—this universal miracle-working *mêlée*.

Two things very necessary to be accomplished, in the estimation of the apostles, were, first, to show that Christ outdid the heathen Gods, and even the prophets, in the display of the wonder-exciting miraculous power, and thus proved his divinity; and second, that the prophecies had been fulfilled in his coming and his practical life. And there is reason to believe all the New Testament miracles are founded on and grew out of prophecy. For, although we do not find prophecies in the Old Testament for every miracle related of Christ, yet it is probable, if we had the Book of God, "the Book of Jehu," "the Like of Hezekiah," and other lost books mentioned in the Old Testament, we should find the supposed prophecy for every miracle of the New Testament. We should there find the key to every miracle. The true explanation of the matter seems to be, that the apostolic writers, looking through the Old Testament, and finding texts therein which they believed to be prophetic of the display of the miraculous power of Jesus, and passages which they religiously believed foreshadowed his coming and mission, or some important event in his history, they were impressed with the deepest conviction that God would not suffer any prophecy to go unfulfilled. But when they sat down to write the history of their Messiah, long after his death, they found they had not the evidence before them that the prophecies had been fulfilled. A third of a century had rolled away since his history had been practically before the people. The subject of their narrative had long since gone to "the house of many mansions," and left not a note, or scratch of a pen, of any act of his life behind him. And the current of time had washed away, or partially obliterated, nearly every event of his earthly career. The witnesses had nearly all left the stage of action, and their voices were forever hushed in the silent tomb. What was to be done in such an emergency? It was all-important to show that the prophecies had been fulfilled to the letter in his practical life. This quandary, however, did not beset them long. The difficulty was easily surmounted. Every religious country, including Judea, was full of miraculous legends and astonishing prodigies appertaining to the terrestrial movements of their Gods and demigods, some of which had floated down on the stream of tradition from time immemorial. And all had become blended, confounded, and mixed up together, until it was impossible to know whence they originated, where they belonged, or to what God they appertained. These miraculous stories were so numerous, and so varied in character, that there was no little difficulty in finding which seemed to be the fulfillment of any Messianic prophecy that had been or might be found in the Old Testament; and thus of the hundreds of miraculous stories afloat, one was picked out and assumed to be the fulfillment of the prophecy. With the countless number of such stories before them, which had been for half a century current in the community, they set themselves to work to select and reject, prune and remodel, honestly believing that this miracle was intended to fulfill this prophecy, and that miracle that prophecy, &c. And accordingly we now find it so stated in the New Testament. As, for example, a story had long been going the rounds that the parents of a young God had to flee with him out of the country, to save his life from being destroyed by its jealous ruler. This they supposed must of course refer to Jesus, because they had found a supposed prophecy of such an event in the Jewish bible, when a more thorough acquaintance with history would have taught them that the story did not refer to the ruler of Judea (Herod), but to Cansa, an ancient, jealous, despotic king, who ruled India at a much earlier period. And the story of the darkness at the crucifixion they incorporated as a part of the history of Jesus, because they had seen a text in Joel which they supposed presaged such an event, while, if they had been well versed in oriental history, they would have known that it had long been recorded as the last chapter in the earthly drama of the Hindoo God Chrishna. And so of the other miracles now found related as a part of the history of Jesus. A historical investigation of the matter would have shown the Gospel writers that they were a part of the written history of other and more ancient Gods, and had never formed a part of the practical life of Jesus, or been realized in his experience. This is a more charitable and honorable explanation of the matter than that found in the assumption of some other writers, that every miracle was constructed for the occasion—that it is a sheer fabrication; and yet there are some plausible grounds for this solution of the case.

These critical writers tell us there was a religious persuasion deeply enstamped upon the minds of all religious countries, that God often justified a departure from the truth—the conscientious or veracious faculty being in that age but feebly developed. And the bible itself is full of

187

evidence to establish the allegation. The prophets often disclose it, and the apostles were their strict imitators. Ezekiel represents God as saying, "If a prophet is deceived, I the Lord deceived that prophet." (Ezek. xiv. 9.) And Jeremiah asks God, "Wilt thou be to me as a liar?" (Jer. xv. 8.) While the writer of Kings represents God as putting a lying spirit into the mouth of his own prophets, (i Kings xxii. 23.) And most certainly if God himself might thus habitually depart from the truth, it was an ample warrant for his apostles, as well as the prophets, to adopt the same expedient. The case of Paul lying for the glory of God, which we have cited from Romans iii. 4, proves they were morally capable of doing this. Mosheim tells us that among the early Christians, "it was an almost universally adopted maxim, that it was an act of virtue to deceive and lie, when by so doing they could promote the interest of the church." (Mosh. vol. i. p. 198.) And Mr. Higgins informs us that "great numbers, of every age and of every religion, have been guilty of systematic frauds and falsehoods to support their religions, to an extent of which we can have no conception. They not only practiced it, but they reduced it to system. They avowed it, and they justified it by declaring it to be meritorious to lie in a good cause." (Ana. vol. i. p. 143.) The reader who can hesitate to credit these statements only betrays his ignorance of the moral weakness of human nature, and the imperfect growth in that era of the veracious faculty, which consequently had but a feeble voice in the councils of the mind. Even the most pious and devout professors of religion did not consider a rigid conformity to truth necessary, or morally obligatory, in their labors to promote the glory of God and the salvation of souls. And when direct falsehood was not resorted to, the writer still allowed himself to color, magnify, and invent largely; that is, to draw copiously upon the resources of his imagination, in the way of supplying omissions and defects, and filling out missing links in the chain of history. And hence it is that all ancient sacred history is so profusely inlaid with stories and statements manifestly fabricated for the occasion, without any historical support, and therefore wholly incredible. Let the Christian reader not, however, misapprehend us by supposing we wish to drive him to the extreme alternative of accepting this as the true explanation, or as indicating the real origin of the incredible stories and senseless miraculous feats interwoven into the Gospel life of Jesus. We only offer it as a plausible, but not as the probable explanation. The above citations from the Scriptures and other history prove most clearly that sacred writers were morally capable of fabricating or manufacturing history to supply assumed omissions. And this explanation is twofold more reasonable than to accept the miracles as real occurrences, for such a belief would be at war with common sense, and prostrate our reason beneath our feet. But there is no necessity of adopting lying hypotheses, while the borrowing theory is amply adequate to account for every Gospel miracle. There is not a miraculous story or incredible legend incorporated in the New Testament as a part of the history of Jesus, that was not afloat in some shape or form, on the wings of tradition in nearly every religious country, ages before his birth. The model for each and every miracle was already constructed, was already in the market, and already a part of the history or tradition of other and older Gods. And all that was wanted to make it appear as a part of the history of the Christian's deified Jesus, was to fill in names and dates. Yes, history with a hundred tongues proclaims it as the real explanation of the incredible and the impossible in the history of Jesus Christ. And the evidence is so voluminous and so overwhelming to disprove the common Christian dogma which makes the son of Joseph and Mary a miracle-working God (a portion of which we have presented under the several propositions of this chapter), that it really demolishes the last timber in the Christian fabric, and leaves it a heap of ruins. And we are certain that if we could divest the Christian reader's mind, for a few moments, of an inherited and fostered prejudice, he would see that our explanation is much more rational, more probable, more beautiful than the popular belief, which degrades the illustrious Judean reformer to a level with the heathen thaumaturgist, and gives him the same undignified reputation as a miracle-worker.

But we are sometimes told we are under as much moral obligation to believe in the miracles reported of Jesus, as to believe in any other portion of his history; that we must accept his Gospel history as a whole, or reject it in toto. But this is manifestly a false assumption, and one easily exploded. No person who is acquainted with Grecian history doubts that Alexander the Great was born in Macedonia, and founded a city in Egypt bearing his own name. Yet not one of those readers will credit for a moment what one of his biographers relates of him, that he stopped the sun in its course, or that he had no human father. We all accept Pythagoras as a real entity, while we reject the story of his walking on the air. Are we morally bound to accept Romulus and Remus, founders of Rome, as mere fabulous beings, because their biographers relate the incredible story of their being suckled by a wolf? Many other illustrations might be given in proof of the falsity of the assumption that because a portion of a man's biography is found to be incredible, the whole must be rejected as false, as unworthy of credence. This would be to annihilate history. For no biography of any person, and no history of any nation, can be accepted as plenarily pure, unmixed truth. There is always more or less chaff with the grain, and it is our privilege and our duty to separate them. And by so doing we not only confer a favor on the cause of truth, but add to the luster and honor of the name of the deceased reformer; and especially is this true of the renowned Judean philanthropist and reformer. Much more lovely and beautiful would his evangelical history stand before the world if stripped of the wild, the weird, and the miraculous. Much more interesting is he when viewed and venerated as a man than when worshipped as a God, guilty of the frequent violation of his own laws, by the display of the miracle-working power.

And much more beautiful and much more rational is the doctrine which accepts every event that ever occurred as the legitimate and harmonious operation of the great machinery of nature, than as the smart trick, the lawless caprice or wild feat, of an arbitrary, wonder-exciting God, performed not to make the people better, more moral or more righteous (for miracles cannot do this), but merely to make them gape and stare, and shout, What a smart God we have got!

And then the belief in miracles involves an utter repudiation of all law, all order, and all system, and introduces in their stead chaos, anarchy, and universal confusion. It is simply "the doctrine of chance." which all orthodox Christendom professes to deprecate and execrate as the quintessence of atheism. But they make a mistake; "chance" is more legitimately the fruit of miracle than of atheism; an assertion which we will here briefly prove.

If the sun may be arrested in his course through the heavens, "the moon turned into blood," and "the stars fall from the heaven,"—sticks turned into serpents, water into blood, and dust into lice,—all of which orthodox Christians profess to believe were witnessed in the days of Moses and Christ, then everything is thrown upon the wheel of chance; everything is involved in uncertainty. If the course of nature could be arrested, or the natural qualities of objects changed by the prayer of a prophet, patriarch, or apostle, then the food set before us to eat may suddenly, in compliance with the prayers of some absent saint, become a deadly poison; the clothes we wear may be instantly transformed into virulent adders, which may inflict the fatal sting before we suspect it; some favorite servant of God (a Moses or an Elijah) might be this moment praying to God to stop the dews from falling, or the rain from descending for the next three months, or three years, as the latter is reported as doing (see James v. 17), so that we could not plant with any certainty that the seed would grow, or that we should be rewarded by a crop. Such would be the incertitude, such the "chance" against us in everything in which we might engage, if it were true that God ever intercepts the action of his laws by working a miracle, that we should eventually become discouraged by this chaos of "chance," the wheels of industry would stop, and the car of civilization go backward. If it were true, as taught by orthodox Christians, that "God in his providence," or "God in the dispensation of his providence," often "visits people with sickness," then it would be useless to study the laws of health with a view of complying with them. For we could not know in any case whether our sickness had been brought upon us by, an "overruling providence," or by our own imprudence. Our inventives to study and comply with these laws, if there could be any, would consequently be very weak indeed, for we might comply with every physiological requisition, and yet there would be several "chances," against us that to-morrow we may be stretched upon a "sick bed and rolling pillow by the visitation of God." Thus the doctrine of miracles is shown to be pre-eminently the doctrine of "chance."

The doctrine of miraculous agency makes God an imperfect being, by implying that his laws were defective in their original construction, that by mistake he left some emergency unprovided for, and now has to supply the omission by an afterclap exercise of power. Or if his laws were originally perfect, then the working of a miracle would disturb them, and make them imperfect; if originally imperfect, then God himself must have been imperfect, and hence no God at all. Think of a wonderworking God violating, suspending, or intercepting his own laws. Such a God would be a puerile, short-sighted being, that only ignorant and uncultivated minds could admire and adore.

The age of miracles, however, is gone. The belief in divine prodigies has receded before the advancing genius of civilization. It has died away in the exact ratio of the progress of science and general intelligence. And a thorough acquaintance with nature's laws will banish the last vestige of such a belief. Hence it is that the most illiterate and ignorant nations and tribes have always been able to recount the longest list of miraculous prodigies achieved by a disorderly God, who seems to have taken pleasure in violating his own laws, or suspending them, for the most trivial purposes.

Yes, the time is approaching when the belief in a "miraculous interposition" or "special providences" must pass away under the lights of science and civilization, and be numbered amongst the things which have been and can be no more, and men will cherish more noble and elevated ideas of the great Ruler of the universe, who is infinite in order, infinite in wisdom, ay, infinite in all his attributes and virtues, ever unchangeably the same.

II. Prophecy, the second Pillar of the Christian Faith, proves as much for Heathenism and Spiritualism.

Truthful prophecy, attested to be such by its fulfillment, is assumed to be one of the basic pillars and one of the main proofs of the truth of the Christian religion. But the following consideration will show that this assumption has no logical force, or real, tangible foundation.

First. Every ancient system of religion had its prophets and seers, who professed to be able to foresee events of the future. And we find but little difference in the proofs each one has left to the world that they possessed this power, if we except the Greeks and Romans, some of whom evidently excelled all the Jewish prophets in their ability to take cognizance of events lying behind the curtain of time. Tacitus, the Latin historian, prophesied the downfall of the Roman empire and its attendant calamities more than five hundred years before its occurrence, which was fulfilled to the letter. And Solon, one of the seven wise men of Greece, foresaw and foretold a series of calamities which befell the Athenians two hundred years before they were realized. A still more remarkable example is furnished in the history of Marcus Tullius Cicero, who, writing of the future, with his mind fixed on the west, about 50 B. C., exclaimed, "There will arise after many ages (if we may credit the Sibyline oracles), a hero who will deliver his oppressed countrymen from bondage"—a prophecy most signally fulfilled in the life of General Washington. Many other examples of heathen prophecy and their fulfillment might be cited, if we had space for them.

Second. The history of modern spiritualism furnishes many cases of future events being predicted long before they took place. In fact, many of the most important events of modern times which have occurred in this and other countries, were foreseen and foretold by spiritual seers known as "seeing mediums," when there was not the slightest probability that such events would ever occur. We will cite one or two cases, by way of proof and illustration. A few years ago John P. Coles, of New York, known as a spiritual medium, prophesied, when under spirit control, that Nicholas of Russia would shortly have difficulty with his secretary Menzicoff, and just three months from that time would die—a prediction that was fulfilled to the very letter and to the very hour. And yet there was not the slightest probability, externally indicated, at the time the prophecy was uttered, that either of these events would ever be realized. And this prophecy, let it be noted, was published in the New York Times at least two months before it was verified, thus proving that the prediction was not an "afterclap" affair, but preceded the event. Take another example. The serious calamity which befell the ill-fated steamer known as the Arctic, which was lost at sea a number of years ago, with all on board, was prophetically described in minute detail, by a spirit medium, several months before it occurred; and was seen and described by another medium, while taking place more than a thousand miles distant. The proof is at our command. And the late disastrous war was foreseen and described by Cora Tappan, of New York, and other mediums, and its principal events pointed out long before the war broke out—a fact which is now a matter of history. These are only a few cases out of hundreds that might be cited of a similar character, drawn from the practical history of modern spiritualism. If, then, prophecy can do anything toward the truth or divine emanation of the Christian religion, it must do the same for the heathen and spiritual systems. And thus proving too much, it proves nothing at all.

Third. The Jewish prophecies not fulfilled. We have examined critically the various texts of the Christian bible called prophecies, and find that, if claimed as predictions of the future events beyond the powers of the natural mind to foresee, they have all failed. But few of them have been fulfilled in any sense, and those few required no divine prescience to foresee the result. Many events have transpired in every country, which the natural sagacity of the most observant minds in that country had anticipated as the result of natural causes, such as the ravages and downfall of cities and the overthrow of empires by the merciless hand of war. The Jewish prophet, fostering a spirit of envy and enmity towards Egypt, Babylon, and other superior kingdoms, because they had been overpowered by them and long held in subjection to their superior sway, were always prophesying evil things of these principalities. And though some of the evils which constituted the burden of prophecy might have been reasonably anticipated as natural occurrences, it is a signal fact they never transpired at all,—such as the total destruction of Babylon, Tyre, Damascus, and other cities belonging to those hostile kingdoms the Jews so much envied and execrated. Look, for proof, at the case of Damascus. The prophets Isaiah, Jeremiah, and Ezekiel, all poured out their fulminatory thunders upon this city. Isaiah declared it should be a "ruinous heap." (Isa. xvii. I.) And Jeremiah predicted its destruction by fire. (Jer. xlix. 27.) And yet, notwithstanding these predictions of ruin, Damascus still stands as "one of the paradises of the earth," as one writer styles it, with a population, according to Burckhart, of not less than two hundred and fifty thousand, being one of the most magnificent and prosperous commercial cities on the globe. Instead of being blotted out of existence, as the Jewish prophets prayed and predicted, it has suffered less by ravages of war and the scythe of time than almost any other city of the east. It has stood nearly three thousand years without becoming a "ruinous heap," or being consumed by fire or destroyed by war. (Jer. xlix. 26.) And the prophecy against Tyre has most signally failed also. Ezekiel declared it should be destroyed by Nebuchadnezzar, and never be found again. (Ezek. xxvi.-xxix.) But two hundred and fifty years after Nebuchadnezzar's time Alexander found it a strong commercial city. And it still contains a population of five thousand or more. St. Jerome, of the fourth century, declared it to be then the finest city of Phoenicia, and was astonished that Ezekiel's prophecy had so utterly failed.

And Isaiah's famous prediction against Babylon furnishes another proof of the utter failure of Jewish prophecy. He declared, after predicting its destruction, "It shall never be inhabited, neither shall it be dwelt in from generation to generation, neither shall the Arabian pitch tent there." (Isa. xiii. 20.) Of course he desired it should be so. But, unfortunately for his credit as a prophet, it never suffered such a calamity. On the contrary, according to Layard and Rawlinson, British commissioners who recently visited the place, it now presents "all the activity of a hive of bees" (to use Layard's language), and contains several thousand inhabitants, though its name is, since rebuilt, called Hillah. And thus the prophecy is falsified. "No," exclaims a good Christian brother, in forlorn hope, it may be fulfilled yet. But if he will examine the language of the prophecy, he will find he is entirely cut off from this "saving clause." The prophet says, "Her time is near to come, and her days shall not be prolonged." (Isa. xiii. 22.) Thus it is evident the prophecy was to be fulfilled in that age and generation. The failure, then, is absolute and indisputable. And these are but mere samples of the complete failure of every text called a prophecy, when applied to the prognostication of future events. Numerous texts can be found in the prophets auguring evil for Egypt, which have made no approximation toward fulfillment. Ezekiel prophesied "the fall of Egypt," "the desolation of Egypt," "the destruction of Egypt," &c., not one of which calamities has ever been realized in her experience. Prophecies respecting the restoration of the lost tribes and the perpetuity of the Israelitish throne are complete failures; also all "the Messianic prophecies," so called. (See Chap. II.) With respect to the prophecy on Babylon, it may be further observed that while the prophet declares, "Neither shall the Arabian pitch tent there" (Isa. xiii. 22), Layard declares that is the very thing they did do while he was there. He says he saw a number of Arabian tents pitched on the ground; thus proving a failure of the prophecy all round in every particular. (See note page Fourth). The bible itself is a witness that truthful prophecy can do nothing toward authenticating a religion, or toward proving the prophet divinely inspired. The same damaging concession is made here as in the case of miracles, that a heathen and an unbeliever could and did succeed as well as the true disciples of the faith. The proof of this statement is found in the history of Balaam. His figurative representation of a star coming out of Jacob and a scepter out of Judah (see Numb. chap. xxiv.) is often quoted by Christian writers as presaging or prefiguring the coming of Christ,—thus making a heathen and an unbeliever the oracle of a Messianic prophecy, and a heathen, too, of sinful and ungodly habits. So that the Christian subterfuge is not available here, that "God might make a righteous man of any nation the vehicle of prophecy." For we have the express declaration of the bible itself that he was not a righteous man, but the very reverse. Peter tells us, "He loved the wages of unrighteousness," at the very time this prophecy so called was uttered (see 2 Peter ii. 13), which prostrates forever the Christian plea the "he might have possessed the true spirit of prophecy by virtue of being a righteous man," and drives us to the admission that an unconverted savage and ungodly heathen unbeliever could make a true prophecy. It not being necessary, then, to be a Jew, or a Christian, or a believer, or even a moral man, to foresee or foretell the far-off important events of the future, the argument falls forever to the ground that the fulfillment of the Jewish prophecies, if admitted to have been fulfilled, could do anything toward proving the truth or divine acceptance of the religion of the bible, or its superiority over any heathen or oriental religion then or subsequently known to history, as they all present the same evidence of being endowed with the true spirit of prophecy. All argument for Christianity based on the prophecies, or "the gift of prophecy," is, then, forever at an end, as it has been shown that the power to foretell future events is not restricted by the bible itself to any nation, to any religion, to any faith, to any belief, or to any moral or religious qualification. What, then, is prophecy worth, or what does it prove? Another case, and one similar to that of Balaam in its essential points, is found in the New Testament. Caiaphas, though not claiming to be any part of a believer, utters a prophecy in the interest of the Christian religion for which the bible itself gives him full credit as a prophet. Here, then, is another case of a heathen stealing the Christian's thunder, and another proof that the spirit of true prophecy has never been confined to any nation or any religion; and hence, according to the teachings of the bible itself, does nothing at all toward establishing the exalted claims of Christianity, or toward proving its superiority over other systems of religion.

III. Moral Precepts the third Pillar of the Christian Faith.

It is declared, in view of the many wise precepts which issued from the mouth of Jesus Christ, that "he spake as never man spake." (John vii. 46.) If this were true, then Gods must have been very numerous prior to the Christian era. For there is not one of the moral maxims or preceptive commands which he gave utterance to that cannot be found literally or substantially in the older bibles of other nations, or the writings of the Greek philosophers, and the religious dissertations of heathen moralists, who gave out moral and religious lessons for the instruction of the world long prior to the birth of Christ. Even the Golden Rule, which Christian writers, ignorant or oriental history, have erroneously ascribed to Jesus Christ, and lauded him as being the author of, is found variously expressed in the writings of several heathen or oriental nations. We find it in the Chinese bible at least five hundred years older than ours, almost word for word as Jesus uttered it. We will here present it as expressed by different writers.

1. Golden Rule by Confucius, 500 B. C.

"Do unto another what you would have him do unto you, and do not to another what you would not have him do unto you. Thou needest this law alone. It is the foundation of all the rest."

2. Golden Rule by Aristotle, 385 B. C.

"We should conduct ourselves toward others as we would have them act toward us."

3. Golden Rule by Pittacus, 650 B. C.

"Do not to your neighbor what you would take ill from him."

4. Golden Rule by Thales, 464 B. C.

"Avoid doing what you would blame others for doing."

5. Golden Rule by Isocrates, 338 B. C.

"Act toward others as you desire them to act toward you."

6. Golden Rule by Aristippus, 365 B. C.

"Cherish reciprocal benevolence, which will make you as anxious for another's welfare as your own."

7. Golden Rule by Sextus, a Pythagorean, 406 B. C.

"What you wish your neighbors to be to you, such be also to them."

8. Golden Rule by Hillel, 50 B. C.

"Do not to others what you would not like others to do to you."

Here is the Golden Rule proclaimed by seven heathen moralists and a Jew long before it was republished by the founder of Christianity; thus proving it to be of heathen origin, and proving that it does not transcend the natural capacity of the human brain to originate, and hence needs no God to reveal it. Indeed, it is one of the most natural sentiments of the human mind. "Would I like to be treated thus?" is the first thought which naturally arises in the mind of a person when maltreating a neighbor; thus showing that the Golden Rule is a spontaneous utterance of the moral feelings of the human mind.

LOVE AND KIND TREATMENT OF ENEMIES.

Love to enemies is considered to be another praiseworthy precept, which Christ has erroneously the credit of being the author of. We have heard the declaration made in the Christian pulpit, that Jesus Christ was the first moral teacher who inculcated love to enemies; a most transcendent error, as the following historical citations will show. Most of the religious books and religious teachers of the ancient oriental heathen breathe forth a spirit of love and kindness toward enemies.

The following is from the old Persian bible, the Sadder:—

1.

> "Forgive thy foes, nor that alone;
> Their evil deeds with good repay;
> Fill those with joy who leave thee none,
> And kiss the hand upraised to slay."

The Christian bible would be searched in vain to find a moral sentiment or precept superior to this. Certainly it is the loftiest sentiment of kindness toward enemies that ever issued from human lips, or was ever penned by mortal man. And yet it is found in an old heathen bible. Think of "kissing the hand upraised to slay." Never was love, and kindness, and forbearance toward enemies more sublimely expressed than in the old Persian ballad.

2. "Treat thine enemy as though a friend, and he will become thy friend," was expressed by Publius Syrus, a Roman slave, which is a wiser admonition than that of Christ, "Love thine enemy," as it is a moral impossibility.

3. "All nature cries aloud, 'Shall man do less than heal the smiter, and the railer bless?'" (Hafiz, a Mahomedan.)

4. "Bridle thine anger, and forgive thine enemy; give unto him who takes from thee." (Koran, Mahomedan bible.)

5. "Let no man be offended with those who are angry at him, but reply gently to those who curse him." (Code of Menu.)

6. "Let him endure injuries, and despise no one." (Ibid.)

7. "Commit no hostile action for your own preservation." (Ibid.)

8. "To be revenged on enemies, become more virtuous." (Diogenes.)

9. "To strike a man, or vex him with words, is a sin." (Zend-Avesta, Persian bible.)

10. "Even the intention to strike is a sin." (Ibid.)

11. "Desire not the death of thine enemy." (Confucius.)

12. "Acknowledge benefits, but never revenge injuries." (Ibid.)

13. "We may dislike an enemy without desiring revenge." (Ibid.)

14. "Pardon the offenses of others, but never your own." (Publius Syrus.)

15. "The noble spirit cures injustice by forgiving it." (Ibid.)

16. "It is much better to be injured than to kill a man." (Pythagoras.)

17. "You can accomplish by kindness what you cannot by force." (Publius Syrus.)

18. "Better overlook an injury than avenge it." (Publius Syrus.)

19. "It is enough to think ill of an enemy without avenging it." (Publius Syrus.)

20. "It is a kingly spirit to return good deeds for evil ones." (Ibid.)

21.

```
"Learn for yon orient shell to love thy foe,
And store with pearls the hand that brings thee woe;
Flee, like yon rock, from base, vindictive pride,
Emblaze with gems the wrist that rends thy side."

(Hafiz.)
```

22. "To revenge yourself on an enemy, make him your friend." (Pythagoras.)

23. "It is not permitted to a man who has received an injury to revenge it by doing another." (Socrates, in his Crito.)

24. "Seek him who turns thee out, and pardon him who injures thee." (Koran.)

25. "Return not evil for evil." (Socrates.)

26. "Endure all things if you would serve God." (Sextus.)

27. "Desire to be able to benefit your enemies." (Ibid.)

28. "Receive an injury rather than do one." (Publius Syrus.)

29. "Be at war with men's vices, but at peace with their persons." (Ibid.)

30. "Cultivate friendship for an enemy." (Pittacus.)

31. "Be kind to your friends that they may continue so, and to your enemies that they may become so." (Ibid.)

32. "Prevent injuries if possible; if not, do not revenge them." (Ibid.)

33. "An enemy should not be hated, but cured." (Seneca.)

34. "To act unkindly toward an enemy will increase his hate." (Antonius.)

35. "Be to everybody kind and friendly." (Ibid.)

36. "Speak evil of no one, not even your enemies." (Pittacus.)

Thus it will be observed that love and kindness toward all mankind, both friends and enemies, is not confined to the teachings of Christ or to the Christian religion, as many have erroneously supposed, but is unquestionably a natural sentiment of the moral instinct or moral impulses of the human mind, and hence is no proof that their teacher is either a God or divinely inspired.

And we have in our possession nearly eight hundred more precepts (see vol. ii.) from the pens or mouths of the ancient heathen, enjoining just and kind treatment of women, and setting forth nearly all the duties of life, and teaching the immortality of the soul, &c. And these precepts breathe the same lofty moral sentiment and moral feeling as those quoted above. How ignorant and how conceited must be the Christian professor who supposes all goodness is confined to Christianity, or that it even possesses any great superiority over other religious systems! And how completely the three foregoing parts of this chapter, "Miracles," "Prophecies," and "Precepts," prostrate the divine claims of Christianity, and leave not an inch of ground for them to rest upon!

CHAPTER XXXV. LOGICAL OR COMMON SENSE VIEW OF THE DOCTRINE OF DIVINE INCARNATION

THE incarnation of an infinite God is a shocking absurdity, and an infinite impossibility. We ask in all solemn earnestness, and in the name of the intuitive monitions of an unshackled reason and an unbiased conscience, can any man in his sober senses, who has been in the habit of reflecting before he believes, entertain for a moment the monstrous absurdity that the Almighty and Infinite Maker of the universe was once reduced to a little wailing infant, lying in senseless and helpless weakness on the lap of its mother, unable to walk a step, or lisp a word, or do aught but cry with pain or for nourishment stored in the mother's breast? What! Almighty God fallen from his burnished, dazzling throne in the lofty heavens, and reduced to helpless, senseless babyhood! Omnipotence shorn of all power but to breathe, and cry, and smile! What! that Omniscient Being, who "leads one world by day, and ten thousand more by night," becoming suddenly transformed into a human bantling, which knows no higher enjoyment that that of being "pleased with a rattle, and tickled with a straw!" Who can believe it? Ay, who dare believe it, if he would escape the charge of blasphemy? Then say not that "the man Christ Jesus," though standing at the top of the ladder of moral manhood, and high above the common plane of humanity, was yet a God—"the Infinite Ruler of the infinite universe." Who can believe that that Being, whose existence stretches to an eternity beyond human conception, yea, whom "the heaven of heavens cannot contain," was ever cooped up in a human body, reduced so near to nothing in dimensions as to be susceptible (as was Jesus) of being weighed in scales, and measured with a yardstick?

We ask again, Who, from the deepest depths of his inmost, enlightened consciousness, can believe such revolting, such atheistical doctrine as this? Or who will venture to descend still lower, and conceive of an Almighty, Omnipresent Being, who fills all space above, around, and beneath, "from infinity below to yon fixed star above," and millions upon millions of miles beyond it, sinking and dwindling to that mere mite, speck, or monad state and condition comprehended in the initiatory step of embryonic existence? And then think of the Almighty, Omnipotent Creator of the universe lying in a manger with four-footed beasts and creeping things, sleeping with oxen and asses in a stable. Next he is seen an urchin on the street playing with marbles and jack-knives, absorbed and forgetful of the world around him. Who can believe that awfully majestic Being, who is represented by his own inspired book as being so transcendently grand and awe-inspiring that "no man san see him and live" (Ex. xxxiii. 20), was not only daily seen by hundreds and thousands, but was on such familiar terms with men, that they regarded him as their companion, and equal, and even sometimes coolly reprimanded him for supposed misdemeanors and errors? Could they believe this to be Almighty God? Impossible! Impossible! And then who can believe that that infinite Being, whom we have been taught to regard as absolutely and eternally unchangeable, could become subject to hunger and thirst (as did Jesus)? Or who can believe that the eternally and unceasingly watchful Omnipotent Deity, whose eye, we are told, "never slumbers," could sink into unconscious sleep, become "to dumb forgetfulness a prey," night after night, for thirty years, oblivious, and unconscious of the world around him? Think of a being of incomprehensible majesty, dignity, and power, able to "shake the heavens and the earth also," being unable to protect himself from insult, and was therefore derided and "spit upon," and finally overcome by his enemies, as is related of Jesus. Can any man believe, who has not made shipwreck of his senses, or banished Reason from her courts, that God 'Almighty, who comprehends in himself the most absolute and boundless perfection of goodness and wisdom, was tempted by demons, devils, and crawling serpents? Who can believe that the Lord, who owns "the cattle upon a thousand hills" (Psalm 1. io), and the countless host of worlds besides, that wheel their course through infinite space, had not "where to lay his head"? Who can believe that that was the all-wise, omnipotent, and omnipresent God, possessing all power in heaven above and the earth beneath, who was betrayed by weak, finite mortals? What! the Almighty Creator betrayed by a puny being of his own creation into the hands of his disobedient and rebellious children? Why could he not, if possessing "power to lay down his life, and take it up again" (John x. 17), cause that all these children of his (as we must assume they were, if he was Almighty God, and hence the Father of all) should love him, instead of hating him? Can any man believe that Jesus was possessed with omnipotent power while standing to be whipped (scourged) by Pontius Pilate, or that he possessed a power above that of finite mortals while in the act of praying, with such extreme ardor that the sweat dropped from his face, that the cup of death might pass from his lips, or while calling for an angel to support him in the hour of his mortal dissolution? or that He, "by whom all things exist," could cease himself to exist, by dying upon the cross between malefactors? Think of this, reader! and think of the eternal Creator, the infinite Deity, the omnipotent Jehovah, the Maker of worlds as numberless as the sands upon the sea-shore for multitude, fainting, bleeding, dying, and pouring out his own blood to appease his own wrath;

198

dying an ignominious death to satisfy an implacable revenge! Away with such insulting mockery, such blasphemous flummery! It can only find place in the dark chambers of an unenlightened mind.

Well has Watts said of Locke's skepticism,—

```
"Reason could scarcely sustain to see,
Or bear the infant Deity:
A ransomed world, a bleeding God,
And heaven appeased by flowing blood,
Were themes too painful to be understood."
```

Yes, and too painful to be believed, too, Mr. Watts! Here we have a "bleeding God," an "infant Deity," and a vengeful God, appeased by murder and streams of "flowing blood." Gracious heavens! Whose reason does not revolt at such a picture? Whose soul does not sicken at the thought, and who would not prefer, infinitely prefer, to sink to annihilation, if not to perdition itself, to being thus saved by navigating a river of blood?? Dr. South hits off some of the absurdities involved in the Christian doctrine of the incarnation so forcibly and so lucidly, that we cannot resist the temptation to subjoin——here a few extracts from his sermon on the subject' "But now," says this Christian clergyman, "was there ever any wonder comparable to this, to behold the Lord (Jesus Christ) thus clothed in flesh, the Creator of all things, humbled, not only to the company, but also to the cognation, of his creatures? It is as if one should imagine the whole world not only represented upon, but also contained in, one of our own artificial globes, or the body of the sun enveloped in a cloud as big as a man's hand, all of which would be looked upon as astonishing impossibilities, and yet is as short of the other as the finite is of the infinite, between which the disparity is immeasurable. It is, as it were, to cancel the essential distances of things, to remove the bounds of nature, to bring heaven and earth, and what is more, both ends of the contradiction, together. Men cannot persuade themselves that a Deity and infinity should lie within so narrow a compass as the dimensions of a human body; that omnipotence, omnipresence should ever be wrapped in swaddling clothes, and debased to the homely usages of a stable and a manger; that the glorious Artificer of the whole universe, who spread out the heaven like a curtain, and laid the foundations of the earth, could ever turn carpenter, and exercise an inglorious trade in a little cell. They cannot imagine that He who once created and at present governs the world, and shall hereafter judge the world, should be abased in all his concerns and relations, be scourged, spit upon, mocked and at last crucified. All which are passages which lie extremely close to the notions of conceptions which reason has made to itself of that high and impossible perfection that resided in the divine Creator." (Sermon, 1665.) Dr. South, it will be observed, admits that the doctrine of the divine incarnation involves many palpable absurdities and contradictions, and lies directly across the path of reason. Fatal admission to the doctrine of the deityship of Christ, but true, as his own elucidation of the subject demonstrates. To the author, since he first subjected the question to a logical scrutiny, and looked at it with an unbiased mind, it presents difficulties insurmountable, and absurdities innumerable. He can imagine nothing more transcendently shocking, revolting, and dwarfing to the mind, both morally and intellectually, than the thought of believing that a being born of and suckled by a woman, and possessing the mere form and dimensions of a man, can be regarded as the great Almighty and Omnipotent God, the Creator of unnumbered worlds, millions of which are larger than this planet, on which Jesus was born.

And then, reader, look for a moment at some of the many childish incongruities and logical difficulties this giant absurdity drags with it. It represents Almighty God as coming into the world through the hands of a midwife, as passing through the process of gestation and parturition. It insults our reason with the idea that the great, infinite Jehovah could be molded into the human form—a thought that is shocking to the moral sense, and withering, cramping, and dwarfing to the intellectual mind, imposing upon it a heavy drag-chain which checks its expansion, and forbids its onward progress. Christians tell us that the human and the divine were united in "the man Christ Jesus." But this is a monstrous absurdity, which no truly rational and unbiased mind can accept for an instant—that of hitching, splicing, tying, or dovetailing together finite man with the infinite Jehovah, that of amalgamating and commingling human foibles with divine perfection. Think of wedding mortal weakness to omnipotent power, local man with the omnipresent Deity! Think of compounding the creature and the Creator in one and the same being! Think of the omnipresent "I AM," whose illimitable existence stretches far away throughout the expansive arena of a boundless universe, occupying a dwelling within the narrow confines of the human temple! As well essay to crowd the universe into your pocket, or the Himalayas Mountains into a thimble. On the other hand, think of a small compound of flesh, blood, and bones, a few feet in dimensions, and weighing perhaps not more than one hundred and fifty pounds avoirdupois, containing that infinite, omnipresent Being, whom, we are told (we repeat the quotation), "the heaven of heavens cannot contain"! And more than all, kind reader, I ask you if you can accept for a moment, without the immolation of your common sense, and the trampling of your reason beneath you feet, the monstrous thought that that mighty and almighty Architect who who created the countless myriads upon myriads of ponderous worlds, which now roll in majestic order, and eternal rotation along the great cerulean causeway of heaven, that mighty Architect who, from time beyond human computation, has been rolling out orb after orb, world after world, if not myriads at a time, ten thousand times, ten thousand of which would dwindle our little pygmy, Lilliputian planet into insignificance, if compared with it in size.

I ask, and drive home the query to your inward consciousness, and the inmost temples of your sacred reason:

Can you believe, after a moment's reflection, that a Being who is too vast, infinitely too vast in power and ubiquity to be grasped by the human understanding, did become (as did the finite and humble Jesus) a helpless, senseless, unconscious, human infant; a suckling, crying, squalling babe, powerless of speech, and unable to walk? Ay, worse, more startling still, we are shocked with the thought that this mighty World-builder, this infinite, omnipotent Creator, was reduced so near to the verge of nonentity, so near to the last glimmering spark or speck of existence, and the world so near without a God, as to become an inanimate foetus—a monad in the matrix of a human virgin? Shocking the thought! Blasphemous the doctrine! Believe it who will; believe it who can! We cannot; we would not; we are infinitely beyond it. Such a belief may be deposited by educational tradition in the affections, but to enter the temple of Reason, it never did, it never can. She never unbarred her doors to admit such monstrous, such enormous incongruities. and all these logical absurdities, and a thousand more, grow legitimately out of the doctrine of the divine incarnation,—out of the postulate which would (following in the line of the pagan superstitions) elevate the finite, humble, mortal Jesus to the throne of heaven, the exclusive prerogative of Almighty God. Come away, my Christian friends, from such disparaging, such dishonorable views of the Deity, such blasphemous caricatures of Almighty God. Come away from such morally darkening and such intellectually dwarfing superstitutions, the moldering relics of oriental mythology, the expiring embers of childish credulity and tradition, which originated far back in the dark cradle of human existence, in the infancy of an undeveloped age, ruled by ignorance, superstition, and priestcraft. Yet millions of people laying claim to sense and intelligence, even now profess to believe it. Talk not to me of infidelity or blasphemy for denying the divinity or Godhead of Jesus Christ. The blasphemy lies in the other direction. The infidelity is with the opposite party. It is with those who thus make the dignity and character of Deity the sport of childish I baubles, the game of priestly tawdryism. And be assured, dear friends, one and all, that coming generations will mark the man who now worships "the man Christ Jesus" as being "very God" as an idolater, if not a blasphemer—for worshipping a finite man for an infinite God, even though the motives for such worship may be as pure as the pearly stream that issues forth from the golden fount which rolls and sparkles beneath the throne of Almighty God.

        Note. The words Creator, Maker, &c., are used from a
        Christian standpoint Science knows no Creator.

CHAPTER XXXVI. PHILOSOPHICAL ABSURDITIES OF THE DOCTRINE OF THE DIVINE INCARNATION

THERE is a philosophical principle underlying the doctrine of the Divine Incarnation, whose logical deductions completely overthrow the claim of Jesus of Nazareth to the Godhead, and which we regard as settling the question as conclusively as any demonstrated problem in mathematics. This argument is predicated upon the philosophical axiom, that two infinite beings of any description of conception, cannot exist, either in whole or in part, at the same time; and per consequence, it is impossible that the Father and Son should both be God in a divine sense, either conjointly or separately. The word infinite comprehends all; it covers the whole ground; it fills the immensity of the universe, and fills it to repletion! so that there is no room left for any other being to exist. And whoever and whatever does exist must constitute a part of this infinite whole.

Now, the Christian world concedes (for it is the teaching of their Scriptures), that the Father is God, always and truly, perfect, complete, and absolute; that there is nothing wanting in him to constitute him God in the most comprehensive and absolute sense of the term; that he is all we can conceive of as constituting God, "the one only true God" (John xvii. 3), and was such from all eternity, before Jesus Christ was born into the world; and Paul puts the keystone into the arch by proclaiming, "To us there is but one God, the Father." (1 Cor. viii. 6.) Hence we have here a logical proposition (despite the sophistry of Christendom) as impregnable as the rocks of Gibraltar, that the Father alone is or can be God, which effectually shuts out every other and all other beings in the universe from any participation in the Godhead with the Father. And thus this parity of reasoning demonstrates that the very moment you attempt to make Christ God, or any part of the Godhead, you attempt a philosophical impossibility. You cannot introduce another being as God in the infinite sense until the first-named infinite God is dethroned and put out of existence, and this, of course, is a self-evident impossibility. It it were not such, then we should have two Gods, both absolute and infinite. On the other hand, if that other being (who with the Christians is Jesus Christ, with the Hindoos Chrishna, with the Budhists Sakia, &c.) is introduced as only a part of the infinite and perfect God, then it is evident to every mind with the least philosophical perception, that some change or alteration must take place in the latter before such a union can be effected. But such a change, or any alteration, in a perfect infinite being would at once reduce him to a changeable and finite being, and thus he would cease to be God. For it is a clear philosophical and mathematical axiom, that a perfect and infinite being cannot become more than infinite. And if he could and should become less than infinite, he would at once become finite, and thus lose all the attributes of the Godhead. To say or assume, then, that Christ was God in the absolute or divine sense, and the Father also God absolute, and yet that there is but one God, or that the two could in any manner be united, so as to constitute but one God, is not only a glaring solecism, but a positive contradiction in terms, and an utter violation of the first axiomatic principles of philosophy and mathematics. It also asserts the illogical hypothesis, that a part can be equal to the whole; it first assumes the Father to be absolutely God, then assumes the Son also to be absolutely God, and finally assumes each to be only a part, and has to unite them to make whole and culminates the theological farce. Such is Christian ratiocination.

Again, it is conceded by Christians, that the Father is an omnipresent being; and we have shown that it is a mathematical impossibility for two omnipresent beings, or two beings possessing any infinite attributes, to exist at one and the same time. Hence the clear logical deducsequence, not God. Again, we have another philosophical maxim or axiom familiar to every schoolboy, that no two substances or beings can occupy the same place at the same time; the first must be removed before the second can by any possibility be introduced, in order thus to make room for the latter. But as omnipresent means existing everywhere, there can be no place to remove on omnipresent being to, or rather there can be no place or space he can be withdrawn from in order to make room for another being, without his ceasing to be omnipresent himself, and thereby ceasing to be God.

It is thus shown to be a demonstrable truth that the omnipresence of the Father does and must exclude that of the Son, and thus exclude the possibility of his apatheosis or incarnated deityship. In other words, it is established as a scientific principle upon a philosophical and mathematical basis, that Jesus Christ was not and could not be "the great I AM," "the only true God."

We will notice one other philosophical absurdity involved in the doctrine of the divine incarnation—one other solecism comprehended in the childish notion which invests the infinite God with finite attributes. It is a well-established and well-understood axiom in philosocomplete God; and thereby that the Son could not be omnipresent, and that "the less cannot be made to contain the greater." A pint bottle cannot be made to contain a quart of wine. For the same reason a finite body cannot contain an infinite spirit. Hence philosophy presses the conclusion that "the man Christ Jesus" could not have comprehended in himself "the Godhead bodily," inasmuch as it would have required the infinite God to be incorporated in a finite human body. We are therefore compelled to reject the doctrine of the incarnate divinity, the belief in the deityship of Jesus Christ, because (with many other reasons enumerated elsewhere) it involves a direct tilt against some of the plainest principles of science, and challenges, ay, virtually overthrows, some of the fundamental laws of both natural and moral philosophy. No philosopher, therefore, does, or can believe in the absolute divinity of Jesus Christ.

CHAPTER XXXVII. PHYSIOLOGICAL ABSURDITIES OF THE DOCTRINE OF THE DIVINE INCARNATION

THERE is also a physiological principle (discovered by the author) comprised in the doctrine of the Divine Incarnation fatal in its practical and logical application to the divinity of Jesus Christ, and all the other incarnate or flesh-invested Gods of antiquity. It is evidently fraught with much logical force. It is based upon the law of mental and physical correspondence. As is the physical conformation, so is the mentality, is a law of analogy which pilots us to nearly all our practical knowledge of the natural world. A knowledge of either serves as an index to the other.

When we observe an animal possessing that physical form and construction peculiar to its species, we expect to find it practically exhibiting the nature, character, disposition, and habits peculiar to that class of animals. If it possesses, for example, the conformation of a sheep, we infer at once that it has the disposition of a sheep, and we are never disappointed in this conclusion. And when we encounter an animal with the tiger form, we expect to see exhibited the tiger spirit. If it possesses the well-known physical conformation of the tiger, we are never deceived or misled when we assign it a predatory disposition. If it is a tiger form, it is sure to be a tiger in character and habits. And so of all the genera and species of animals that range upon the face of the globe. We may travel through the whole field of animated nature, and observe the infallible operation of this beautiful law of correspondence till we come, however, to the crowning work of God, called Man. Here we find this law, this beautiful chain of analogy, broken by the doctrine of the "divine incarnation." God becomes a man, at least is made to exhibit every external appearance of a man. All external distinction between God and man is thus obliterated. So that the very first being we meet in the street or on the highway possessing the form, size, and physical conformation of a man, and presenting every other external appearance of being a man, may nevertheless be a God. And no less is this objection practically exemplified, and not less is the infraction of this beautiful law of analogy observable in the case of Jesus Christ, than in the numerous other incarnate Gods and demigods of antiquity. Being in appearance a man, how was he to be, or how could he be, visually distinguished from a man? Or how could those men who were cotemporary with him, know, as they approached him, or as they approached each other, whether they were meeting a man or a God? Seeing that "he was found in fashion as a man" (Phil. ii. 8), either he might be mistaken for a man, or they for a God. They were constantly liable to be confounded. If, then, the infinite deityship was lodged in the person of Jesus Christ, it is evident that that important fundamental law of nature—"as is the form, so is the character"—was utterly annulled, prostrated, annihilated, and banished from the world by the act. So that all was, and is henceforth and forever, chaos, confusion, and uncertainty. For if the principle can be violated in one instance, it may be in another, and in thousands of cases, ad infinitum. If one case could be allowed to occur, the principle is established, and nature's universal chain of analogy is broken and destroyed; for to intercept the law is to "break the tenth and ten thousandth link alike."

Hence it is evident that if a being resembling a man may be a God, an animal resembling a cow may be a horse, and yonder stick a poisonous adder; and fatal may be the consequences, in thousands of instances, in judging or inferring the nature and character of an animal by its form and size. A supposed innocent animal might be a deadly enemy, or vice versa. Can we then believe, or dare we believe, a doctrine so atheistical in its tendencies as that the Infinite Diety was incorporated in the person of the meek and lowly Jesus, when it would thus set at naught, violate, prostrate, and utterly cancel from the world one of God's own fundamental laws, and one of the essential principles of natural science, and banish forever the co-ordinate harmony of the universe, and thus inaugurate a state of universal disorder, incertitude, anarchy, and misrule into the otherwise beautifully law-governed, well-regulated domain of nature? Certainly, most certainly not! If the incarnation of the Deity, should or could take place, there should be something strikingly peculiar, ay, infinitely peculiar, in his figure, size, and general appearance, in order to make him susceptible of being distinguished from the human. Otherwise, men would be liable to be constantly mistaking and worshiping each other for the Great Almighty and Ubiquitous God, and thus constantly blundering into idolatry. And we actually find several cases reported in the Scriptures (mark the fact well) of men, ay, the saints themselves, being led into this error; being led to commit "the high-handed sin of idolatry" in consequence of their previous acceptance of the belief in a man-God—that is, a God of human size and type. St. John, in two instances, was in the act of worshipping a being possessing the human form, whom he mistook for the omnipotent and omnipresent God. (See Rev. xix. 10, and xxii. 4.) Having, perhaps, been taught that "the fullness of the Godhead dwelt bodily in Christ Jesus," he probably mistook the being he met for Him, and hence offered to worship him. If, then, Christ's own "inspired disciples" could thus be betrayed into "the sin of idolatry" by having abolished the infinite distinction between the divine and the human, we surely find here a very weighty argument against such a leveling and equalizing doctrine. And certainly nothing could be better calculated to promote "the sin of idolatry" than thus to obliterate the broad, the infinitely grand line of demarkation between the infinite God and his finite creature man. Indeed, may we not here find the very origin and the cause of the now general prevalence of idolatry in pagan countries? Is it not directly traceable to the demolition of the broad, high, and insurmountable wall of distinction which ought forever to stand between a God of infinite attributes, and a being caged up in the human form? Certainly, most certainly it is. Hence here I would ask, How can Christians, after subscribing to the doctrine, "that the fullness of the Godhead dwelt bodily in the man Christ Jesus" (as Paul very appropriately calls him), condemn the people of any age or nation for worshiping as God their fellow-beings—that is, beings with the human form? Certainly the man who could believe that the infinite God could be comprehended or incorporated in the person of Jesus, could easily be brought to believe that the Grand Lama of Thibet is a proper object of divine worship. He only lacks the substitution of names. Substitute the Grand Lama for that of Jesus Christ, and the thing is done. And idolatry thus becomes an easily established institution, and its abolition in any country an absolute moral impossibility.

CHAPTER XXXVIII. A HISTORICAL VIEW OF THE DIVINITY OF JESUS CHRIST.

A MOST fatal distrust is thrown upon the miraculous portions of the history of Jesus Christ, as found in his Gospel narratives, by the discovery of the fact (brought to light through recent archaeological researches), that the same marvelous feats, the same miraculous incidents, which were recorded in his life, were long previously ingrafted into the sacred biographies of Gods and demigods no less adored and worshipped as beings possessing divine attributes. We shall leave the reader to account for the long list of astonishing coincidences, as we proceed to recapitulate and abridge from previous chapters, the almost innumerable parallel incidents running through the legendary history of the many demigods and sin-atoning saviors of antiquity. The historical vouchers are given. We shall first direct attention to the long string of corresponding events recorded in the sacred histories of ancient Hindoo Gods, as compared with those of Jesus Christ at a much later period.

As far back as 1200 B. C., sacred records were extant and traditions were current, in the East, which taught that the heathen Savior (Chrishna) was, 1st, Immaculately conceived and born of a spotless virgin, "who had never known man." 2d, That the author of, or agent in, the conception, was a spirit or ghost (of course a Holy Ghost). 3d, That he was threatened in early infancy with death by the ruling tyrant, Cansa. 4th, That his parents had, consequently, to flee with him to Gokul for safety. 5th, That all the young male children under two years of age were slain by an order issued by Cansa, similar to that of Herod in Judea. 6th, That angels and shepherds attended his birth. 7th, That his birth and advent occurred on the 25th of December. 8th, That it occurred in accordance with previous prophecy. 9th, That he was presented at birth with frankincense, myrrh, &c. 10th, That he was saluted and worshipped as "the Savior of men," according to the report of the late Christian Missionary Huelith, That he led a life of humility and practical moral usefulness. 12th, That he wrought various astounding miracles, such as healing the sick, restoring sight to the blind, casting out devils, raising the dead to life, &c. 13th, That he was finally put to death upon the cross (i. e., crucified) between two thieves. 14th. After which he descended to hell, rose from the dead, and ascended back to heaven "in the sight of all men," as his biblical history declares. For hundreds of other similar parallels, including his doctrines and precepts, see Chapter XXXII.

Now, all these were matters of the firmest belief, more than three thousand years ago, in the minds of millions of the most devout worshippers that ever bowed the knee in humble prayer to the Father of Mercies. The reader can draw his own deduction.

And then we have presented similar brief lists of parallels in Chapter XXIII., comprised in a comparative view of the miraculous lives of the Judean and Egyptian Saviors, Christ, Alcides, Osiris, Tulis, &c. In this analogous exhibition, it will be observed the Egyptian Gods are reported, as remotely as 900 B. C, as performing, besides several of the miraculous achievements enumerated above, other miracles equally indicative of divine power, such as converting water into wine, causing "rain to descend from heaven," &c. And on the occasion of the crucifixion of Tulis we are told "the sun became darkened and the moon refused to shine."

We find, also, several well-authenticated instances of raising the dead to life, in works portraying the miraculous achievements of the Egyptian Gods, the relation being given in such specific detail in some cases that the names of the reanimated dead are furnished. Tyndarus and Hypolitus were instances of this kind, both (according to Julius) having been raised from the dead. Descending the line of history, until we arrive at the confines of Grecian theology, we find here the same train of marvelous events recorded in the histories of their virgin-born Gods, as we have shown in Chapter XXXIII., such as their healing the sick and the cripples, causing the blind to see, the lame to walk, the dead to be resuscitated to life, &c. And cases, as we have shown, are reported of their reading the thoughts of their disciples, as Jesus did those of the woman of Samaria. Apollonius declares he knew many Hindoo saints to perform this achievement with entire strangers.

Likewise Apollonius of Tyana and Simon Magus, both cotemporary with Jesus Christ, we have arranged in the historic parallel (see Chapter XXXIII.), with their long train of miracles, constituting an exact counterpart with those related in the Gospel history of Christ, and including in Apollonius's case, besides those specified in the histories of the Gods above named, the miracle of transfiguration, the resurrection from the dead, his visible ascent to heaven, &c., while Simon Magus was very expert in casting out devils, raising the dead, allaying storms, walking on the sea, &c.

But without recapitulating further, we will recite some new historic facts not embraced in any of the preceding chapters of this work, and tending to demonstrate still further the universal analogy of all religions, past and present, in their claims for a miraculous power for their Gods and incarnate Saviors. The "New York Correspondent," published in 1828, furnishes us the following brief history of an ancient Chinese God, known as Beddou:—

"All the Eastern writers agree in placing the birth of Beddou 1027 B. C. The doctrines of this Deity prevailed over Japan, China, and Ceylon. According to the sacred tenets of his religion, 'God is incessantly rendering himself incarnate,' but his greatest and most solemn incarnation was three thousand years ago, in the province of Cashmere, under the name of Fot, or Beddou. He was believed to have sprung from the right intercostal of a virgin of the royal blood, who, when she became a mother, did not the less continue to be a virgin; that the king of the country, uneasy at his birth, was desirous to put him to death, and hence caused all the males that were born at the same period to be put to death, and also that, being saved by shepherds, he lived in the desert to the age of thirty years, at which time he opened his commission, preaching the doctrines of truth, and casting out devils; that he performed a multitude of the most astonishing miracles, spent his life fasting, and in the severest mortifications, and at his death bequeathed to his disciples the volume in which the principles of his religion are contained."

Here, it will be observed, are some very striking counterparts to the miraculous incidents found related in the Gospel history of Jesus Christ. And no less analogous is the no less well-authenticated story of Quexalcote of Mexico, which the Rev. Mr. Maurice concedes to be, and Lord Kingsborough and Niebuhr (in his history of Rome) prove to be much older than the Gospel account of Jesus Christ According to Maurice's "Ind. Ant.," Humboldt's "Researches in Mexico," Lord Kingsbor-ough's "Mexican Ant.," and other works, the incarnate God Quexalcote was born (about 300 B. C.) of a spotless virgin, by the name Chimalman, and led a life of the

206

deepest humility and piety; retired to a wilderness, fasted forty days, was worshipped as a God, and was finally crucified between two thieves; after which he was buried and descended into hell, but rose again the third day. The following is a part of Lord Kingsborough's testimony in the case: "The temptation of Quexalcote, the fast of forty days ordained by the Mexican ritual, the cup with which he was presented to drink (on the cross), the reed which was his sign, the 'Morning Star,' which he is designated, the 'Teoteepall, or Divine Stone,' which was laid on his altar, and which was likewise an object of adoration,—all these circumstances, connected with many others relating to Quexalcote of Mexico, but which are here omitted, are very curious and mysterious." (Vol. vi. p. 237, Mexican Ant.)

Again "Quexalcote is represented, in the painting of Codex Borgianus, as nailed to the cross." (See Mex. Ant. vol. vi. p. 166.) One place in this work represents him as being crucified in the heavens, one as being crucified between two thieves. Sometimes he is represented as being nailed to the cross, and sometimes as hanging with the cross in his hands. The same work speaks of his burial, descent into hell, and his resurrection; while the account of his immaculate conception and miraculous birth are found in a work called "Codex Vaticanus."

Other parallel incidents could be cited, if we had space for them, appertaining to the history of this Mexican God. And parallels might also be constructed upon the histories of other ancient Gods,—as that of Sakia of India, Salivahana of Bermuda, Hesus, or Eros, of the Celtic Druids, Mithra of Persia, Hil and Feta of the Mandaites, &c.

But we will close with the testimony of a French philosopher (Bagin) on the subject of deific incarnations. This writer says, "The most ancient histories are those of Gods who became incarnate in order to govern mankind. All those fables are the same in spirit, and sprang up everywhere from confused ideas, which have universally prevailed among mankind,—that Gods formerly descended upon earth."

Now, we ask the Christian reader,—and it will be the first query of every man whose religious faith has not made shipwreck of his reason,—"What does all this mean? How are you going to sustain the declaration that Jesus Christ was the only son and sent of God, in view of these historic facts? Where are the superior credentials of his claim? How will you prove his apparently legendary history (that is, the miraculous portion of his history) to be real, and the others false?" We boldly aver it cannot be done. Please answer these questions, or relinquish your doctrine of the divinity of Jesus Christ.

CHAPTER XXXIX. THE SCRIPTURAL VIEW OF CHRIST'S DIVINITY.

THE monstrous scientific paradox (as coming ages will regard it) comprehended in the conception of an almighty, omnipresent, and infinite Being, "the Creator of innumerable worlds," ("by him [Christ] were all things made that were made," John i. 3-10), being born of a frail and finite woman, as taught by both the oriental and Christian religion, is so exceedingly shocking to every rational mind, which has not been sadly warped, perverted, and coerced into the belief by early psychological influence, that we would naturally presume that those who, on the assumption of the remotest possibility of its truth, should venture to put forth a doctrine so glaringly unreasonable and so obviously untenable, would of course vindicate it and establish it by the strongest arguments and by the most unassailable and most irrefragable proofs; and that in setting forth a doctrine so manifestly at war with every law and analogy of nature and every principle of science, no language should have been used, nor the slightest admission made, that could possibly lead to the slightest degree of suspicion that the original authors and propagators of this doctrine had either any doubt of the truth of the doctrine themselves, or were wanting in the most ample, the most abundant proof to sustain it. No language, no text, not a word, not a syllable should have been used making the most remote concession damaging to the validity of the doctrine, so that not "the shadow of a shade of doubt" could be left on any mind of its truth. Omnipotent indeed should be the logic, and irresistible the proof, in support of a thesis or a doctrine which so squarely confronts and contradicts all the observation, all the experience, the whole range of scientific knowledge, and the common sense of mankind. How startling then, to every devout and honest professor of the Christian faith ought to be the recent discovery of the fact, that the great majority of the texts having any bearing upon the doctrine of the divinity of Jesus Christ,—a large majority of the passages in the very book on which the doctrine is predicated, and which is acknowledged as the sole warranty for such a belief,—are actually at variance with the doctrine, and actually amount to its virtual denial and overthrow. For we find, upon a critical examination of the matter, that at least three-fourths of the texts, both in the Gospels and Epistles, which relate to the divinity of Christ, specifically or by implication either teach a different and a contrary doctrine, or make concessions entirely fatal to it, by investing him with finite human qualities utterly incompatible with the character and attributes of a divine or infinite Being. How strange, then, how superlatively strange, that millions should yet hold to such a strange "freak of nature," such a dark relic of oriental heathenism, such a monstrously foolish and childish superstition, as that which teaches the infinite Creator and "Upholder of the universe" could be reduced so near to nonentity, as was required to pass through the ordinary stages of human generation, human birth, and human parturition, —a puerile notion which reason, science, nature, philosophy, and common sense, proclaim to be supremely absurd and self-evidently impossible, and which even the Scriptures fail to sustain,—a logical, scriptural exposition, of which we will here present a brief summary:—

1. The essential attributes of a self-existing God and Creator, and "Upholder of all things." are infinitude, omnipotence, omniscience, and omnipresence, and any being not possessing all these attributes to repletion, or possessing any quality or characteristic in the slightest degree incompatible with any one of these attributes, cannot be a God in a divine sense, but must of necessity be a frail, fallible, finite being.

2. Jesus Christ disclaims, hundreds of times over, directly or impliedly, the inherent possession of any one of these divine attributes.

3. His evangelical biographers have invested him with the entire category of human qualities and characteristics, each one of which is entirely unbefitting a God, and taken together are the only distinguishing characteristics by which we can know a man from a God.

4. Furthermore, there issued from his own mouth various sayings and concessions most fatal to the conception of his being a God.

5. His devout biographers have reported various actions and movements in his practical life which we are compelled to regard as absolutely irreconcilable with the infinite majesty, lofty character, and supreme attributes of an a mighty Being.

6. These human qualities were so obvious to all who saw him and all who became acquainted with him, that doubts sprang up among his own immediate followers, which ultimately matured into an open avowal of disbelief in his divinity in that early age.

7. Upon the axiomatical principles of philosophy it is an utter and absolute impossibility to unite in repletion the divine and the human in the same being.

8. And then Christ had a human birth.

9. He was constituted in part, like human beings, of flesh and blood.

10. He became, on certain occasions, "an hungered," like finite beings.

11. He also became thirsty (John xix. 28), like perishable mortals.

12. He often slept, like mortals, and thus became "to dumb forgetfulness a prey."

13. He sometimes became weary, like human beings. (See John iv. 6.)

14. He was occasionally tempted, like fallible mortals. (Matt. iv. 1.)

15. His "soul became exceeding sorrowful," as a frail, finite being. (Matt. xxvi. 38.)

16. He disclosed the weakness of human passion by weeping. (John xi. 35.)

17. He was originally an imperfect being, "made perfect through suffering." (Heb. ii. 10.)

18. He "increased in wisdom and stature" (Luke ii. 52); therefore he must have possessed finite, changeable, mortal attributes.

19. And he finally died and was buried, like all perishable mortals. He could not possibly, from these considerations, have been a God. It is utterly impracticable to associate with or comprehend, in a God of infinite powers and infinite attributes, all or any of these finite human qualities.

20. Dark, intellectually dark, indeed, must be that mind, and sunk, sorrowfully sunk in superstition, that can worship a being as the great omniscient, omnipotent, and omnipresent "I AM," who possessed all those qualities which were constitutionally characteristic of the pious, the noble, the devout, the Godlike, yet finite and fallible Jesus, according to his own admissions and the representations of his own interested biographers.

21. The only step which the disciples of the Christian faith have made toward disproving or setting aside these arguments, objections, and difficulties, is that of assigning the incarnate Jesus a double or twofold nature—the amalgamation of the human and divine; a postulate and a groundless assumption, which we have proved and demonstrated by thirteen arguments, which we believe to be unanswerable, is not only absurd, illogical, and impossible, but foolish and ludicrous in the highest degree. (See vol. ii.)

22. This senseless hypothesis, and every other assumption and argument made use of by the professors of the Christian faith to vindicate their favorite dogma of the divinity of Jesus, we have shown to be equally applicable to the demigods of the ancient heathen, more than twenty of whom were invested with the same combination of human and divine qualities which the followers and worshippers of Jesus claim for him.

23. Testimony of the Father against the divinity of the Son. The Father utterly precludes the Son from any participation in the divine essence, or any claim in the Godhead, by such declarations as the following: "I am Jehovah, and beside me there is no Savior." (Isaiah xliii. 11.) How, then, we would ask, can Jesus Christ be the Savior? "I, Jehovah, am thy Savior and thy Redeemer." Then Christ can be neither the Savior nor Redeemer. "There is no God else beside me, a just God and a Savior; there is none beside me." (Isaiah xiv. 21.) So the Father virtually declares, according to "the inspired prophet Isaiah," that the Son, in a divine sense, cannot be either God, Savior, or Redeemer. Again, "I am Jehovah, thy God, and thou shalt not acknowledge a God beside me." (Hosea xiii. 4.) Here Christ is not only by implication cut off from the Godhead, but positively prohibited from being worshipped as God. And thus the testimony of the Father disproves and sets aside the divinity of the Son.

24. Testimony of the mother. When Mary found, after a long search, her son Jesus in the temple, disputing with the doctors, and chided or reproved him for staying from home without the consent of his parents, and declared, "thy father and I sought thee, sorrowing" (Luke ii. 48), she proclaimed a twofold denial of his divinity. In the first place it cannot be possible that she regarded her son Jesus as "that awful Being, before whom e'en the devout saints bow in trembling fear," when she used such language and evinced such a spirit as she did. "Why hast thou thus dealt with us?" (Luke ii. 48) is her chiding language. And then, when she speaks of Joseph as his father, "thy father and I," she issues a declaration against his divinity which ought to be regarded as settling the question forever. For who could know better than the mother, or rather, who could know but the mother, who the father of the child Jesus was? And as she acknowledges it was Joseph, she thus repudiates the story of the immaculate conception, which constitutes the whole basis for the claim of his divinity. Hence the testimony of the mother, also, disproves his title to the Godhead.

25. Testimony or disclaimer of the Son. We will show by a specific citation of twenty-five texts that there is not one attribute comprehended in or peculiar to a divine and infinite Being, but that Christ rejects as applicable to himself—that he most conclusively disclaims every attribute of a divine Being, both by precept and practice, and often in the most explicit language.

26. By declaring, "The Son can do nothing of himself" (John v. 19), he most emphatically disclaims the attribute of omnipotence. For an omnipotent Being can need no aid, and can accept of none.

27. When he acknowledged and avowed his ignorance of the day of judgment, which must be presumed to be the most important event in the world's history, he disclaimed the attribute of omniscience. "Of that day and hour knoweth no man, neither the Son, but the Father only." (Matt. xxiv. 36.) Now, as an omniscient Being must possess all knowledge, his avowed ignorance in this case is a confession he was not omniscient, and hence not a God.

28. And when he declares, "I am glad for your sakes I was not there" (at the grave of Lazarus), he most distinctly disavows being omnipresent, and thus denies to himself another essential attribute of an infinite God.

29. And the emphatic declaration, "I live by the Father" (John vi. 57), is a direct disclaimer of the attributes of self-existence; as a being who lives by another cannot be self-existent, and, per consequence, not the infinite God.

30 He disclaims possessing infinite goodness, another essential attribute of a supreme divine Being. "Why callest thou me good? there is none good but one, that is God." (Mark x. 18.)

31. He disclaim divine honors, and directed them to the father. "I honor my Father." (John viii. 49.) "I receive not honor from men." (John v. 41.)

32. He recommended supreme worship to the Father, and not to himself. "The true worshippers shall worship the Father in spirit and in truth." (John iv. 21.)

33. He ascribed supreme dominion to the Father. "Thine is the kingdom, and the power, and the glory forever." (Matt. vi. 13.)

34. It will be seen, from the foregoing text, that Christ also acknowledges that the kingdom is the Father's. A God without a kingdom would be a ludicrous state of things.

35. He conceded supreme authority to the Father.

"My doctrine is not mine, but his that sent me." (John vii. 16.)

36. He considered the Father as the supreme protector and preserver of even his own disciples. "I pray that thou shouldst keep them from the evil." (John xvii. 15.) What, omnipotence not able to protect his own disciples?

37. In fine, he humbly acknowledged that his power, his will, his ministry, his mission, his authority, his works, his knowledge, and his very life, were all from, and belonged to and were under the control of, the Father. "I can do nothing of myself;" "I came to do the will of him that sent me." "The Father that dwelleth within me, he doeth the work," &c. "A God within a God," is an old pagan Otaheitan doctrine.

38. He declared that even spiritual communion was the work of the Father. (See John vi. 45.)

39. He acknowledged himself controlled by the Father. (See John v. 30.)

40. He acknowledged his entire helplessness and dependence on the Father. "The Son can do nothing of himself, but what he seeth the Father do." (John v. 19.)

41. He acknowledged that even his body was the work of his Father; in other words, that he was dependent on his Father for his physical life. (See Heb. xvi. 5.)

42. And more than all, he not only called the Father "the only true God" (John xvii. 3), but calls him "my Father and my God." (John xx. 17.) Now, it would be superlative nonsense to consider a being himself a God, or the God, who could use such language as is here ascribed to the humble Jesus. This text, this language, is sufficient of itself to show that Christ could not have laid any claim to the Godhead on any occasion, unless we degrade him to the charge of the most palpable and shameful contradiction.

43. He uniformly directed his disciples to pray, not to him, but the Father. (See Matt. vi. 6.)

44. On one occasion, as we have cited the proof (in Matt. xi. 11), he even acknowledged John the Baptist to be greater than he; while it must be patent to every reader that no man could be greater than the almighty, supreme Potentate of heaven and earth, in any sense whatever.

45. Testimony of the disciples. Another remarkable proof of the human sireship of Jesus is, that one of his own disciples—ay, one of the chosen twelve, selected by him as being endowed with a perfect knowledge of his character, mission, and origin—this witness, thus posted and thus authorized, proclaims, in unequivocal language, that Jesus was the son of Joseph. Hear the language of Philip addressed to Nathanael. "We have found him of whom Moses, in the law and the prophets, did write—Jesus of Nazareth, the son of Joseph." (John i. 45.) No language could be more explicit, no declaration more positive, that Jesus was the son of Joseph. And no higher authority could be adduced to settle the question, coming as it does from "headquarters." And what will, or what can, the devout stickler for the divinely paternal origin of Jesus Christ do with such testimony? It is a clincher which no sophistry can set aside, no reasoning can grapple with, and no logic overthrow.

46. His disciples, instead of representing him as being "the only true God," often speak of him in contradistinction to God.

47. They never speak of him as the God Christ Jesus, but as "the man Christ Jesus." (1 Tim. ii. 5.) "Jesus of Nazareth, a man approved of God." (Acts ii. 23.) It would certainly be blasphemy to

speak of the Supreme Being as "a man approved of God." Christian reader, reflect upon this text. "By that man whom he (die Father) hath ordained" (Acts xvii. 3), by the assumption of the Godhead of Christ, we would be presented with the double or twofold solecism, 1st. Of God being "ordained" by another God; and 2d. That of his being blasphemously called a "man."

48. Paul's declaration has been cited. that "unto us there is but one God—the Father." (1 Cor. iv. 8.) Now, it is plain to common sense, that if there is but one God, and that God is comprehended in the Father, then Christ is entirely excluded from the Godhead.

49. If John's declaration be true, that "no man hath seen God at any time" (John iv. 12), then the important question arises, How could Christ be God, as he was seen by thousands of men, and seen hundreds of times?

50. God the Father is declared to be the "One," "the Holy One," "the only One," &c., more than one hundred times, as if purposely to exclude the participation of any other being in the Godhead.

51. This one, this only God, is shown to be the Father alone in more than four thousand texts, thirteen hundred and twenty-six of which are found in the New Testament.

52. More than fifty texts have been found which declare, either explicitly or by implication, that God the Father has no equal, which effectually denies or shuts out the divine equality of the Son. "To whom will ye liken me, or shall I be equal with, saith the holy One." (Isaiah xl. 25.)

53. Christ in the New Testament is called "man," and "the Son of man," eighty-four times,— egregious and dishonorable misnomers, most certainly, to apply to a supreme and infinite Deity. On the other hand, he is called God but three times, and denominates himself "the Son of God" but once, and that rather obscurely.

54. The Father is spoken of, in several instances, as standing in the relation of God to the Son, as "the God of our Lord Jesus Christ" (Acts iii. 2.) "Ye are Christ's, and Christ is Gods." (i Cor. xi. 3.) Now, the God of a God is a polytheistic, heathen conception; and 1 no meaning or interpretation, as we have shown, can be I forced upon such texts as these, that will not admit a plurality of Gods, if we admit the titles as applicable to Christ, or that his scriptural biographers intend to apply such a title in a superior or supreme sense.

55. Many texts make Christ the mere tool, agent, image, servant, or representative of God, as Christ, "the image of God" (Heb. i. 3), Christ, the appointed of God (Heb. iii. 1), Christ, "the servant of God" (Matt. xii. | 18), &c. To consider a being thus spoken of as himself the supreme God, is, as we have demonstrated, the very climax of absurdity and nonsense. To believe "the servant of God" is God himself,—that is, the servant of himself,—and that God and his "image" are the same, is to descend within one step of buffoonery.

56. And then it has been ascertained that there are more than three hundred texts which declare, either expressly or by implication, Christ's subordination to and dependence on the Father, as, "I

can do nothing of myself;" "Not mine, but his that sent me;" "I came to do the will of him that sent me" (John iv. 34); "I seek the will of my Father," &c.

57. And more than one hundred and fifty texts make the Son inferior to the Father, as "the Son knoweth not, but the Father does" (Mark viii. 32); "My Father is greater than I;" "The Son can do nothing of himself" (John v. 19), &c.

58. There are many divine titles applied to the Father which are never used in reference to the Son, as "Jehovah," "The Most High," "God Almighty," "The Almighty," &c.

On the other hand, those few divine epithets or titles which are used in application to Jesus Christ, as Lord, God, Savior, Redeemer, Intercessor, &c., it has been shown were all used prior to the birth of Christ, in application to beings known and acknowledged to be men, and some of them are found so applied in the bible itself; as, for example, Moses is called a God in two instances, as we have shown, and cited the proof (in Ex. iv. 16, vii. 1), while the title of Lord is applied to men at this day, even in Christian countries. And instances have been cited in the bible of the term Savior being applied to men, both in the singular and plural numbers. (See 2 Kings xiii. 5, and Neh. ix. 27.) Seeing, then, that the most important divine titles which the writers of the New Testament have applied to Jesus were previously used in application to men, known and admitted to be such, it is therefore at once evident that those titles do nothing toward proving him to be the Great Divine Being, as the modern Christian world assume him to be, even if we base the argument wholly on scriptural grounds. While, on the other hand, we have demonstrated it to be an absolute impossibility to apply with any propriety or any sense to a divine infinite omnipotent Being those finite human qualities which are so frequently used with reference to Jesus throughout the New Testament. And hence, even if we should suppose or concede that the writers of the New Testament did really believe him to be the great Infinite Spirit, or the almighty, omnipotent God,'we must conclude they were mistaken, from their own language, from their own description of him, as well as his own virtual denial and rejection of such a claim, when he applied to himself, as he did in nine cases out of ten, strictly finite human qualities and human titles (as we have shown), wholly incompatible with the character of an infinite divine Being. We say, from the foregoing considerations, if the primitive disciples of Jesus did really believe him to be the great Infinite, both their descriptions of him and his description or representation of himself, would amply and most conclusively prove that they were mistaken. At least we are compelled to admit that there is either an error in applying divine titles to Jesus, or often an error in describing his qualities and powers, by himself and his original followers, as there is no compatibility or agreement between the two. Divine titles to such a being as they represent him to be, would be an egregious misnomer. We say, then, that it must be clearly and conclusively evident to every unbiased mind, from evidence furnished by the bible itself, that if the divine titles applied to Jesus were intended to have a divine significance, then they are misapplied. Yet we would not here conclude an intentional misrepresentation in the case, but simply a mistake growing out of a misconception, and the very limited childish conception, of the nature, character, and attributes of the "great positive Mind," so universally prevalent in that semi-barbarous age, and the apparently total ignorance of the distinguishing characteristics which separate the divine and the human. We will illustrate: some children, on passing through a wild portion of the State of Maine recently, reported they encountered a bear; and to prove they could not be mistaken in the animal, they described it as being a tall, slight-built animal, with long slender legs, of yellowish auburn hue, a short, white, bushy tail, cloven feet, large branchy horns, &c. Now, it will be seen at once that, while their description of the animal is evidently in the main correct, they had simply mistaken a deer for a bear, and hence misnamed the animal.

In like manner we must conclude, from the repeated instances in which Christ's biographers have ascribed to him all the foibles, frailties, and finite qualities and characteristics of a human being, that if they have in any instance called him a God in a divine sense, it is an egregious misnomer. Their description of him makes him a man, and but a man, whatever may have been their opinion with respect to the propriety of calling him a God. And if the two do not harmonize, the former must rule the judgment in all cases. The truth is, the Jewish founders of Christianity entertained such a low, narrow, contracted, and mean opinion of Deity and the infinite distinction and distance between the divine and the human, that their theology reduced him to a level with man; and hence they usually described him as a man.

CHAPTER XL. A METONYMIC VIEW OF THE DIVINITY OF JESUS CHRIST

IF Jesus Christ were truly God, or if there existed such a co-equal and co-essential oneness between the Father and the Son that they constituted but one being or divine essence, then what is true of one is true of the other, and a change of names and titles from one to the other cannot alter the sense of the text. Let us, then, substitute the titles found applied to the Son in the New Testament, to the Father, and observe the effect:—

"My Son is greater than I." (John vii. 28)

"God can do nothing of himself." (John v. 19.)

"I must be about my Son's business." (Luke i. 49.)

"The kingdom of heaven is not mine to give. but the Son's." (Matt. xx. 23.)

"I am come in my Son's name, and ye receive me not" (John v. 43.)

"God cried, Jesus, why hast thou forsaken me?" (Matt. xiii. 28.)

"No man hath seen Jesus at any time." (1 John i. 5-)

"Jesus created all things by his Son." (Eph. iii. 9.)

"God sat down (in heaven) at the right hand of Jesus." (Luke xxii. 69.)

"There is one Jesus, one mediator between Jesus and men." (Gal. iii. 20.)

"Jesus gave his only begotten Father." (1 John iv. 9)

"God knows not the hour, but Jesus does." (Mark viii. 32.)

"God is the servant of Jesus." (Mark xii. 18.)

"God is ordained by Jesus." (Acts xvii. 31.)

"The head of God is Christ." (Eph. i. 3.)

"We have an advocate with Jesus, God the righteous." (1 John ii. 1.)

"Jesus gave all power to God." (Matt, xxviii. 18.)

"God abode all night in prayer to Jesus." (Luke vi. 12.)

"God came down from heaven to do the will of Jesus." (John vi. 38.)

"Jesus has made the Father his high priest." (Heb. x. 24.)

"Last of all, the Son sent the Father." (Matt. xxi. 39.)

"Jesus will save the world by that God whom he hath ordained."

"Jesus is God of the Father." (John xx. 17.)

"Jesus hath exalted God, and given him a more excellent name." (Phil. ii. 9.)

"Jesus hath made God a little lower than the angels." (Heb. ii. 9.)

"God can do nothing except what he seeth Jesus do." (John v. 19.)

Now, the question arises, Is the above representation a true one? Most certainly it must be, if Jesus and the Father are but one almighty Being. A change of names and titles cannot alter the truth nor the sense.

To say that Chief Justice Chase has gone south; Secretary Chase has gone south; Governor Chase has gone south; Ex-Senator Chase has gone south, or Salmon P. Chase has gone south, are affirmations equally true and equally sensible, because they all have reference to the same being; the case is to plain to need argument.

The above reversal of names and titles of Jesus and the Father may sound very unpleasant and rather grating to Christ-adoring Christians, simply because it is the transposition of the tides of two very scripturally dissimilar beings, instead of being, as generally taught by orthodox

216

Christians, "one in essence, one in mind, one in body or being, and one in name," as the Rev. Mr. Barnes affirms. Most self-evidently false is his statement, based solely on scriptural ground. If Jesus is "very God," and there is but one God, then the foregoing transposition cannot mar the sense nor altar the truth of one text quoted.

CHAPTER XLI. THE PRECEPTS AND PRACTICAL LIFE OF JESUS CHRIST; HIS TWO HUNDRED ERRORS

THE exaltation of men to the character and homage of divine beings has always had the effect to draw a vail over their errors and imperfections, so as to render them imperceptible to those who worship them as Gods. This is true of nearly all the deified men of antiquity, who were adored as incarnate divinities, among which may be included the Christian's man-God, Jesus Christ. The practice of the followers of these Gods has been, when an error was pointed out in their teachings, brought to light by the progress of science and general intelligence, to bestow upon the text some new and unwarranted meaning, entirely incompatible with its literal reading, or else to insist with a godly zeal on the correctness of the sentiment inculcated by the text, and thus essay to make error pass for truth. In this way millions of the disciples of these Gods have been misled and blinded, and made to believe by their religious teachers and their religious education, that everything taught by their assumed-to-be divine exemplars is perfect truth, in perfect harmony with science, sense, and true morals. Indeed, the perversion of the mind and judgment by a religious education has been in many cases carried to such an extreme as to cause their devout and prejudiced followers either to entirely overlook and ignore their erroneous teachings, or to magnify them into God-given truths, and thus, as before stated, clothe error with the livery of truth. This state of things, it has long been noticed by unprejudiced minds, exists amongst the millions of professed believers in the divinity of Jesus Christ. Hence the errors, both in his moral lessons and his practical life, have passed from age to age unnoticed, because his pious and awe-stricken followers, having been taught that he was a divine teacher, have assumed that his teachings must all be true; and hence. too, have instituted no scrutiny to determine their truth or falsity. But we will now proceed to show that the progress of science and general intelligence has brought to light many errors, not only in his teachings, but in his practical life also. In enumerating them, we will arrange them under the head

MORAL AND RELIGIOUS ERRORS.

1. The first moral precept in the teachings of Christ, which we will bring to notice, is one of a numerous class, which may very properly be arranged under the head of Moral Extremism. We find many of his admonitions of this character. Nearly everything that is said is oversaid, carried to extremes—thus constituting an overwrought, extravagant system of morality, impracticable in its requisitions; as, for example, "Take no thought for the morrow." (Matt, v.) If the spirit of this injunction were carried out in practical life, there would be no grain sown and no seed planted in

spring, no reaping done in harvest, and no crop garnered in autumn; and the result would be universal starvation in less than twelve months. But, fortunately for society, the Christian world have laid this positive injunction upon the table under the rule of "indefinite postponement."

2. Christ's assumed-to-be most important requisition is found in the injunction, "Seek ye first the Kingdom of God, and his righteousness, and all else shall be added unto you." (Matt. vi. 33.) His early followers understood by this injunction, and doubtless understood it correctly, that they were to spend their lives in religious devotion, and neglect the practical duties of life, leaving "Providence" to take care of their families—a course of life which reduced many of them to the point of starvation.

3. The disciple of Christ is required, "when smitten on one cheek," to turn the other also that is, when one cheek is pommeled into a jelly by some vile miscreant or drunken wretch, turn the other, to be smashed up in like manner. This is an extravagant requisition, which none of his modern disciples even attempt to observe.

4. "Resist not evil" (Matt. v. 34) breathes forth a kindred spirit. This injunction requires you to stand with your hands in your pocket while being maltreated so cruelly and unmercifully that the forfeiture of your life may be the consequence—at least Christ's early followers so understood it.

5. The disciple of Christ is required, when his cloak is formally wrested from him, to give up his coat also. (See Matt. v.) And to carry out the principle, if the marauder demands it, he must next give up his boots, then his shirt, and thus strip himself of all his garments, and go naked. This looks like an invitation and bribe to robbery.

6. "Lay not up for yourselves treasures on earth." (Matt. vi. 19.) This is another positive command of Christ, which the modern Christian world, by common consent, have laid on the table under the rule of "indefinite postponement," under the conviction that the wants of their families and the exigencies of sickness and old age cannot be served if they should live up to such an injunction.

7. "Sell all that thou hast,... and come and follow me," is another command which bespeaks more piety than wisdom, as all who have attempted to comply with it have reduced their families to beggary and want.

8. "If any man love the world, the love of the Father is not in him." Then he must hate it, as there are but the two principles, and "from hate proceed envy, strife, evil surmisings, and persecution." Evidently the remedy in this case for "worldly-mindedness" is worse than the disease.

9. "He that cometh to me, and hateth not father, mother, brother, and sister, &c., cannot be my disciple." (Luke xiv. 26). This breathes forth the same spirit as the last text quoted above. Many learned expositions have been penned by Christian writers to make it appear, that hate in this case does not mean hate. But certainly it would be a slander upon infinite wisdom to leave it to be inferred that he could not say or "inspire" his disciples to say exactly what he meant, and to say it so plainly as to leave no possibility of being misunderstood, or leave any ground for dispute about the meaning.

10. "Rejoice and be exceeding glad" when persecuted. (Matt. v. 4.) Now, as a state of rejoicing is the highest condition of happiness that can be realized, such advice must naturally prompt the religious zealot to court persecution, in order to obtain complete happiness, and consequently to pursue a dare-devil life to provoke persecution.

11. "Whosoever shall seek to save his life, shall lose it," &c. (Luke xvii. 33.) Here is displayed the spirit of martyrdom which has made millions reckless of life, and goaded on the frenzied bigot to seek the fiery fagot and the halter. We regard it as another display of religious fanaticism.

12. "Ye shall be hated of all men for my name's sake." (Matt. x. 12.) How repulsive must have been their doctrines or their conduct! No sensible religion could excite the universal hatred of mankind. For it would contain something adapted to the moral, religious, or spiritual taste of some class or portion of society, and hence make it and its disciples loved instead of hated. And then how could they be "hated of all men," when not one man in a thousand ever heard of them? Here is more of the extravagance of religious enthusiasm.

13. "Shake off the dust of your feet" against those who cannot see the truth or utility of your doctrines. (Matt. x. 14.) Here Christ encourages in his disciples a spirit of contempt for the opinions of others calculated to make them "hated." A proper regard for the rules of good-breeding would have forbidden such rudeness toward strangers for a mere honest difference of opinion.

14. "Take nothing for your journey, neither staff, nor scrip, nor purse" (Mark vi. 8); that is "sponge on your friends, and force yourselves on your enemies," the latter class of which seem to have been much the most numerous. A preacher who should attempt to carry out this advice at the present day would be stopped at the first toll-gate, and compelled to return. Here is more violation of the rules of good-breeding, and the common courtesies of civilized life.

15. "Go and teach all nations," &c. Why issue an injunction that could not possibly be carried out? It never has been, and never will be, executed, for three-fourths of the human race have never yet heard of Christianity. It was not, therefore, a mark of wisdom, or a superior mind, to issue such an injunction.

16. "And he that believeth and is baptized shall be saved; but he that believeth not shall be damned." What intolerance, bigotry, relentless cruelty, and ignorance of the science of mind are here displayed! No philosopher would give utterance to, or indorse such a sentiment. It assumes that belief is a creature of the will, and that a man can believe anything he chooses, which is wide of the truth. And the assumption has been followed by persecution, misery, and bloodshed.

17. "All things whatsoever ye shall ask in prayer, believing, ye shall receive." (Matt. xxi. 22.) Here is an entire negation of natural law in the necessity of physical labor as a means to procure the comforts of life. When anything is wanted in the shape of food or raiment, it is to be obtained, according to this text, by going down on your knees and asking God to bestow it. But no Christian ever realized "all things whatsoever asked for in prayer," thought "believing with all his heart" he should obtain it. The author knows, by his own practical experience, that this

declaration is not true. This promise has been falsified thousands of times by thousands of praying Christians.

18. "Be not called rabbi." "Call no man your father." (Matt, xxiii.) The Christian world assume that much of what Christ taught is mere idle nonsense, or the incoherent utterings of a religious fanatic; for they pay no more practical attention to it than the barking of a dog. And here is one command treated in this manner: "Call no man father." Where is the Christian who refuses to call his earthly sire a father?

19. "Call no man master." (Matt, xxiii.) And yet mister, which is the same thing, is the most common title in Christendom.

20. He who enunciates the two words, "'Thou fool.' shall be in danger of hell fire." (Matt, xxii.) Mercy! Who, then, can be saved? For there is probably not a live Christian in the world who has not called somebody a "fool," when he knew him to be such, and could not with truthfulness be called anything else. Here, then, is another command universally ignored and "indefinitely postponed."

21. "Swear not at all, neither by heaven nor earth." (Matt, v.) And yet no Christian refuses to indulge in legal, if not profane, swearing which the text evidently forbids.

22. "Men ought always to pray." (Luke xviii.) No time to be allowed for eating or sleeping. More religious fanaticism.

23. "Whosoever will be chief among you let him be your servant" (Matt. xx. 27); that is, no Christian professor shall be a president, governor, major-general, deacon, or priest. Another command laid on the table.

24. "Love your enemies." (Matt. v. 44.) Then what kind of feeling should we cultivate toward friends? And how much did he love his enemies when he called them "fools," "liars," "hypocrites," "generation of vipers," &c.? And yet he is held up as "our" example in love, meekness, and forbearance. But no man ever did love an enemy. It is a moral impossibility, as much so as to love bitter or nauseating food. The advice of the Roman slave Syrus is indicative of more sense and wisdom—"Treat your enemy kindly, and thus make him a friend."

25. We are required to forgive an enemy four hundred and ninety times; that is, "seventy times seven." (Matt, vii.) Another outburst of religious enthusiasm; another proof of an overheated imagination.

26. "Be ye perfect, even as your Father in heaven is perfect." (Matt. v. 48.) Here is more of the religious extravagance of a mind uncultured by science. For it is self-evident that human beings can make no approximation to divine perfection. The distance between human imperfection and a perfect God is, and ever must be, infinite.

27. Christ commended those who "became eunuchs for the kingdom of heaven's sake" (Matt. xix. 12)—a custom requiring a murderous, self-butchering process; destructive of the energies of

life and the vigor of manhood, and rendering the subject weak, effeminate, and mopish, and unfit for the business of life. It is a low species of piety, and discloses a lamentable lack of a scientific knowledge of the true functions of the sexual organs on the part of Jesus.

28. Christ also encouraged his disciples to "pluck out the eye," and "cut off the hand," as a means of rendering it impossible to perpetrate evil with those members. And we would suggest, if such advice is consistent with sound reasoning, the head also should be cut off, as a means of more effectually carrying out the same principle. Such advice never came from the mouth of a philosopher. It is a part of Christ's system of extravagant piety.

29. He also taught the senseless, oriental tradition of "the unpardonable sin against the Holy Ghost"—a fabulous being who figured more anciently in the history of various countries. (See Chapter XXII.) No philosopher or man of science could harbor such childish misconceptions as are embodied in this tradition, which neither describes the being nor explains the nature of the sin.

30. We find many proofs, in Christ's Gospel history, that he believed in the ancient heathen tradition which taught that disease is caused by demons and evil spirits. (See Luke vii. 21, and viii. 2.)

31. Many cases are reported of his relieving the obsessed by casting out the diabolical intruders, in imitation of the oriental custom long in vogue in various countries, by which he evinced a profound ignorance of the natural causes of disease.

32. Christ also taught the old pagan superstition that "God is a God of anger," while modern science teaches that it would be as impossible for a God of perfect and infinite attributes to experience the feeling of anger as to commit suicide; and recent discoveries in physiology prove that anger is a species of suicide. and that it is also a species of insanity. Hence an angry God would be an insane God—an omnipotent lunatic, "ruling the kingdom of heaven," which would make heaven a lunatic asylum, and rather a dangerous place to live.

33. And Christ's injunction to "fear God" also implies that he is an angry being. (See Luke xxiii. 40.) But y past history proves that "the fear of God" has always been the great lever of priestcraft, and the most paltry and pitiful motive that ever moved the human mind. It has paralyzed the noblest intellects, crushed the elasticity of youth, and augmented the hesitating indecision of old age, and finally filled the world with cowardly, trembling slaves. No philosopher will either love or worship a God he fears. "The fear of the Lord" is a very ancient heathen superstition.

34. The inducement Christ holds out for leading a virtuous life by the promise of "Well done, thou good and faithful servant," bespeaks a childish ignorance of the nature of the human mind and the true science of life. It ranks with the promise of the nurse of sugar-plums to the boy if he would keep his garments unsoiled. (For the remainder of the two hundred errors of Christ, see Vol. II.)

221

There are many other errors found in the precepts and practical life of Jesus Christ (which we are compelled to omit an exposition of here), such as his losing his temper, and abusing the money-changers by overthrowing their counting-table, and expelling them from the temple with a whip of cords when engaged in a lawful' and laudable business; his getting mad at and cursing the fig tree; his dooming Capernaum to hell in a fit of anger; his being deceived by two of his disciples (Peter and Judas), which prompted him to call them devils; his implied approval of David, with his fourteen crimes and penitentiary deeds, and also Abraham, with his falsehoods, polygamy, and incest, and his implied sanction of the Old Testament, with all its errors and numerous crimes; his promise to his twelve apostles to "sit upon the twelve thrones of Israel" in heaven, thus evincing a very limited and childish conception of the enjoyments of the future life; his puerile idea of sin, consisting in a personal affront to a personal God; his omission to say anything about human freedom, the inalienable rights of man, &c.

THE SCIENTIFIC ERRORS OF CHRIST.

That Jesus Christ was neither a natural or moral philosopher is evident from the following facts:—

1. He never made any use of the word "philosophy."

2. Never gave utterance to the word "science."

3. Never spoke of a natural law, or assigned a natural cause for anything. The fact that he never made use of these words now so current in all civilized countries, is evidence that he was totally ignorant of these important branches of knowledge, the cultivation of which is now known to be essential to the progress of civilization. And yet it is claimed his religion has been a great lever in the advancement of civilization. But this is a mistake—a solemn mistake, as elsewhere shown. (See Chap. XLV.)

4. Everything to Christ was miracle; everything was produced and controlled by the arbitrary power of an angry or irascible God. He evidently had no idea of a ruling principle in nature or of the existence of natural law, as controlling any event he witnessed. Hence he set no bounds to anything, and recognized no limits to the possible. He believed God to be a supernatural personal being, who possessed unlimited power, and who ruled and controlled everything by his arbitrary will, without any law or any limitation to its exercises. Hence he told his disciples they would have anything they prayed for in faith; that by faith they could roll mountains into the sea, or bring to a halt the rolling billows of the mighty deep. He evidently believed that the forked lightning, the out-bursting earth-shaking thunder, and the roaring, heaving volcano were but pliant tools or obsequious servants to the man of faith. And he displays no less ignorance of the laws of mind than the laws of nature; thus proving him to have been neither a natural, moral, nor mental philosopher. He omitted to teach the great moral lessons learned by human experience, of which he was evidently totally ignorant.

5. He never taught that the practice of virtue contains its own reward.

6. That the question of right and wrong of any action is to be decided by its effect upon the individual, or upon society.

7. That no life can be displeasing to God which is useful to man.

8. And he omitted to teach the most important lesson that can engage the attention of man, viz.: that the great purpose of life is self-development.

9. That no person can attain or approximate to real happiness without bestowing a special attention to the cultivation and exercise of all the mental and physical faculties, so far as to keep them in a healthy condition. None of the important lessons above named are hinted at in his teachings, which, if punctually observed, would do more to advance the happiness of the human race than all the sermons Christ or Christna ever preached, or ever taught.

10. And then he taught many doctrines which are plainly contradicted by the established principle of modern science, such as,—

11. Diseases being produced by demons, devils, or wicked spirits. (See Mark ix. 20.)

Christ nowhere assigns a natural cause for disease, or a scientific explanation for its cure.

12. His rebuking a fever discloses a similar lack of scientific knowledge. (See Luke iv. 39.)

13. His belief in a literal hell and a lake of fire and brimstone (see Matt, xviii. 8) is an ancient heathen superstition science knows nothing about, and has no use for.

14. His belief in a personal devil also (see Matt. xvii. 88), which is another oriental tradition, furnishes more sad proof of an utter want of scientific knowledge, as science has no place for and no use for such a being.

15. Christ taught the unphilosophica. doctrine of repentance, as he declared he "came to call sinners to repentance" (Matt. ix. 13)—a mental process, which consists merely in a revival of early impressions, and often leads a person to condemn that which is right, as well as that which is wrong. (For proof, see Chapter XLIII.)

16. The doctrine of "forgiveness," which Christ so often inculcated, is also at variance with the teachings of science, as it can do nothing toward changing the nature of the act forgiven, or toward cancelling its previous effects upon society. Science teaches that every crime has its penalty attached to it, which no act of forgiveness, by God or man, can arrest or set aside.

17. But nothing evinces, perhaps, more clearly Christ's total lack of scientific knowledge than his holding a man responsible for his belief, and condemning for disbelief, as he does in numerous instances (see Mark xvi. 16), for a man could as easily control the circulation of the blood in his veins as control his belief. Science teaches that belief depends upon evidence, and without it, it is impossible to believe, and with it, it is impossible to disbelieve. How foolish and unphilosophical, therefore, to condemn for either belief or disbelief!

223

18. The numerous cases in which Christ speaks of the heart as being the seat of consciousness, instead of the brain, evinces a remarkable ignorance of the science of mental philosophy. He speaks of an "upright heart," "a pure heart," &'c., when "an upright liver," "a pure liver," would be as sensible, as the latter has as much to do with the character as the former.

19. And the many cases in which he makes it meritorious to have a right "faith," and places it above reason, and assumes it to be a voluntary act, shows his utter ignorance of the nature of the human mind.

20. And Christ evinced a remarkable ignorance of the cause of physical defects, when he told his hearers a certain man was born blind, in order that he might cure him. (Matt. vii. 22.)

21. And Christ's declaration, that those who marry are not worthy of being saved (see Luke xx. 34), shows that he was very ignorant of the nature of the sexual functions of the human system.

22. Nothing could more completely demonstrate a total ignorance of the grand science of astronomy than Christ's prediction of the stars falling to the earth. (See Luke xxi. 25.)

23. And the conflagration of the world, "the gathering of the elect," and the realization of a fancied millennium, which he several times predicted would take place in his time, "before this generation pass away" (Matt, xxiv. 34), proves a like ignorance, both of astronomy and philosophy.

24. And his cursing of the fig tree for not bearing fruit in the winter season (see Matt. xxi. 20), not only proves his ignorance of the laws of nature, but evinces a bad temper.

25. Christ indorses the truth of Noah's flood story (see Luke xvii. 27), which every person at the present day, versed in science and natural law, knows is mere fiction, and never took place.

And numerous other errors, evincing the most profound ignorance of science and natural law, might be pointed out in Christ's teachings, if we had space for them. It has always been alleged by orthodox Christendom, that Christ's teaching and moral system are so faultless as to challenge criticism, and so perfect as to defy improvement. But this is a serious mistake. For most of his precepts and moral inculcations which are not directly at war with the principles of science, or do not involve a flagrant violation of the laws of nature, are, nevertheless, characterized by a lawless and extravagant mode of expression peculiar to semi-savage life, and which, as it renders it impossible to reduce them to practice, shows they could not have emanated from a philosopher, or man of science, or a man of evenly-balanced mind. They impose upon the world a system of morality, pushed to such extremes that its own professed admirers do not live it out, or even attempt to do so. They long ago abandoned it as an impracticable duty. We will prove this by enumerating most of its requisitions, and showing that they are daily violated and trampled under foot by all Christendom. Where can the Christian professor be found who, 1. "takes no thought for the morrow" or, 2. who "lays not up treasure on earth," or, at least, tries to do it; or, 3. who "gives up all his property to the poor;" or who, "when his cloak is wrested from him by a robber," gives up his coat also; or who calls no man master or mister (the most common title in Christendom); or who calls no man father (if he has a father); or who calls no man a fool (when he knows he is a fool); or who, when one cheek is pommeled into a jelly by some vile miscreant or drunken wretch, turns the other to be battered up in the same way; or who prays without ceasing; or who rejoices when persecuted; or who forgives an enemy four hundred and ninety times (70 times 7); or who manifests by his practical life that he loves his enemies (the way he loves him is to report him to the grand jury, or hand him over to the sheriff); or who forsakes houses and land, and everything, "for the kingdom of heaven's sake." No Christian professor lives up to these precepts, or any of them, or even tries to do so. To talk, therefore, of finding a practical Christian, while nearly the whole moral code of Christ is thus daily and habitually outraged and trampled under foot by all the churches and every one of the two hundred millions of Christian professors, is bitter irony and supreme solecism. We would go five hundred miles, or pay five hundred dollars, to see a Christian. If a man can be a Christian while openly and habitually violating every precept of Christ, then the word has no meaning. These precepts, the Christian world finding to be impossible to practice, have unanimously laid upon the table under the rule of "indefinite postponement." They are the product of a mind with an ardent temperament, and the religious faculties developed to excess, and unrestrained by scientific or intellectual culture. A similar vein of extravagant religious duty is found in the Essenian, Budhist, and Pythagorean systems. As Zera Colburn possessed the mathematical faculty to excess, and Jenny Lind the musical talent, Christ in like manner was all religion. And from the extreme ardor of his religious feeling, thus derived, sprang his extravagant notions of the duties of life. This peculiarity of his organization explains the whole mystery.

CHRIST AS A MAN, AND CHRIST AS A SECTARIAN.

To every observant and unbiased mind a strange contrast must be visible in the practical life of Jesus Christ when viewed in his twofold capacity of a man and a priest. While standing upon the broad plane of humanity with his deep sympathetic nature directed toward the poor, the unfortunate, and the downtrodden, there often gushed forth from his impassioned bosom the most sublime expressions of pity, and the strongest outburst of commiseration for wrongs and sufferings, and his noble goodness and tender love yearned with a throbbing heart to relieve them. But the moment he put on the sacerdotal robe, and assumed the character of a priest, that moment, if any one crossed his path by refusing to yield to his requisitions of faith, or dissented from his religious creed, his whole nature was seemingly changed. It was no longer, "Blessed are ye," but "Cursed are ye," or "Woe unto you." Like the founders of other religious systems, he was ardent toward friends and bitter toward enemies, and extolled his own religion, while he denounced all others. His way was the only way, and all who did not walk threin, or conform thereto, were loaded with curses and imprecations, and all who could not accomplish the impossible mental achievement of believing everything he set forth or urged upon their credence, and that, too, without evidence, were to be eternally damned. All who climbed up any other way were thieves and robbers. All who professed faith in any other religion than his were on the road to hell. Like the oriental Gods, he taught that the world was to be saved through faith in him and his religion. All who did not honor him were to be dishonored by the Father. And "without faith (in him and his religion), it is impossible to please God." He declared that all who were not for him were against him; and all who were not on the same road are "heathens and publicans." His disciples were enjoined to shake off the dust from their feet as a manifestation of displeasure toward those who could not conscientiously subscribe to their creeds and dogmas. Thus we discover a strong vein of intolerance and sectarianism in the religion of the otherwise, and in other respects, the kind and loving Jesus. Though most benignantly kind and affectionate while moving and acting under the controlling impulses of his lofty manhood, yet when his ardent religious feelings were touched, he became chafed, irritated, and sometimes intolerant. He then could tolerate no such thing as liberty of conscience, or freedom of thought, or the right to differ with him in religious belief. His extremely ardent devotional nature, when roused into action in defense of a stereotyped faith, eclipsed his more noble, lofty, and lovely traits, and often dimmed his mental vision, thus presenting in the same individual a strange medley, and a strange contrast of the most opposite traits of character. That such a being should have been considered and worshipped as a God, and for the very reason that he possessed such strange, contradictory traits of character, and often let his religion run riot with his reason, will be looked upon by posterity as one of the strangest chapters in the history of the human race. But so it is. Extraordinary good qualities, though intermingled with many errors and human foibles, have deified many men.

Note. One Christian writer alleges, in defense of the objectionable precepts of Jesus Christ, that "He taught some errors in condescension to the ignorance of the people." If this be true, that he taught both truth and falsehood, then the question arises, How can we know which is which? By what rule can we discriminate them, as he himself furnishes none? Or how are we to determine that he taught truth at all? And then this plea would account for and excuse all the errors found in the teachings of the oriental Gods. If it will apply in one case, it will in the other. And thus it proves too much.

CHAPTER XLII. CHRIST AS A SPIRITUAL MEDIUM

THERE are many incidents related in the life of Christ, which, when critically examined, furnish abundant evidence that he was what is now known as a spiritual medium. He unquestionably represented, and often practically exhibited, several important phases of modern mediumship.

1. The many instantaneous cures which he wrought, as reported in his Gospel narrative, performed in the same manner that "spirit doctors" now heal the sick, prove that he was an excellent "healing medium."

2. His declaration to Nathanael, "When thou wast under the fig tree, I saw thee," and his recounting to the woman of Samaria the deeds of her past life (acts similar to which are now performed every day by spiritualists), are evidence that he was also a "clairvoyant medium."

3. His walking on the water (if the story is true), as D. D. Home has frequently, within the past few years, walked or floated on the air in the presence of many witnesses (including men of science, royal personages, and members of parliament), entitles him to the appellation of a "physical medium."

4. And the circumstance of his pointing his disciples to the mark of the spear in his side, and the print of the nails in his hands, while amongst them as a spirit, has led many spiritualists to

226

conclude he was also a "medium for materialization." His spirit was made to present the peculiar marks which had been inflicted upon his physical body, cases parallel to which are now witnessed every day by modern spiritualists. Hundreds of cases have occurred of departed spirits presenting themselves to their friends with all the peculiar marks which their physical bodies had long worn while in the earth life. And the former physical wounds have often been exhibited by the spirit in the same manner Christ exhibited his. And thus spiritualism explains the phenomenon which otherwise would be entirely incredible.

5. And there is yet another phase of mediumship which Christ often exhibited in his practical life. He claimed to have frequent intercourse with some invisible being, whom he called "the Father." But as modern science has settled the question of the personality of God in the negative, we are led to conclude that Christ, like many eminent persons since his time, mistook some finite spirit for the great infinite but impersonal Father spirit—though his attendant invisible companion was probably a spirit of a very high order. And the great beauty and grandeur of his life are exhibited by his frequent intercourse with and dependence upon this his "guardian spirit." He declared he did nothing of himself, so dependent was he upon his invisible guide. And the strongest proof that he had a spirit companion, which he often looked to for counsel and aid, and that this was the being he called the Father, is furnished by the fact, that when he prayed to the Father, his petition was answered by an angel spirit. (See Luke xxii. 44.) And there is no account and no evidence of any invisible or spiritual being ever presenting itself to him but an angel or spirit. That he should have supposed this spirit to be the great infinite Father God was very natural. Thousands since, and some before his time, committed a similar mistake. The author has known several persons who had long had intercourse with some invisible being they supposed to be God, who have recently, by the light afforded by modern spiritualism, become entirely convinced that they had simply mistaken a finite spirit for the great Infinite Spirit. And did Christ live in our day, he would probably be rescued from a similar error in the same way. In conclusion, we will remark that it was doubtless his frequent displays of several very remarkable phases of spiritual mediumship that contributed much to lead the people into the error of supposing him to be God. And this fact will yet be known.

CHAPTER XLIII. CONVERSION, REPENTANCE, AND "GETTING RELIGION" OF HEATHEN ORIGIN

THEIR NUMEROUS EVILS AND ABSURDITIES.

OF all the follies ever enacted or exhibited under the sun, and of all the ignorance of history, science, and human nature ever displayed in the history of the human race, that which stands out in bold relief, as pre-eminent, is the fashionable custom of conversion, or "getting religion." When the evidence lies all around us as thick as the fallen leaves of autumn, clustering on the pages of history, and proclaimed by every principle of mental science, that what is called conversion is nothing but a mental and temperamental or nervous phenomenon—a psychological process—how can we rank those amongst intelligent people who still claim it to be "the power of God operating upon the soul of the sinner"? Ignorance is the only plea that can acquit them of the charge of imbecility. The number who daily fall victims to this priestly delusion in various parts of the country may be reckoned by thousands. We propose in this chapter to exhibit some of the evils and absurdities of this widespread delusion and religious mono-mania. To do so the more effectually, we will arrange the presentation of the subject under four separate heads. We will attempt to show,—

1. Its historical errors.

2. Its logical errors.

3. Its philosophical or scientific errors.

4. Its moral evils.

1st. *Its Historical Errors.*—Can we conceive it possible that the thousands of priests who are now employed in "converting souls to God" are so ignorant of history as not to know that it is an old pagan custom? that it was prevalent in heathen countries long before a single soul was converted to Christianity, and is carried on to some extent now, both among pagans and Mahomedans? From such facts it would appear (viewing the matter from the Christian stand-point) that God is indifferent as to what kind of religion, or what sort of religious nonsense, people are converted to, or whether it is truth or error they embrace, or whether it is a true religion or a false one they imbibe, so he gets them converted. According to Mr. Higgins, the practice of converting people from one sect to another by the popular priesthood was prevalent under the ancient Persian system, and was carried on there quite extensively more than three thousand years ago; and the process was essentially the same as that now in vogue amongst modern Methodists, and the effect the same. At their large revival meetings the whole congregation would sometimes become so affected under the eloquent ministrations of the officiating priest, as to cry, and shout, and prostrate themselves upon the ground, which was afterward found to be drenched with their tears; and on these occasions they would confess their sins to each other, and to their priests; and yet those very sins they condemned were, perhaps, amongst the best acts of their lives, while their real crimes were overlooked and justified, instead of being condemned, thus showing that an honest, just, and sensible God could have had nothing to do with it. And we have reports of similar scenes witnessed more recently among the Mahomedans. Major Denham furnishes us an account of some "revival meetings" he attended a few years since in Arabia, carried on by one of the Mahomedan sects. On one occasion the effect of the discourse of the preacher upon the audience in the way of "converting souls to God" was so powerful, that he could only convince himself that he was not in a Methodist revival meeting by a knowledge of his geographical position. The preacher's name was Malem Chadily, and here is a specimen of some of his language. "Turn, turn, sinner, unto God; confess he is good, and that Mahomet is his prophet; wash, and become clean of your sins, and paradise is open before you: without this nothing can save you from eternal fire." During this earnest appeal (says the major), tears flowed plentifully, and everybody appeared to be affected. One of his hearers, becoming converted, shouted, "Your words pierce my soul," and fell upon the floor. Now let it be borne in mind, that Mahomet is stigmatized and condemned by the Christian churches as "a false prophet," and his religion denounced as "a system of fraud," "a false religion," &c. Of course, then, Christians will not argue, nor admit, that conversion, and "getting religion," in this case, is the work of God. A just God would have nothing to do in converting people to "a false religion." What explanation shall we adopt for it then? To assume it to be the work of the devil (the dernier resort for all religious difficulties), and conversions among Christians the work of God, when both are so clearly and obviously alike, is to insult common sense. To assume that two things, exactly alike in character, can be exactly and diametrically unlike in origin, is a scientific paradox which no person of common intelligence can swallow, or accept for a moment. Both, then, we must admit, have the same origin. This train of argument leads us to speak of—

2d. *The Logical Absurdities of the Doctrine of Conversion.*—There are several circumstances which point, unmistakably as the needle to the pole, to the mundane origin of the phenomenon of conversion.

The character of many of the priestly conductors who "run the battery," is sufficient of itself to preclude the hypothesis of any divine agency in the matter. The most powerful revivalist we ever knew, the priest who could convert an audience the quickest, and bring down sinners to the mourners' bench faster than any other clergyman we ever heard "dealing out damnation" to the people, was a broad-shouldered, muscular, stentorian-voiced circuit rider of the "Buckeye State," who, as was afterward learned, was guilty of perpetrating some of the blackest crimes that ever blotted the page of human history, at the very time of his most successful career in the way of "convicting souls of sin, and converting them to God." He was apprehended by the officers of the law in the midst of one of his most flourishing revivals, under the twofold charge, i. Of being the father of an illegitimate child, the young mother of which was a member of his church; 2. Of defrauding one of his neighbors in a trade, to the amount of nearly a thousand dollars—both of which charges he was convicted of. A similar case, but possessing some worse features, occurred a few years since in the county in which the author now resides. A preacher, who had had criminal connection with a young woman of his church, in order to conceal his guilt resorted to the damnable expedient of administering poison to his victim shortly before his illicit intercourse with her would have been made manifest by the birth of a child, thus committing a double murder. He was apprehended for the crime while carrying on "a most glorious revival," as it was styled by some of the deluded congregation. Now to ascribe the irresistible power which these two preachers exerted over their audience (in the way of "converting them to God") to a divine source, as they claimed for it, would be to trifle with common sense, common decency, and all honorable conceptions of a God. These reverend scamps often instituted the high claim of being "called of God" to their ministerial labors. But if we concede the claim, we should have to conclude that God knew but little about them, for he certainly would not knowingly employ such moral outlaws upon such an important mission.

Having thus briefly spoken of the character of some of the actors and agents in the work of conversion, we will now glance at the character of some of the religions and religious ideas, and moral course of conduct, to which the sinner is converted. It is evident that if an All-wise God had anything to do in the process of converting people to any system of religion, he would also convert them to correct moral habits. But in many cases, after conversion they are no nearer right in this respect, and in some cases further from it than before being thus sanctified. In some cases their religion becomes worse, their religious ideas less sensible, and their moral conduct more objectionable, by "the change of heart" in "getting religion." Mr. Spencer informs us that the Vewas, a sect or tribe of the Feegees, often cry for hours under conviction for sin. And what is that sin? Why, the neglect to offer sacrifices to their God. And those sacrifices consist in human beings, sometimes their own children. And their conviction, conversion, and repentance only make them more diligent in practicing this crime. It is evident, then, that their religion is at war with their humanity, and the former always triumphs in the contest. They are addicted to cannibalism, infanticide, and polygamy. But as the process of "getting religion" never makes anybody more intelligent, the "change of heart," with the Vewas, never changes their views, or opens their eyes to see the enormity of their crimes. In "getting religion" people get neither sense, knowledge, nor morality. They get neither a larger stock, nor an improved quality, of either. Their moral conduct is not often sensibly improved, materially or permanently.

3d. *Scientific Errors, and Scientific Explanations of Conversion.*—The phenomena of conversion and "getting religion" are so easily explained in the light of science and philosophy, and that explanation is susceptible of so many proofs and demonstrations, that it seems remarkably strange that any persons claiming to be intelligent, and situated in the focal, scientific light of the nineteenth century, should still be hampered with the delusion that such phenomena are the direct display of the power of God. It requires but little investigation and reflection to convince any person that what is called conversion, and "repentance for sin," is nothing but the revival of early educational impressions resuscitated by the influence of mind on mind. No person has ever been known to get or embrace a religion he was not biased in favor of prior to the time of his conversion, unless we except a few weak-minded persons negative to any influence, and convertible to any religion the priest may urge upon their attention. A very strong proof of this statement is furnished by the history of the Christian missionary enterprise. The reports of travelers and sojourners in India show, that with two hundred years' labor, and two hundred missionaries in the field during a part of that period, the churches have not succeeded in converting one in ten thousand of the Hindoos to the Christian religion—unless we except those who, while children, were sent to Christian schools instituted by the missionaries for the special purpose of converting and warping the young mind, and welding it to the Christian faith before It should receive an unchangeable and unyielding bias in favor of another religion. So fruitless has been the effort to convert to Christianity those who were already established in the religion of the country, that, according to the estimate of Colonel Dow, each convert, on an average, has cost the missionary enterprise not less than ten thousand dollars. An intelligent Hindoo, while lecturing recently in London, made the remarkable statement, that conversions which are made to the Christian religion are not amongst the intelligent or learned classes, but are confined to the low, ignorant, and superstitious classes, "who have not sense or intelligence enough to perceive the difference between the *religion they are converted to, and that which they are converted from.*" And the effort to convert the Mahomedans, Chinese, Persians, and the disciples of other religions has been attended with the same fruitless results—all seeming to warrant the conclusion that God can do but little toward converting any nation to Christianity which has always been biased in favor of another religion. The reason why people are so easily converted from one sect to another in Christian countries is owing to the fact that their religious convictions are unsettled. The members of the different Christian sects are all mixed up together in the various settlements throughout the country, and are brought in daily contact with each other in the busy scenes of life.

230

Hence the children have the seeds of Methodism, Presbyterianism, Baptistism, Quakerism, and various other isms implanted in their minds in very early life. And which one of these will ultimately predominate depends upon what priest they fall victims to first. Having thus the germs of so many religious isms implanted in their minds, they are easily shifted about, and converted from one sect to another. And this shuttlecock process is called "getting religion," while, if they had lived in a country where only one form of religion exists, they would be as hard to convert as Mahomedans and Hindoos.

Repentance.—Much importance is attached by the orthodox churches to the act of getting religion in the dying hour,—called "death-bed repentance,"—as if the person were better capable of discriminating between right and wrong when his brain is deranged with fever, and his whole system racked with disease and pain, than when in health. Such repentance can do nothing more than prove the honesty of the dying man or woman. For very often their doctrines, or religious belief, will be found no nearer right, and sometimes more erroneous after repentance than before, as repentance merely consists in the return to early impressions—the revival of former convictions, which may be either right or wrong, and are about as likely to be the latter as the former. No instance can be found of a person condemning a wrong act, or a wrong course of life, in his dying moments, unless he had previously believed it to be wrong, or if he had always believed it to be right. How much, then, does repentance do toward deciding what is right and what is wrong? Mahomedanism we know to be deeply fraught with error, but we never read nor heard of an instance of the many millions who had been educated to believe it is right, condemning it on their death-beds, or repenting for not having embraced Christianity, and led the life of a Christian, or for adoring Mahomet instead of Jesus Christ. On the contrary we have a well-authenticated instance of a Mahomedan (a Mr. Merton) who had embraced Christianity, and lived the life of a Christian for many years, renouncing it all, and returning to his primitive faith, when he was taken sick and became apprehensive he was going to die: his early religious impressions, returning involuntarily, wiped out his Christianity, and he died glorying in Mahomedanism. And we have an equally well authenticated case of an Indian of the Choctaw tribe, who had been taught to believe from early life that the white man was his natural enemy, and that it was his right and duty to kill him, repenting on his death-bed for having a short time previously neglected, when the opportunity presented, to despatch a "pale face" he met in his travels. Instead of killing him, he yielded for the moment to the impulse of his better feelings, and passed him by. But on reviewing his past life at the approach of death, he came to the conclusion he had sinned in omitting to kill this man, and he grieved and lamented sorely over this dereliction of apprehended duty. Here we have a case of repentance sanctioning murder. Must we, therefore, conclude that murder is morally right, or a righteous act? Certainly, according to orthodox logic.

Their religious tracts assume that repentance is always for the right, and is *prima facie* evidence of being right. If not, what does it prove, or what moral value is it? According to orthodox teaching, being "a murderer at heart," he was as consignable to perdition as if he had committed the act. There is no escaping the conclusion, therefore, that his repentance landed him in hell, or else proves murder to be right according to orthodox logic.

We have known Quakers to leave their dying testimony against water baptism; and Baptists, with their last breath, declare it is right, and a sin to neglect it. Which is right? Who can tell? We have

231

also known Quakers to condemn dancing in their dying hours, but Shakers never; because one had been taught that it is wrong, and the other that it is right. And which testimony must we accept? Mahomedans often, when approaching the confines of time, repent (sometimes in tears) for not having lived out more rigidly the injunctions of the Koran, but never regret not having been Christians. They often call upon Mohamet to aid them through the gates of death: but not one of the million who die every year ever calls upon Jesus Christ. What, then, does such a conflicting jargon of death-bed repentance prove? What good can grow out of it, or what moral value can possibly attach to it? It establishes simply two principles,—

1st. That repentance grows out of education.

2d. That it depends entirely upon previous convictions as to what it may sanction, and what it may condemn.

No Christian ever repents in favor of Mahomedan-ism; and no Mahomedan ever lifts up his dying voice in favor of Christianity as being superior to his own religion; and no Hindoo has ever been known to indulge in death-bed lamentation for not having previously embraced either Christianity or Mahomedanism; because their earlier education never turned their minds in that direction. The mind has to be educated over again before it can embrace a new religion, or even condemn a wrong act, which, up to that period, it had always believed to be right.

Hence it is evident repentance may lead a person to condemn what is right and sanction what is wrong. How profoundly ignorant of religious history and mental science must those persons therefore be who attach any importance to those diseased and often incoherent utterances, called "death-bed recantations," or who believe a thing the sooner because sanctioned by a dying man or woman, or that they do anything toward proving what is right or what is wrong with respect to either our belief or our moral conduct! And yet we find the orthodox churches printing every year, through their tract societies, stories of death-bed repentance in tract form, and scattering them over the country by the million. As they prove nothing but the honesty of the dying man or woman, they are not worth the paper on which they are printed.

The phenomenon of repentance is simply the operation of a natural law, by which the last impressions made upon the mind are generally cancelled from the memory first, by the progress of fever and disease, thus leaving the earlier impressions to rule the judgment. The person is then virtually a child, controlled by his early youthful convictions, with which, if his late belief and conduct disagree, it causes a mental conflict, called repentance. Thus, instead of being the visitation of God, as Christians claim, repentance is shown to be the product of natural causes. The conclusion is thus established beyond disproof, that the mental processes called conversion, repentance, and "getting religion" are simply natural psychological operations, depending upon education, organization, and intelligence. They depend also upon intellect and scientific knowledge. For persons of large intellectual brains, or extensive scientific culture, never fall victims to these mental derangements. Hence those priests who claim God as their author are either deplorably and inexcusably ignorant, or lacking in moral honesty.

CHAPTER XLIV. THE MORAL LESSONS OF RELIGIOUS HISTORY.

1. The most important lesson deducible from all the religious systems, commemorated in history, and noticed in this work, is, that all religious conceptions, whether in the shape of doctrine, precept, prophecy, prayer, religious devotion, or a belief in miracles, are a spontaneous outgrowth of the moral and religious elements of the human mind. And to assign them a higher origin is to ignore the developments of modern science, and insult the highest intelligence of the age.

2. From the elevated scientific plane occupied by the most enlightened portion of the present age, there is no difficulty in finding a satisfactory solution for every event, every occurrence, and every performance recorded in any of the numerous bibles which have long been afloat in the world, and which have always constituted the sole basis for the claim to a divine origin of all the religious systems of the past; so that such a claim can be no longer vindicated by historically intelligent people.

3. We have shown in this work that all the miraculous incidents related in the history of Jesus Christ as a proof of his divinity can find a more rational explanation than that which assigns them to divine agency. Some of them are now known to lie within the natural capacity of the human mind to achieve, others are explained by recently discovered natural laws. Another class are now well understood mental or nervous phenomena. Other stories, now regarded by the Christian world as referring to miraculous achievements, were probably designed by the writer as mere fable or metaphor. All the events in Christ's history, we have shown, are susceptible of a hundred fold more rational explanation than that which regards them as the feats of a God in violation of his own laws.

4. We have also shown that the same marvelous incidents now found incorporated in the Gospel history of Jesus Christ were related long previously as a part of the sacred history of other Gods; such as being miraculously conceived and born of a virgin; born on the 25th of December; visited in infancy by angels and shepherds;' threatened by the ruler of the country; being of royal lineage; receiving the same divine titles; performing the same miracles, &c.

In a word, we have shown that various heathen Gods and Demigods had, long before Christ's advent, filled the same chapter in history now reported of him in the Christian New Testament. All these stories of the heathen Gods prove as conclusively as any scientific problem can be demonstrated by figures, that the same stories related of Jesus Christ have no other foundation than that of heathen tradition. And will the Christian world, then, hereafter stultify their common sense by ignoring these facts of history so fatal to their claims? Past history points to an affirmative answer to this question, as we will illustrate.

In the early history of this country, several reports were published of showers of blood being seen to fall in some of the sea-coast states, which were regarded as a divine judgment. But the use of the telescope revealed the fact that it was the ordure of butterflies, as those insects were seen at the time in vast swarms. But the devout Christian, whose faith in his religion has always been proof against the demonstrations of science, would give it up. He would not accept the butterfly explanation, but continued to teach his children that it came from God out of heaven as a manifestation of displeasure toward the sins of the people. And it now remains to be seen whether Christian professors at the present day will manifest a similar folly by standing out against the demonstrated truths and facts of this work.

5. We here cite it as the last and most sorrowful lesson of history, that no facts, no proofs, no demonstrations of science can eradicate religious errors from the human mind, if instilled in early life, and never disturbed till the possessor arrives at mature age or middle life.

CHAPTER XLV. CONCLUSION AND REVIEW.

IN writing the concluding chapter of this work, the author deems it proper to re-state some points, and elaborate others, and anticipate some objections to some of the positions advanced. Each division of the subject will be marked by a separate figure, and treated in a brief and succinct manner, as follows:—

1. Several persons, who examined this work before it went to press, have expressed the opinion that it must exert a powerful influence in the way of producing an entire revolution in the religion of orthodox Christendom sooner or later. But this must of course be the work of time, as moral revolutions are not the work of a day. When the human system has been long prostrated with chronic disease, no system of medication can restore it at once to health. The same principle governing the mind makes it morally impossible to eradicate its deeply-seated moral and religious errors in a day by even the presentation of the most powerful and convincing truths and demonstrations that can be brought to bear or operate upon the human judgment. The mind instinctively repels everything (no difference how true or how beautiful) that conflicts with its long-established opinions and convictions. The fires of truth usually require much time to burn their way through those incrustations of moral and religious error which often environ the human mind as the products of a false education. But when they once enter, the work of convincement is complete.

2. It has been stated that the resemblance between Christianity and the more ancient heathen systems is complete and absolute throughout in all their essential doctrines, and principles, and precepts. And if it shall be found, on a critical reading of this work after it comes from the press, that there is one feature of Christianity which has not been traced to pagan origin, or that any points of resemblance have been omitted, they will be supplied in an appendix.

3. It has been stated that a transfiguration is related of Chrishna of India (1200 B. C.) in the Hindoo bible (the Baghavat Gita), which is strikingly similar to that of Christ. We will here present the proof. "Abandoning the mortal form, he (Chrishna) appeared to his disciples in all the divine eclat of his Divine Majesty, his brow encircled with such a brilliant light that Adjouma and the other disciples, unable to bear it, fell with their faces in the dust, and prayed the Lord (Chrishna) to pardon their unworthiness. He replied, 'Have you not faith in me? Know ye not, that whether present or absent in body, I will be ever present with you to guard and protect you?'" (Gaghavat Gita.) How remarkable this to the story of Christ's transfiguration!

4. Some readers, perhaps, will be surprised to observe that we have named so many crucified gods to whom some writers assign a different death. But we have followed, as we believe, the best authorities in doing so.

5. In our work, "The Bibles of Bibles," we have shown that the score of bibles which have been extant in the world teach essentially the same doctrines, principles, and precepts. There are to be found in the old pagan bibles the same grand and beautiful truths mixed up with the same mind-enslaving errors and deleterious superstitions as those contained in the Christian bible. And the same exalted claim is set up by the disciples of each for their respective holy books—that of being a direct revelation from God, and inspired at the fountain of infinite wisdom. And all were exalted, adored, and idolized by their respective admirers, as containing a perfect embodiment of truth, without any admixture of error. The ancient Persians carried their bibles in their bosoms, and read them and prayed over them daily. The Hindoos often read their bible through on their bended knees, and sometimes committed it all to memory. The Baghavat has the following text: "The most important of all duties is to study the Holy Scriptures, which is the word of Brahma and Chrishna, revealed to the world.' Some of the Mahomedans claim that immortal life can only be obtained by reading the Koran, and that the reading of it is essential to the progress and practice of good morals, and the advancement of civilization; and that it will ultimately reform and civilize the world. Both they and the Hindoos, like the Christian world, have numerous commentaries, explaining the obscure texts of their bibles, and aiming to reconcile their teachings with reason and science. And the disciples of all bibles had a mode of doing away with the immoral teachings, and concealing the worst features of their sacred books by bestowing on them a spiritual meaning, as Christians do theirs, thus dressing up error in the guise of truth. The Hindoo bible, the Mahomedan bible, and other holy books, consign those who disbelieve in their teachings to eternal damnation, denouncing them as infidels. In this respect, also, they are like the Christian's bible.

6. "But then, after all (as some good pious Christian will probably exclaim after reading this work), the bible and Christianity are essential to the progress of good morals, and the advancement of the cause of civilization, and the civilized world would sink into a state of heathen darkness, demoralization, and savagism without them; for every enlightened nation owes its present moral and intellectual greatness to the Christian bible and the Christian religion, and would relapse into barbarism without them." This is a mistake, a most egregious mistake, my good brother Christian, as the following facts of history will show:—

1. There are heathen nations now existing who never saw a bible, and others which flourished in the past, before our bible was written, who nevertheless attained to a higher state of morals, and a

higher state of civilization in some respects, than any Christian nation known to history. A whole volume of facts might be adduced, if we had space for them, drawn from the ablest and most reliable authorities, to prove that India, Egypt, Greece, and other countries had reached a high state of civilization centuries before Christianity or any of its founders were even heat'd of, or made their appearance in the world. India was distinguished for her teaming, her laws, her legislation, her civil courts, her judicial tribunals, her astronomers, her poets, her philosophers, her writers, her moralists, her libraries, her men of literature, and her good morals before Moses was found in the bulrushes.

Jacolliot says, "India gave civilization to the world." Egypt borrowed of India, the Greeks of the Egyptians, and the Jews and Christians are indebted to the Greeks for both their morals and their civilization. Dubois, a Christian missionary, in his "Memoirs of India," testifies that "kindness, justice, humanity, good faith, compassion, disinterestedness, and in fact nearly all the moral virtues, were familiar to the ancient Brahmans and Hindoos, and they taught them both by precept and example." Can as much be said of any Christian nation? Certainly not. And the Rev. D. O. Allen says they were distinguished for all the arts and refinement of civilized life—thus placing them on the highest plane of civilization and moral elevation. And other nations might be referred to. Egypt had her vast temples of science, Chaldea her astronomical observatories, and Greece her distinguished academies of learning, her profound philosophers, and her high-toned moral writers and moral teachers, while the Jews, "God's holy people." were in a state of semibarbarism. So affirms the Rev. Albert Barnes.

2. No advancement has often been made in morals or civilization in any country by the introduction of the Christian bible or the Christian religion. It is the arts and sciences which accompany or follow the bible which do the work. A proof of this statement is found in the fact, that no improvement takes place in the morals of the people by the introduction of the bible till the arts and sciences are also introduced amongst them. On the contrary, the morals of many deteriorate by reading the bible alone, because it sanctions as well as condemns every species of crime then known to society. (For proof see Chap. XXXIX. of this work.) That India has become corrupted and sunk in morals since the introduction of the Christian bible, is admitted by the Rev. D. O. Allen, for twenty-five years a missionary in that country. But science, especially moral science, imparts a different influence. It explains the nature of crimes, and teaches and demonstrates that a life of honesty and virtue can alone produce true and real happiness, while the bible augments the temptation to commit sin by teaching that "it is a sweet morsel to be rolled under the tongue," and that its punitive effects may be entirely escaped by an act of divine forgiveness. But science, either directly or by the enlightening of the mind, teaches and convinces the wrong-doer that there is no escape from the evil effects of a wrong or wicked act, and that sin is not a "sweet morsel," but ultimately a *bitter pill.* And thus it arrests the demoralizing effects of this pernicious doctrine of the Christian bible.

3. It may startle some of the bible devotees to be told that their sacred book, instead of being a prompter to civilization and good morals, is really a hindrance to those ends; and that consequently nations without bibles advance faster in these respects than those who are well supplied with this book. But the facts of history seem to establish this as a fact. As a proof we will contrast the present condition of heathen Japan with that of Christian Abyssinia. Colonel Hall and Dr. Oliphant both testify that no drunkenness, no fighting, no quarreling, no thefts, no

robberies, no rapes, no fornication, no domestic feuds or broils, and no fraudulent dealing take place in Japan. No locks or keys are used, for none are needed. There is no disposition to steal, or even to cheat, or overreach in dealing. But in Christian Abyssinia, on the other hand, according to Mr. Goodrich, where bibles and churches are numerous, and preaching and praying are heard every day, nearly all the crimes above enumerated are daily committed. The people go naked, eat raw flesh, cheat, lie, and murder, and practice polygamy. Such a thing as a legitimate child, he tells us, is not known. And thus it has been for fifteen hundred years, while in the daily practice of reading their bible. The arts and sciences have never been introduced amongst them. And this fact explains the cause of their continued moral degradation.

4. According to Noah Webster, the cultivation of the arts and sciences is essential to the progress of civilization and good morals. But bible religion knows nothing about the arts and sciences. It don't even use the words. Paul uses the word science only once, and then to condemn it. But Jesus omits any allusion to science, philosophy, or natural law. So thoroughly convinced were the early disciples of the Christian faith that the teachings of their bible are inimical to the arts and sciences, that they destroyed works of art wherever they could find them, and opposed with a deadly aim every new discovery in the sciences.

5. As bibles represent only the morals and state of society in the age in which they are written, and are not allowed to be altered or transcended, they thus hold their disciples back in all coming time, and compel them to teach and practice the morals of that semi-barbarous age as found taught in their bibles. And thus bibles prevent the moral growth of the people as effectually as the Chinese wooden shoes prevent the growth of the feet. For a fuller exposition of this matter, see The Bible of Bibles, Chap. XIV.

237